IN THE FOOTSTEPS OF CAESAR: WALKING ROAMN ROADS — IN — BRITAIN

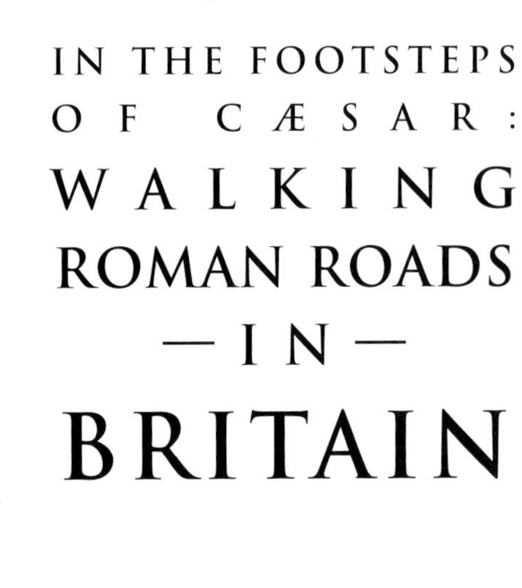

IN THE FOOTSTEPS OF CÆSAR: WALKING ROMAN ROADS — IN — BRITAIN

HELEN LIVINGSTON

PHOTOGRAPHS BY FRANK HASKEW

BCA

LONDON NEW YORK SYDNEY TORONTO

Photographs by Frank Haskew unless otherwise credited

This edition published 1995 by BCA
by arrangement with Ian Allan Publishing
an imprint of Ian Allan Ltd,
Terminal House, Station Approach,
Shepperton, Surrey TW17 8AS

CN 2341

Printed by Ian Allan Printing Ltd, Coombelands House,
Addlestone, Weybridge, Surrey KT15 1HY.

Jacket: *All photographs by Frank Haskew except view of Hadrian's Wall (top right) by Bruce Herrod and gold coin of the Emperor Claudius, courtesy of the National Museum of Wales.*

Title Page: *Condicote Lane lies along Ryknild Street.*

Half Title Page: *The western way on Longridge, north of Ribchester, where the road changes alignment sighted on Tryfan, 28 miles away.*

ACKNOWLEDGEMENTS

Many people have helped with the preparation of this book, and I would like to thank in particular the following people: my mother and sister for moral support and help; the staff at Ian Allan, especially Simon Forty, Peter Waller, Nick Grant and Sophie Mogg; Stephen and Miranda Aldhouse-Green; Linda Hart, Derek and Julia Parker and Rebecca King; Richard Lockett for his invaluable assistance; David and Ann Christie and Tony and Blana Haskew for accommodation and sustenance when we needed them most. Lastly I wish to thank my husband, Frank Haskew, without whose help this book would not have been written.

I would also like to thank the following museums for permission to reproduce photographs: the National Museum of Wales, the Grosvenor Museum at Chester, Verulamium Museum at St Albans and Colchester Museum.

Helen Livingston

KEY TO MAPS

● town
✷ legionary fortress

General chapter maps (except Chapter 4)

● town
○ smaller Roman settlements
☆ non-Roman places
✷ fort
✷ legionary fortress — permanent
✧ legionary fortress — temporary
— Roman road
34 walk/cycle ride locations (plus identifying number)
– – – trackway in use in Roman times

DOVER all Roman sites
Heath all non-Roman sites

London (Chapter 4)

═ Roman roads, course known
===== Roman roads, course inferred
=:=:= pre-Roman trackways

Route Maps (one for each walk/cycle ride)

Roman road — visible
Roman *agger* visible
Roman cutting visible
modern road
modern road on Roman line
Modern footpath on Roman line

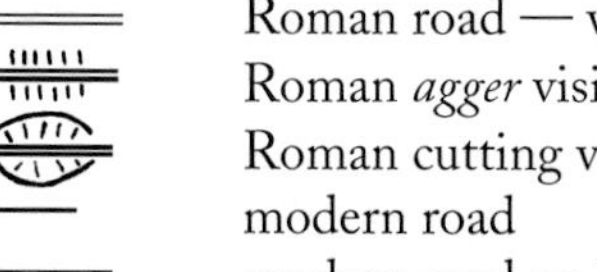

numbered points on walk/cycle ride
direction of walk/cycle ride

Top: *The Welsh Watling Street, now in use as a main entrance.*

Above: *The Colchester Vase showing a gladiatorial scene. Colchester Museum*

CONTENTS

ALL ROADS LEAD TO ROME

The road they fashioned pays homage yet
To a splendour that long lies still:
And we that follow may not forget
The Roman courage, the Roman will:
And dreamers hear when the shadows fall
The stirring sound of their bugle-call;
Men from Africa, men from Gaul
Marching over the Hill!

A. G. PRYS-JONES
Roman Road

Roman roads exert a particularly strong hold on the imagination. They fire us with the grand design of the Romans; to govern the whole world; and possess almost architectural qualities, raised high above the surrounding land and heroically direct. They are by far the most lasting memorial to our days as a Roman province.

Julius Caesar invaded Britain in 55 BC and then again in 54 BC. On both occasions he pushed inland past the site of London. These expeditions, particularly the first, had a profound influence on the Romans, for whom Britain was a weird and wonderful island on the very edge of the world. Caesar had shown the way, but it was not until a century later that the island was conquered under the Emperor Claudius. The Roman army landed in Kent in AD 43 and for nearly 400 years after that Britain was Britannia, the northernmost province of the Roman Empire. Roads built during those years were the vital links which bound this island into the Roman world. These roads not only led to Rome, they led from Rome. The Roman army marched along them, Roman government officials travelled by them, Roman merchandise was moved along them and via their direct lines the Roman way of life was spread. To a great extent the roads were Rome.

ROADS IN BRITAIN BEFORE THE ROMAN INVASION

The network of roads which already existed in Britain when the Romans arrived was far more complex than used to be thought. Iron Age Britain was cultivated and prosperous, with pastures grazed by cattle and fields producing crops for closely spaced farmsteads. A dense network of trackways covered the hills and lowlands alike. There is no truth in the popular image of the ancient Britons as a people living in a land of impenetrable forest and marsh with ridgetop routes keeping to the dry hills.

THE ROMAN ROAD SYSTEM

The Romans, like the Persians before them and Napoleon long after, knew that the secret of holding territory after initial conquest lay in a well planned system of good roads. Along these troops could be deployed speedily and arms and supplies shipped to them. The roads also served to break up the enemy territory: the concept of 'divide and rule'.

So it was that very rapidly military roads were laid across Britain, superimposed on the dense network of Iron Age trackways. The Roman roads ran straight for considerable distances; when new they must have stood out as raw scars across the farmland and through the woodlands. These earliest Roman roads were built for and by the military, laid down behind the advancing army. The routes taken by the conquerors can still be followed today.

During the 400 years of Roman rule there were changes in use. Roads in the south and east of the country developed into civilian routes, their maintenance handed over from the army to the people. Only in the militarised northern zone did the roads remain primarily military in nature.

Some roads were designed in the first place for the trans-

Above: *The agger of Stane Street still carries a main highway at Ockley.*

port of goods. British metals, in particular, were exploited by the Romans and large quantities were exported to Rome and to other parts of the Empire: silver-lead from the Mendips, copper from Anglesey, tin from Cornwall, gold from Mid-Wales and iron from the Forest of Dean and the Weald. Other home-produced goods carried included pottery of various kinds, while imports included French wine, olive oil, Mediterranean marble and high-quality Samian pottery from Gaul.

Not all Roman roads followed completely new routes. Frequently it was possible to adapt the old trackways to Roman use, straightening and upgrading them to Roman standards. The Icknield Way is, perhaps, the best known of these Romanised trackways, but there were many others, possibly far more than we realise as yet. Many of them date from late in the 1st century AD, but some of them, including Akeman Street, were Romanised in the early years of the Roman conquest.

The Romans built nearly 10,000 miles of road in Britain, and they did this remarkably quickly. The main Roman roads in the south and east of the country were constructed within five years of the conquest, from AD 43 to AD 48, while the main northern and western roads were built by the mid-AD 80s. The roads of the succeeding centuries of Roman rule, with the exception of the military ways of Hadrian's Wall and the Antonine Wall, tended to have a peaceful purpose, until the Saxon threat of the 4th century forced the building of roads to serve the new defensive sites of the Saxon Shore.

Many early military routes radiate from London, testifying to its strategic importance as the port on the Thames even in the very early years of Roman rule. London was the hub of the Roman road system and it is possible that distances along British roads were measured from London rather than from the famous Golden Milestone in the Forum at Rome. The London Stone is said to be the milestone now set behind glass in a wall in Fenchurch Street.

Travel in the Roman world was largely on foot and while some people may have travelled on horseback it is not known whether they were permitted to use the roads. In towns officials were carried on litters and sedan chairs. Pack-horses were used to carry certain commodities while heavy wagons transported bulky goods such as corn. Carriages (with four wheels) and carts (with two wheels) were also used.

Evidence from rutted Roman roads shows that in all probability the Romans travelled down the middle of the road, whether driving, riding or on foot. In those less hectic times they were able to pass any oncoming traffic on whichever side was the more convenient.

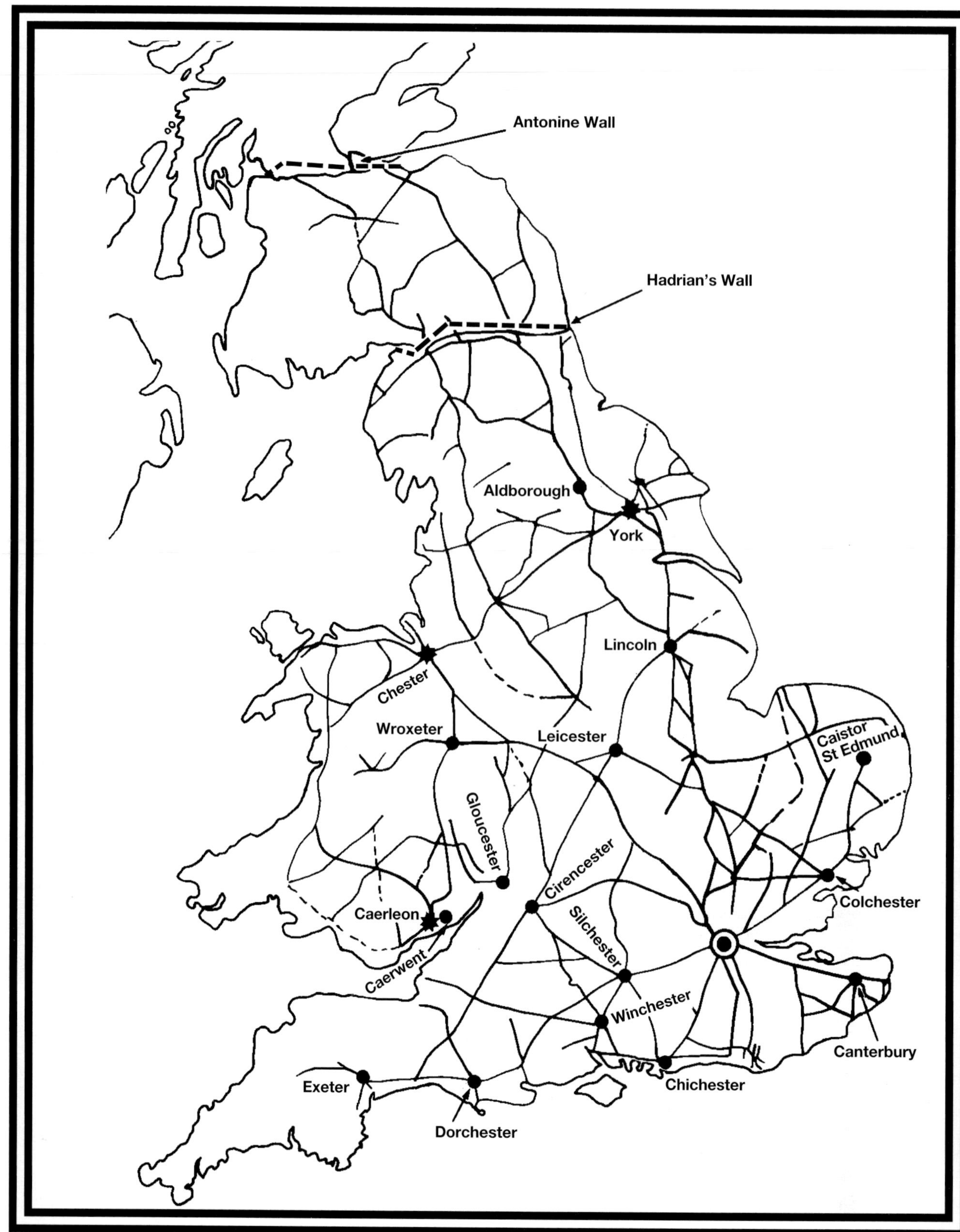

Antonine Wall
Hadrian's Wall
Aldborough
York
Lincoln
Chester
Wroxeter
Leicester
Caistor St Edmund
Gloucester
Cirencester
Silchester
Caerleon
Caerwent
Colchester
Winchester
Canterbury
Chichester
Exeter
Dorchester

SURVEYING AND BUILDING THE ROADS

Surveying Techniques

We do not know how the Romans worked out the alignment between places too far apart to be mutually visible without the aid of a magnetic compass, we can only admire the Roman surveyor's ability. It is probable that latitude and longitude measurements were used to fix the position of the end-points of the road (London and Chichester in the case of Stane Street, for example) and the surveyor then calculated the alignment which follows the shortest distance between them. The Roman road surveyor's next job was a thorough reconnaissance to get to know the terrain along the line of the proposed road.

Once the direct survey line was known and the reconnaissance undertaken the actual course of the road could be determined. Roman roads are laid out in a series of straight lengths with abrupt turns where each new alignment begins. These changes were usually made on high ground giving good visibility both for the laying out of the next stretch and for patrolling the roads when in use. Where necessary the Roman engineer was perfectly capable of diverging from the given alignment to adapt the road to local conditions, to avoid marshy areas and very steep slopes. The Romans possessed a superb knowledge of Britain's geography, manifest time and time again in the routes taken by the roads. The engineers eased the descent of steep hills by zig-zags or by cutting a terrace with a uniform gradient; they drove cuttings through hill crests and carried the roads obliquely to river crossings so as to make use of the best place to ford (the usual method) or to build a bridge.

Actually marking the line of the road on the ground was not difficult if the earlier work had been done satisfactorily. It is likely that the road line was fixed on the ground by relatively unskilled soldiers using movable markers to set out straight lines. We do not know what kinds of marker were used, but the most probable are beacon fires on high points to fix the longer alignments and between them wooden cross-stakes, like those used in modern road building. These would have marked the line across the fields, pasturage and woodlands of the British Iron Age tribes.

The line to be followed by many a Roman road was probably given its final fixing on the ground by ploughing a furrow to mark the course. It would be surprising if archaeologists could unearth much evidence for such a flimsy mark, but faint traces have been found under the roads in several places.

This means of marking the line of the roads reminds us of how little we know of the Romans' attitude to road building. It is likely that some sort of religious ceremony would have accompanied the building of a Roman road, but we have no idea what it might have been. We can, if we like, see the straight alignments of Roman roads and

Above: *Watercolour painting of a Roman street in Pompeii.*

Above:
Roman cutting for the road over Hardknott Pass, Cumbria.

Left:
Richborough Fort, Kent — site of the successful landings of AD43.

the use of a plough to mark the line as simply a reflection of their surveying techniques. It is doubtful if the Romans themselves saw them that way.

Road Construction

The navvying was carried out in part by legionary soldiers and in part by conscripted gangs of locals. The usual method was to build the road on an embankment, known today by the Latin word, *agger*. This was constructed using earth excavated from side-ditches, on one or both sides of the road. Local materials were used which vary considerably from area to area, so that there is no standardisation in *agger* size or construction. It is probable that different stretches of the same road were built by different gangs.

The road surface was laid on the *agger*, but did not use the full width. Large stone slabs were laid first, sometimes with rectangular stones set lengthwise to form a kerb. Above the slabs, stones and then gravel were rammed hard to form the road 'metalling' and the surface given a camber to help drainage. Roman cambers could be steep, sometimes as much as eight inches on a road 18 feet wide.

The roads varied in width. In southern Britain important military and civilian roads were 20–30 feet wide, though they were set on *aggers* of considerably greater width. Two possible standard spacings for the side ditches are 84 feet and 64 feet. In northern Britain the important roads were all military routes, while the topography and hard bedrock frequently prevented the construction of complex *aggers* and side ditches. It seems that these roads had to be at least 12 feet wide between the ditches.

Official posting houses (*Masiones*) were built for official travellers, ensuring them safe board and lodging. Non-official travellers had to make do with the inns, which seem to have suffered a very ill reputation.

Milestones were set up, but frequently these do not give distances, recording only the name of the emperor and the year of his reign. So far some 110 Roman milestones have been found in Britain. The word mile is itself derived from the Latin, *milia passuum*, a thousand paces, for Roman miles were a thousand paces long. A pace was two steps or about five feet, making a Roman mile 1,680 yards long (1,536 metres), slightly less than a statute mile (1,760 yards or 1,609 metres).

Tombs and cemeteries were built beside the roads because burials were not allowed within the walls of towns. Perhaps here, though, we also see another facet of the antique mind that we cannot comprehend. Were the dead laid by the roadside so as to start them on their journey to the next world?

WRITTEN INFORMATION ABOUT THE ROADS

Roman writers tell us little about the roads, though the poet Horace in his first book of *Sermones*, published in 30 BC, tells of a journey he made along the *Via Appia*:

Leaving great Rome, my journey I begin,
And reach Aricia, and a moderate inn ...
... Next Appii Forum, filled e'en nigh to choke,
With knavish publicans and boatmen folk.
This portion of our route, which most get through
At one good stretch, we chose to split in two,
Taking it leisurely ...

Vitruvius, in his *De Architectura*, describes the method for laying open-air paving. This has been confused with road construction and led to the erroneous belief that Roman roads consisted of four layers. In contrast, the poet Statius, writing in about AD 86–96, gives an accurate description of the construction of the *Via Domitiana* in Rome.

Information on the British roads compiled in Roman times is an exciting complement to the story related by archaeology. The 'Antonine Itinerary' is a medieval copy of a book compiled in about AD 210 giving a list of routes with places along them and the distances between them. It is an official document, either the record of an official journey or the plan for such a journey, so the routes shown are not necessarily the most direct. In contrast, the 'Peutinger Table' is a third-century road map in which the Roman Empire is shown as a seemingly endless strip drawn on rolls of parchment. All that survives is a 13th-century copy, but most of Britain is missing as it was on the outside sheet of the roll, which is lost. A small part of south-east England appears on the second roll. The seventh-century 'Ravenna Cosmography' gives British place names in a very corrupt form. It is thought to have been compiled from a now unknown Roman itinerary and from Roman military documents when the remains of the Imperial Library were housed in Ravenna.

Below: *The Roman road to Malton in use as a lane on the Yorkshire Wolds.*

NAMES OF ROMAN ROADS

The Romans frequently named their Italian roads after the builder, as in *Via Appia*, named for Appius Claudius Caecus who ordered its building in 312 BC, and *Via Domitiana* after Emperor Domitian, but we have no information on the Roman names of the British roads. Names associated with them today, such as Ermine Street and Stane Street, are of Saxon, not Roman, origin, while apparently Latin names, like *Via Devana*, are no older than the 18th century, deriving from the enthusiasm for the classical past of the early antiquaries.

THE ROADS AFTER THE ROMANS

The final abandonment by Rome in AD 410 left Britain without a central government and forced to defend herself against the Saxons. The Roman road system, for so long a civilising influence, at once became dangerous, offering a swift means of travel to the invaders. The frightened Romano-British strove to sever their roads, deliberately blocking them where possible. The most famous such blockage is the Bokerley Dyke, which was thrown right across the Roman road south of Salisbury.

The Saxons, Danes and fearsome Vikings overran the Roman province. These peoples brought their own way of life with them and it did not include a centralised road system. Roads were only of local use, and from being the northerly outpost of a great Empire, with lines of communication linking it to the great metropolis of Rome, Britain turned inward, becoming a group of self-sufficient, self-governing kingdoms.

The roads fell into disrepair. Heavy rain damaged culverts; floods carried bridges away and wrecked fords; leaves and soil filled up side-ditches and trees fell, blocking the way. The new settlers, with neither the inclination nor the skill to repair the damage, let well alone. The history of the roads was lost to these people, and frequently giants or Satan were credited with the construction of the old highways. In many places the roads were used as boundaries between adjoining estates and the emerging Dark Age kingdoms. Houses were built on the *aggers*, which provided good, dry sites. The stone remains left behind by the Romans were plundered for building materials, and we find reused Roman tiles, bricks and dressed stones in many a Saxon church. The roads, too, were used as quarries. Only in the uplands did they survive in anything like their original condition, but even in the uplands the road stone was useful for building field walls.

As long-distance travel reasserted itself the Roman roads, somewhat distorted by time and neglect, became the backbone of the road system. The coming of the turnpike roads in the 18th century marked a sea change. Like the Roman roads, the turnpikes were engineered, and some of them followed the lines of pre-existing Roman roads, perpetuating the routes.

One of the most exciting aspects of tracing Roman roads is their ghostly appearance in the names of the places along them. Many of our place names today are of Saxon origin and the Saxons called the Roman roads 'streets'. Where the word street occurs in a place name it probably refers to a Roman road. Thus we have a whole array of names like Ham Street, Thornton-le-Street, Streatham, Stratford and Stretton. Likewise, the word 'stone' or 'stane' probably refers to a Roman road: Stanstead and Stone Street are examples of such names. Frequently the term 'causeway', if not associated with a bridge, refers to the *agger* of a Roman road, as in Long Causeway, Devil's Causeway, Causeway Farm. There are other place names that seem to refer to Roman roads. Two of the oddest are 'Folly', found near Roman road sites where there is no 18th-century construction of that name, and perhaps derived from the verb 'to follow'; and 'Coldharbour', which may relate to Dark Age huts built on or near the dry sites of the roads.

THE ROMAN ROADS TODAY

The Roman roads of Britain have shown a remarkable durability. Some, such as Watling Street (A2, A5) and the trans-Pennine road through the Stainmore Pass (A66) survive as major highways for virtually their entire length. Other major Roman roads seem to have vanished utterly from the face of the earth. Where, for example, were the roads of Cornwall?

By far the largest number of Roman roads fall between these two extremes, followed in places by modern roads, forming part of the present road network. Ermine Street, Stane Street and Dere Street fall into this category.

When we travel by car along these Roman roads, we find that sudden bends take us off the Roman line. At these sharp bends the Roman road frequently continues straight ahead as a track, footpath or line of hedgerows, showing where the road has fallen out of use. Here are delightful green lanes, unfrequented bridleways and field paths which entice us to walk them and experience for ourselves the neat terraceways along hillsides, the causeways across marshy areas and the courageous zig-zags down steep slopes. The long, straight alignments striding purposefully across the land make for perfect exploring, often ascending over high ground to give superb views, and stretch diminishing to the horizon, writing the might and determination of Rome on a landscape which that power forsook sixteen centuries ago.

ROMAN ROADS EXPLORED

I The South East

The Richborough–Canterbury Road
1. 4-mile walk from Richborough to Ash

The Ash–Dover Road
2. 8½-mile walk from Eastry to Dover

The London–Lewes Way
3. 3½-mile walk from Edenbridge to Cowden Pound

The Sussex Greensand Way (Barham–Hardham) and the Middleton Track
4. 8-mile circular walk at Plumpton

The Seaford–Ripe Road
5. 10-mile walk from Seaford to Glynde

Stane Street (London–Chichester)
6. 3¾-mile walk/cycle ride from Epsom to Burford Bridge
7. 6¼-mile walk from Bignor to Halnaker

Below: *Roman milestone on the Stangate, near Hadrian's Wall.*

II The South West

The South Western Highway (London–Exeter)
- 8a. The Port Way: 5-mile walk from White Hill to Clap Gate
- 8b. The Port Way: 12-mile circular walk from White Hill to Clap Gate and back
- 9. Ackling Dyke: 25-mile walk from Old Sarum to Shapwick
- 10. 14-mile cycle ride/drive from Dorchester to Loders

The Charterhouse–Winchester Road
11. 10-mile walk from Old Sarum to Broughton

The Speen–Bath Road
12. 7¾-mile walk from Beckhampton to Sandy Lane

The Winchester–Wanborough Road (including the Chute Causeway)
13. 17½-mile walk/cycle ride from East Anton to Great Bedwyn

The Dorchester–Ilchester Road
14. 4-mile cycle ride/drive from Dorchester to Grimstone

III Eastern England

Ermine Street (London–Lincoln)
15. 8-mile walk/cycle ride from Byard's Leap to Coleby

***Via Devana* (Colchester-Godmanchester)**
16. 9½-mile walk from Horseheath to Cambridge

The Braughing–Godmanchester Road
17. 9½-mile walk from Westmill to Baldock

The Peddars Way (Chelmsford–Holme-next-the-Sea)
18. 20-mile walk from Castle Acre to Holme-next-the-Sea

The Wixoe–Peasenhall Road
19. 8-mile walk from Long Melford to Lavenham

IV London

Watling Street
Ermine Street
The Great Road
The Old Colchester Road
The Silchester Road
The London Akeman Street
Stane Street
The London–Brighton Way
The London–Lewes Way

V The Midlands

Watling Street (London–Wroxeter)
20. 7½-mile circular walk at St Albans

The Foss Way (Axminster–Lincoln)
21. 23-mile walk from Castle Combe to Cirencester

Akeman Street (St Albans–Cirencester)
22. 7½-mile walk from Tackley to North Leigh

The Towcester–Silchester Road
23. 8-mile walk from Toot Baldon to Brightwell-cum-Sotwell

Ryknild Street (Bourton-on-the-Water–Chesterfield)
24. 14½-mile cycle ride/walk from Upper Slaughter to Weston-sub-Edge

The Gartree Road (Godmanchester–Leicester)
25. 6½-mile walk from Glooston to Little Stretton

VI South Wales and the Marches

Welsh Watling Street (Wroxeter–Caerleon)
26. 6½-mile cycle ride/walk from Craven Arms to Leintwardine

The Caerleon–Llanfair Clydogau Road
27. 6-mile circular walk at Brecon
28. 8¾-mile walk from Trecastle to Llandovery

Sarn Helen (Brecon) (Brecon–Neath)
29. 14½-mile walk from Mynydd Illtud to Coelbren

The Dean Road (*Ariconium*–Lydney)
30. 1¾-mile walk from Upper Soudley to Blackpool Bridge

The Tillington–Abergavenny Road
31. 6½-mile walk from Madley to Abbey Dore

Below: *The famous paved surface on Blackstone Edge, near Rochdale, on the Manchester-Ilkley Roman road. The central groove may have been designed for a pole brake on carts and would have been filled with earth.*

VII North Wales and Chester

Sarn Helen (Caerhun–Pennal)
32. 12½-mile walk from Dolwyddelan to Trawsfynydd

Welsh Watling Street (Chester–Wroxeter)
33a. 6-mile circular walk from Chester to Eccleston and back
33b. 6½-mile walk from Chester to Churton

The Chester–Dolgellau Road
34. 11-mile cycle ride/drive from Pen-y-stryt to Corwen

The Chester–Caernarfon Road
35. 6-mile walk from Roewen to Aber

The Chester–Meols Road
36. 4-mile walk up the Wirral from Ledsham to Willaston

VIII Northern England

South Newbald–Malton Road
37. 17½-mile cycle ride/walk from Warter to Malton

Stamford Bridge–Bridlington Road
38. 13-mile walk from Fridaythorpe to Kilham

Wade's Causeway (Malton–Whitby)
39. 14½-mile walk from Wrelton to Grosmont

Ingleton–Brough-by-Bainbridge Road
40. 19½-mile walk from Ingleton to Brough-by-Bainbridge

High Street (Brougham–Windermere)
41. 15½-mile walk from Celleron to Troutbeck

Ambleside–Ravenglass road
42. 7-mile walk from Little Langdale to Hardknott

IX Hadrian's Wall

The Maiden Way (Kirkby Thore–Carvoran)
43. 5-mile walk from Burnstones to Featherstone Common

The Stanegate (Corbridge–Carlisle)
44. 6½-mile cycle ride/drive from Newbrough to *Vindolanda*

Hadrian's Wall Military Way
45. 8½-mile walk from Walltown to Housesteads

X North of Hadrian's Wall

Agricola's Western Way (Carlisle–Inveresk)
46. 8-mile walk from Dolphinton to Ninemileburn

Dere Street (Corbridge–Elginhaugh)
47. 21-mile walk from High Rochester to Jedfoot

The Devil's Causeway (Corbridge–Berwick-upon-Tweed)
48. 5½-mile cycle ride/drive from East Horton to Lowick

The Antonine Wall Military Way (Bridgeness–Old Kilpatrick)
49. 2-mile circular walk at Bearsden

Rome's Farthest North (Camelon–Kirriemuir)
50. 7½-mile walk from Crossgates to Ardunie

Below left: *Roman glass jug. St Albans Museums*

Below right: *The Roman road from Ash to Dover strides over the downs.*

— I —

THE SOUTH EAST

'Do thou (the goddess, Fortuna) preserve our Caesar, soon to set forth against the Britons, furthest of earth's peoples!'

HORACE

Odes 1, XXXV (*c*26 BC)

South East England, the corner of Britain closest to the Continent, has long been the gateway for conquerors: Romans, Saxons and Normans all made their entry here. In later years, other powers one after another attempted an invasion through the South East. Traditionally, the area has also had friendly commercial links with its neighbours, the white bastions of whose lands are visible across the Straits of Dover.

The Romans in South East England

Julius Caesar's British expeditions of 55 and 54 BC mark the beginning of the Roman Empire's intervention in British affairs. Traditionally, Caesar is said to have sailed past the cliffs of Dover and then landed near Deal, to work his way inland across two rivers, probably the Medway and the Thames. On both occasions he lost part of his fleet in a Channel storm and withdrew hastily to the Continent. Caesar was not in Britain long enough to build any roads, though he probably advanced along the line of a British track, later to be Romanised as Watling Street.

After Caesar a century was to elapse before Britain was conquered under Emperor Claudius. In the intervening years trading links were built up with many of the British tribes, and in parts of the South East the invading Roman army was welcomed. There were several reasons for Rome's renewed interest in Britain, including her fabled wealth. Moreover, at that time Rome was an expansionist power; the island whose coast was visible from northern

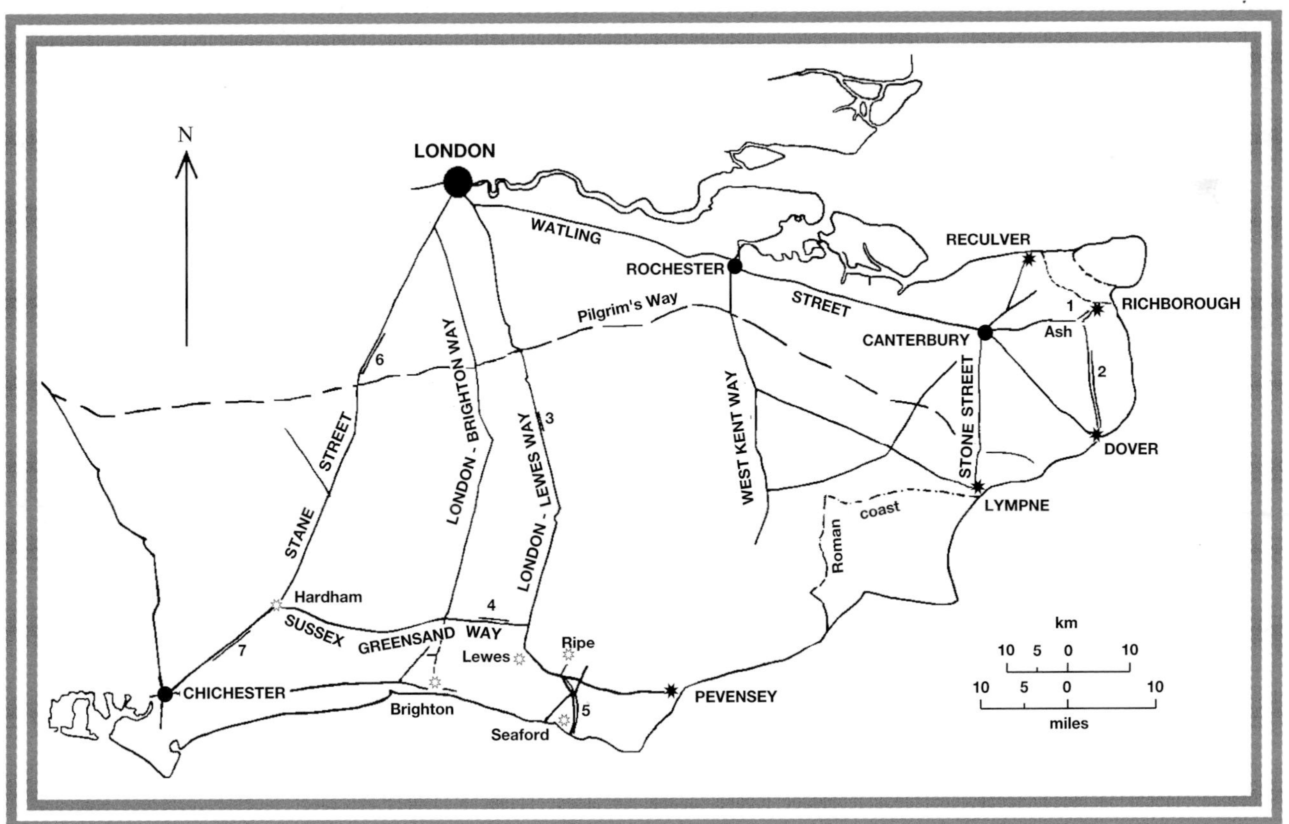

Gaul was sure to attract her attentions. In addition, Claudius, who had recently been proclaimed Emperor, possessed no military prowess, being rather a bookish type who realised from his study of history that to remain in power he needed to maintain the support of the army. In short, the new Emperor needed to find a land to conquer and Britain offered the ideal opportunity. Claudius siezed it with alacrity.

The Romans never attacked neighbouring territory without giving a reason. This time it was provided by a claimant to the throne of one of the British tribes who had appealed to Rome for assistance and whose cause Rome now espoused — a typical Roman ploy to make use of complicated political situations among the tribes they conquered.

So, in AD 43 the invasion commenced under the overall command of a distinguished general, Aulus Plautius. The invasionary force consisted of about 40,000 men, over half of them legionaries, and therefore Roman citizens, in the legions of II

Top: *The South Country: friendly towards the Romans and later a civilized part of the province.*

Above: *Richborough. The massive walls of the Saxon Shore fort overlook the parallel ditches — all that remains of Aulus Plautus' bridgehead fort of AD 43.*

Augusta, IX Hispana, XIV Gemina and XX Valeria, as well as associated auxiliary troops, landed unopposed in Kent, where there were several landing points, with the main contingent coming ashore at Richborough, near Sandwich. The army reassembled and, meeting with no opposition, advanced across Kent, roughly along the line followed by Watling Street, now the A2. The Romans met concerted British resistance at the River Medway, where a two-day battle was fought, most unusual in ancient times. They forced a crossing and pressed on to the Thames, where another battle took place.

At this stage the victorious Roman army paused long enough for the Emperor to hurry over, bringing with him his elephants and other trappings to amaze and terrify the natives. Claudius himself then led his invasionary force into East Anglia and sacked Colchester, the capital of the Catuvellauni — the most powerful British tribe. He received the surrender of many British kings and created several 'client kingdoms' — tribal states allowed a degree of autonomy which then acted as 'buffer states' between a new province and the unconquered barbarians. Claudius returned to Rome and a hero's welcome. He was awarded a triumph by the Senate and a triumphal arch was erected to commemorate his conquest of Britain. Aulus Plautius became Britain's first Roman governor and set about annexing the rest of the island.

During the invasion the Regni of Sussex were strongly pro-Roman and were rewarded by being granted client kingdom status. This allowed them a good deal of freedom and their king, Cogidubnus, continued to rule them. He was accorded considerable honours by the Romans and the great Roman palace at Fishbourne was built for him. It is close to his capital, Chichester, at the head of a navigable creek and the site of an important harbour.

Even during the 1st century AD an opulent Roman lifestyle developed in South East England, particularly along the Sussex coast, which was well endowed with fine villas, the country houses of the well-to-do. Kent also developed rapidly as a favoured place of residence for the noble and the great. Wealth to support luxurious villas came from, among other things, the exploitation of the natural resources of the area, iron and timber from the Weald and corn from the downs. The area was prosperous and peaceful, a far cry from the military north of England, though by the 2nd century the British fleet (*Classis Britannica*) was stationed at Dover (*Dubris*) and Lympne (*Portus Lemanis*) and was involved in the iron and timber industries of the Weald.

By the late 3rd century, though, there was crisis in the Empire. Rome's confidence had been shaken by the incursions of marauding barbarians on her northern and eastern frontiers, while the sea lanes between Britain and the Continent were effectively in the control of Saxon pirates. These cruel but skilled seafarers would sail up rivers to attack peaceful towns and farming communities where there were no soldiers to guard the inhabitants or their property. The problem was immense and the Romans were terrified, a fear expressed as late as the 5th century by Sidonius, in a letter to a friend in the army:

'Please do be very careful — there's no time like the present for a warning. Saxons are the most brutal of enemies, they'll only attack if they have the advantage of surprise — if you see them first they'll slink away. They avoid defended sites, but hit hardest at the unprepared. If they hunt, they'll catch, but if you pursue them they'll escape ...'

None the less, the Romans found a way both to defend the coasts and to protect the sea lanes so that goods could once again travel between Britain and the Continent. In true Roman fashion the system devised was effective and long-lasting. It prolonged the life of Roman Britain for over a hundred years.

Firstly, the high command was altered to meet the changed circumstances and there was scope for the deployment of mobile units to deal with any piratical landings. These troops were stationed at massive forts and fortified harbours built on the southern and eastern coasts of Britain and along the coast of Gaul. A late Roman document, the *Notitia Dignitatum*, gives the name of this extensive and well planned defensive system, these were

Above: *The south coast at Fairlight: South East England has traditionally had close links with the continent across the English Channel.*

the forts of the *litus Saxonicum*, the Saxon Shore. The forts include some of the most exciting surviving sites of Roman Britain, including Portchester Castle, Pevensey Castle, Richborough Fort and Burgh Castle.

The Roman Road Network in South East England

The Roman road system of the South East consists of three parts: the east Kent roads, the roads of the rest of the South East, and Stane Street. In east Kent, roads from the three main Roman ports, Richborough (*Portus Rutupiae*), Dover and Lympne, converge on Canterbury (*Durovernum*), the former capital of the east Kent kingdom, and then forge ahead towards London on a single line, Watling Street. This is a military pattern, born of the successful invasion of AD 43 itself, and was to remain military and political throughout Roman times, since the east Kent ports were the normal ports of entry both for troops and for Roman officials. These are straight, unyielding roads, the superb handiwork of Roman surveyors, skilfully engineered to make the best use of natural features, slicing through annexed territory like a knife.

On the far western boundary of South East England another military road, Stane Street, links London with Chichester, capital of the client kingdom and an important port. This road was the route followed by Vespasian and the II Legion, Augusta, in AD 43 in his push into the South West.

Between Stane Street and the east Kent roads the road system is not of a military nature, but rather is primarily commercial. It was designed for the peaceful exploitation of natural resources and for trade. The roads cross the important timber and iron producing district of the Weald, a region of broken, difficult country, and the prosperous corn producing district of the South Downs. These roads are not as straight as the east Kent roads.

Two important roads led northwards from the South Downs across the Weald to London, linking the corn and

Left: *Fishbourne Roman palace — the famous dolphin mosaic.*

Below: *The broken walls of the Saxon Shore fort at Richborough silently mock the passage of time.*

iron producing districts with the capital. These were the London-Lewes Way and the London-Brighton Way. The existence of both these routes was unsuspected until pioneering work on aerial photographs was undertaken between the wars. Their existence and the discovery of numerous branch roads of Roman origin has dispelled for ever the notion that the Weald was uncharted forest during Roman times. Another important north-south road, the West Kent Way, lies further east, heading through Maidstone and Bodiam to the iron-producing district north of Hastings.

These were connected by cross-country roads, one along the Sussex coast plain and another just to the north of the South Downs: the Sussex Greensand Way. Moreover, the ancient North Downs ridgeway, later the Pilgrim's Way, remained in use throughout Roman times, while the South Downs ridgeway, never as important a route, retained sections of local importance. The Roman road network of the South East was very complete indeed with numerous local roads and trackways infilling the lattice-work of the great roads.

THE ROMAN ROAD FROM RICHBOROUGH TO CANTERBURY

Britain's First Roman Road

This was Britain's first Roman road, laid down by the engineers of the invading army in AD 43. It ran from Richborough, where Aulus Plautius established his bridgehead, to Canterbury where his troops met up with other contingents of the invading army.

Richborough now presents to the world a face rather changed from its appearance in AD 43. Today the view northwards takes in level farmland, the quietly meandering River Stour and the Isle of Thanet. The Romans looked north across an arm of the sea, for in those days Thanet was truly an island and a wide navigable stretch of water, the Wantsum Strait, separated it from the mainland. One end of the strait lay near Reculver, the other between Ramsgate and Sandwich, with Richborough perched on a small, marsh-bound island just off its southern shore.

The beginning of any journey is important, and in exploring the Roman roads of Britain, it is fitting to begin at Richborough and walk to Ash along this road. Not only the invading army, but news, views, Empire-made finery, ideas and Roman civilisation itself travelled this way as Richborough — *Portus Rutupiae* — became the most important port of Roman Britain. It was famous throughout the Empire. It was here that the most important persons arrived; here that Romans built a triumphal monument, 90 feet high and faced with white Italian marble and bronze figures, to commemorate the inclusion of Britain into the Roman Empire; here that a thriving town developed with a range of port industries and here too that, in the twilight of Roman times, the Romano-British built one of the great forts of the Saxon Shore to protect the province from marauding Saxons. The site of *Rutupiae* today is dominated by the massive, tumbledown walls of the Saxon Shore fort which, on this elevated little knoll that was once an island, stand in defiance of all the change that time has wrought.

The road left Richborough fort by the west gate, its course dictated by saltings and the marshy Fleet Channel, and it was built on a causeway. The northern end of the Fleet Channel, where it opened into the Wantsum Strait, is the likely site for a Roman harbour, and as we set out on to the grassy causeway from Richborough Farm the possible site of a Roman quay lies at the bottom of the steep overgrown slope on the right.

Once safely across the channel the road turns south-west near Fleet Farm to head along a ridge of dry land to Cooper Street and then follows a line of footpaths over the fields. It crosses the modern Ash bypass to enter this pleasant Kentish village along a pathway past the playing fields and then between houses, arriving at the main street beneath Griffin Cottage.

Beyond Ash, the Roman road turns west, straight for Canterbury, its line now followed by the A257, though it had to swing south to avoid formerly marshy ground around Ickham before rejoining the straight alignment to Canterbury.

1 A WALK FROM RICHBOROUGH TO ASH

Starting from the point of Aulus Plautius' bridgehead at Richborough this walk follows the first Roman road on British soil past the site of the great Roman harbour of Portus Rutupiae to the road junction at Ash.

Instructions

1. Start at Richborough Fort (English Heritage). Go down the footpath to the east of the fort and follow the path round to the west gate from which the Roman road emerged. Turn on to the Roman road and follow it to Castle Farm. Continue along the lane which comes in from the left to join the Roman line.

2. Turn left through the gate opposite Richborough Farm. Turn right and go downhill following the sign 'public footpath to Ash Street'. You are still on the line of the Roman road. Note the very steep slope on the right, possibly the site of a quay in Roman times. Go downhill into the former Fleet Channel which separated

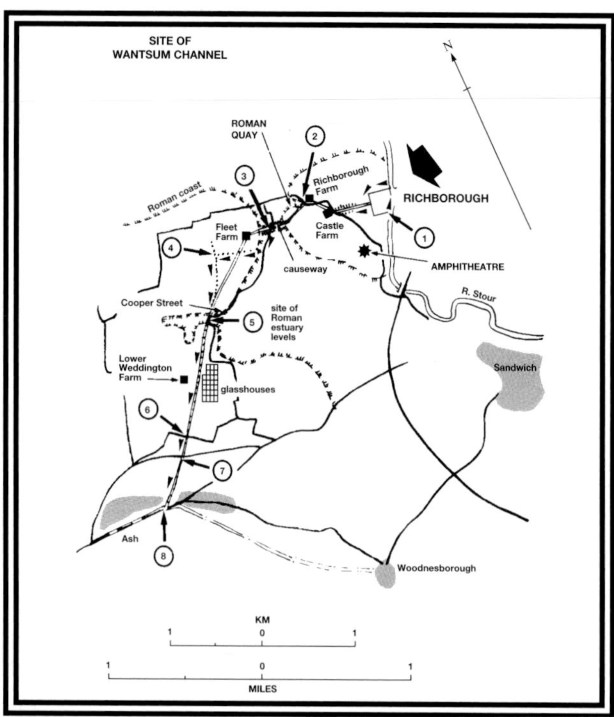

OS maps:
1:50,000 Landranger sheet 179

1:25,000 Pathfinder sheets
1196 [Margate & St Nicholas at Wade]
1212 [Sandwich & Deal]

Distance: 4 miles

Pubs/hostelries:
On the walk: Ash
Nearby: Sandwich Woodnesborough

Roman engineering works:
causeway over the Fleet Channel
site of Roman quay
embankments probably of Roman origin at Cooper Street

Other antiquities:
ditches from Aulus Plautius' bridgehead
foundation of monumental arch — 'Richborough Cross'
Richborough Saxon Shore Fort

Richborough Island from the mainland. Carry on along the noticeable Roman causeway and cross the bridge over the brook.

3. Turn left along the modern road. Turn right up the footpath across the line of the Roman road, not visible today. Keep going till you come to a trackway.

Below: *A sheepfold on the Roman road opposite Richborough Farm, just before the Roman road descends to cross the Fleet Channel by causeway.*

4. Turn left down the trackway to Cooper Street, rejoining the Roman road to cross the bridge. The hamlet of Cooper Street stands on artificially embanked marshland, with a rectangular promontory of land between straight fen ditches.

5. It is possible to follow the line of the Roman road, now dwindled to a line of connecting footpaths, all the way from Cooper Street to Ash, although the road has been ploughed out and the footpaths are not well marked. Cross the bridge and turn right. After a short distance, turn left over a stile and go straight across the field towards the glasshouses. Continue along the overgrown path, skirting to the right around the tomato nurseries which are built across the line of the road.

6. Cross the minor road and continue to the bypass.

7. Continue along the pathway over the field and then beside the playing fields to go along the passageway

between the houses into Ash. The Roman road comes out on to the main street just to your right. Griffin Cottage is now built on it.

8. Finish the walk at Ash.

Left: *Canterbury cathedral now stands within the walls of the Roman town, destination of this road.*

Below: *The hamlet of Cooper Street stands on artificially embanked land and today's marshy hollows were probably open water in Roman times.*

THE ROMAN ROAD FROM ASH TO DOVER

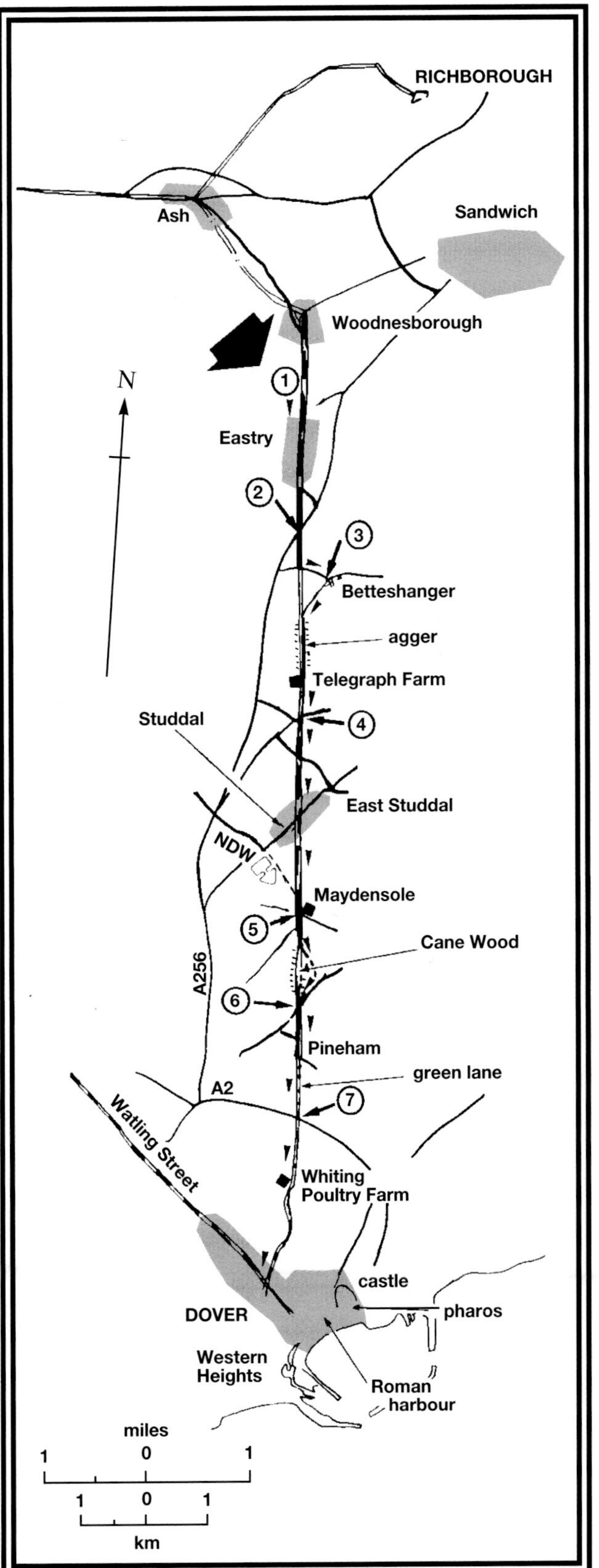

The Roman road from Richborough forked at Ash, one branch heading west to Canterbury and the other heading South East towards Dover and providing a direct land communication between the two prominent ports, the civilian one at Richborough and the naval base at Dover. It was probably built in the mid-AD 40s as a military link between the two ports, both of which were supplying the army at that time.

This Dover road runs South East from Ash, its course no longer visible, to Woodnesborough church, on a prominent hill which was used as a sighting point by the road engineers. Here the road turns south and maintains the same alignment as it hurries along the North Downs all the way to Dover. It passes through Eastry as the modern High Street and then a lane follows the line to Betteshanger. It forges ahead through the parkland as a fine *agger*, though the modern road turns aside. Beyond Betteshanger a line of little lanes and green trackways follow it along the top of the North Downs, an open, windswept route across the grassy chalklands, with expansive views to the sea. When it reaches the edge of the hills above Dover it has arrived, by expert surveying, at the head of a coombe down which it descends to the town and its junction with Watling Street.

Dubris was the most important Roman naval base in Britain, the headquarters of the Roman British fleet (*Classis Britannica*). The Roman harbour lay further inland than the present one, bounded by Castle Street, Russell Street and King Street. The Romans constructed two lighthouses, one on each headland overlooking the harbour, and one of these, the *pharos*, survives close against St Mary's Church within the walls of medieval Dover Castle. At night a beacon-fire would have blazed from its top to guide shipping in the Channel. The other Roman lighthouse, set on the Western Heights, was described by John Leland in the 1530s and stood until the end of the 17th century.

The prosperous town associated with the harbour seems to have been on the western side of the valley and in later Roman times Dover was the site of one of the great forts of the Saxon Shore. Nothing of this fort remains standing, and even its location was lost until rescue archaeology in 1970 identified the site.

2 A WALK FROM EASTRY TO DOVER

A walk from Eastry to Dover over the North Downs on this early Roman road connecting the route centre at Ash, with its easy link to the great port at Richborough, and Dover,

Above: *Betteshanger church.*

headquarters of the Roman navy in Britain. The road now runs along lanes and trackways and is followed in part by the North Downs Way.

Instructions

1. Start at Eastry. Walk south along the Roman road.

2. Cross the Eastry bypass (A256) and continue south along the Roman road, now a lane. At the T-junction the Roman road carried straight on through the grounds of Northbourne Park School (Betteshanger Park), but the right of way does not follow it. Turn left along the minor road past the school entrance.

3. Turn right up the little lane towards Betteshanger church. Keep on the lane past the church and through the belt of trees to rejoin the line of the Roman road which comes in from the right. Head straight across the field on the Roman line and continue past Telegraph Farm and a wood, to reach a minor road.

IOS maps:
1:50,000 Landranger sheet 179

1:25,000 Pathfinder sheets
1212 [Sandwich & Deal]
1232 [Dover]

Distance: 8½ miles

Pubs/hostelries:
On the walk: Eastry, Studdal, Dover

Roman engineering works:
agger visible in places
terraceway

Other antiquities:
Roman lighthouse at Dover
painted house at Dover

4. Go straight across the road beneath the beech trees and keep on along the lane, which bends slightly on and off the straight Roman line. Go over the next crossroads, and continue to the crossroads at Studdal. Go straight over and carry on along the lane, which is joined from the right by the North Downs Way all the way to Dover.

5. At Maydensole Farm go straight over the crossroads and along the lane for 100 yards. Here the modern lane turns to the right off the Roman line. Turn left on to the byway. This crosses the Roman road and then runs parallel to it past Cane Wood, where the Roman *agger* can be seen. It rejoins the Roman line just before reaching the lane.

6. Cross the lane and continue to Pineham. Turn left through Pineham — which is only two farms — and bear right on to the byway along the Roman road.

7. Cross the A2 and continue to Whiting Poultry Farm. Here the Roman road descends down a coombe to Dover. Cross the railway and pass the cemetery. Turn right along Frith Road, still on the Roman line, and follow it into Dover.

Above: *Eastry, where the walk begins.*
Left: *The Roman road south of Telegraph Farm.*

THE LONDON-LEWES WAY

The London-Lewes Way is the best known of the three 'iron routes' that ran south across the Weald to serve the extensive iron mining operations of the region. These routes do not follow the rigid alignment of Roman military highways: heavily laden waggons had to travel them, and so steep climbs and precipitous descents had to be avoided at all costs. Moreover, the nature of the Weald, broken by steep-sided, curving valleys, and crossed by numerous ridges would not allow the layout of any straight road. None the less, the London-Lewes Way was skilfully engineered to keep to as direct a line as possible and it frequently crosses high ground along ridgetops, giving superb views.

This is an early road, built in the second half of the 1st century AD, for iron was exploited early on in Britain's days as a Roman province. Like the London-Brighton Way, this road was designed to pass through the iron

Above: *The Weald is still wooded as it was in Roman times when the forests provided charcoal for the numerous iron furnaces and timber for the Roman navy.*

mining district to the rich corn producing lands of the South Downs, Rome's granary in Britain.

The London-Lewes Way is a 'lost' road, passing through the countryside like a ghost. It branched from the great Watling Street at Peckham, heading to the top of the North Downs at Tatsfield, near Biggin Hill. Here, though the road is no more, its shadow survives. South of Wickham Court the Kent-Surrey boundary faithfully follows the line of the London-Lewes Way. So faithfully, in fact, that where the Roman road crossed a deep coombe at Skid Hill by a sharp V-shaped detour which eased the gradient for waggon traffic, the county boundary, too, makes a V-shaped kink in its otherwise straight line.

The road changes alignment on the crest of the North Downs, and passes through fields and woods, turning to the South East to descend Crockham Hill as a terraceway, initially slightly below the B269 and then merging with it past Earlylands. The B269 on Crockham Hill used to be known as Stone Street, a name redolent of Roman roads! Edenbridge High Street lies on a fine, straight alignment of the Roman road which continues to Cobhambury Farm. Beyond this point it has fallen out of use, coinciding in only a few places with modern roads and doing its best to hide entirely from view. In this way the road undergoes a complete personality change and passes furtively through Holtye to ascend on to Ashdown Forest. Here, among the heath and the pines, it makes a change of alignment to the south-west and picks its way across the heathlands, its *agger* and side ditches visible in places, to make a final change of alignment at Camp Hill and run along the wide Ouse valley to Malling Down near Lewes.

The fame of the London-Lewes Way rests on the preservation at Holtye, near East Grinstead, of a length of

Above: *Looking along the line of the London-Lewes Way on Ashdown Forest.*

Top: *The Roman London-Lewes Way as a private lane near Edenbridge.*

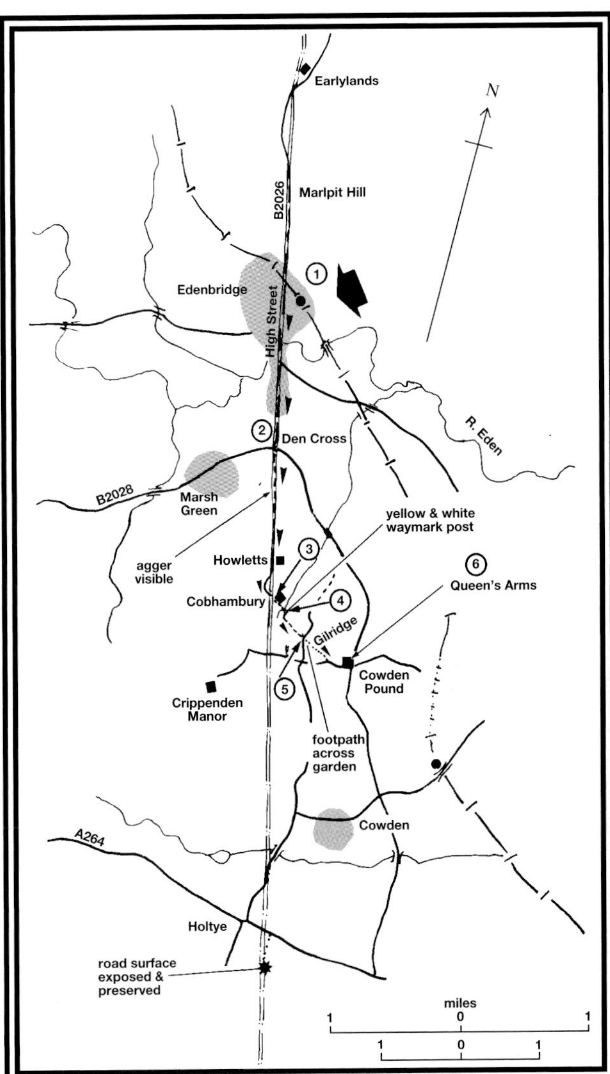

the road showing its rutted surface metalled with iron cinders. Another section of the road, a heath-clad *agger*, is preserved behind a low fence on Ashdown Forest near Camp Hill.

The best walkable stretch of the road includes delightful Edenbridge High Street and passes on to high ground beyond Cobhambury.

3 A WALK FROM EDENBRIDGE TO COWDEN POUND

This is a short, fairly easy walk along a commercial Roman road.

Instructions

1. Start at Edenbridge Town station. Walk west and turn left along the High Street. Continue along the pavement to Den Cross.

2. Keep straight on along the private lane past Howlets Farm to Cobhambury.

3. Cross the stile and go down the field crossing over the Roman line. Go over the stile and down the track into the wooded dell. Bear left with the track over the stream to the waymark post.

OS maps:
1:50,000 Landranger sheets
187 and 188

1:25,000 Pathfinder sheet
1228 [Tonbridge and Edenbridge]

Distance: 3½ miles

Pubs/hostelries:
On the walk: Edenbridge, Cowden Pound

Roman engineering works:
agger visible in places

4. Turn right and go up the path, crossing a plank bridge and bearing to the left into Cobhambury Wood. Continue up the woodland path and cross over the stile near the equestrian centre. Go over another stile on to the private road at Gilridge.

5. Cross the private road and follow the footpath emerging over the corner of a rough field to the stile on to the road. Turn left along the road to Cowden Pound.

6. Finish at the Queen's Arms.

THE SUSSEX GREENSAND WAY AND THE MIDDLETON TRACK

The Sussex Greensand Way was the major cross-country route designed to link the highways running south from London with numerous local roads and tracks. It runs along the greensand ridge of higher, drier land which parallels the steep northern slope of the South Downs within the verdant Vale of Sussex. It follows this ridge as a deliberately planned road, set on several alignments necessitated by the northward curve of both chalk and greensand at

Wolstanbury Hill. It is a well engineered road with no steep climbs or descents such as characterise most cross-country routes, yet almost everywhere it has gone out of use and passes unseen across the fields. Ironically, the ancient ridgeway route which it replaced, and which ran on a swithchback course on the top of the chalk hills, has in part survived and come down to us as the South Downs Way.

Rome's chief source of wealth was agriculture, notwithstanding her mining activities, and in Roman times, as now, the chalky downland soils were favoured for the production of corn. The Sussex Greensand Way ran through a prosperous area with numerous villas, the great estate houses, lying in sheltered locations, and several temples up on the breezy downs.

Above: *The agger of the Sussex Greensand Way runs alongside the track at Plumpton Cross.*

Left: *View across the Weald from the Middleton track on the top of the South Downs. The Sussex Greensand Way crosses middle of the picture from right to left past the line of houses and Streat Church.*

This Roman road branched from the London-Lewes Way at Barcombe Mills, just north of Lewes in the Ouse valley. It runs due west over fields and is briefly in use as a lane at East Chiltington. It is marked by a hollow way on the north side of the lane to Plumpton Cross, while its *agger* runs beside the lane at Plumpton Racecourse towards Streat. It continues unseen north of Ditchling and on through Keymer to cross the Roman London-Brighton Way at Hassocks, north of the present-day crossroads of the A273 and B2116. At this Roman crossroads lay a large Roman cemetery.

At Hurstpierpoint a new alignment was

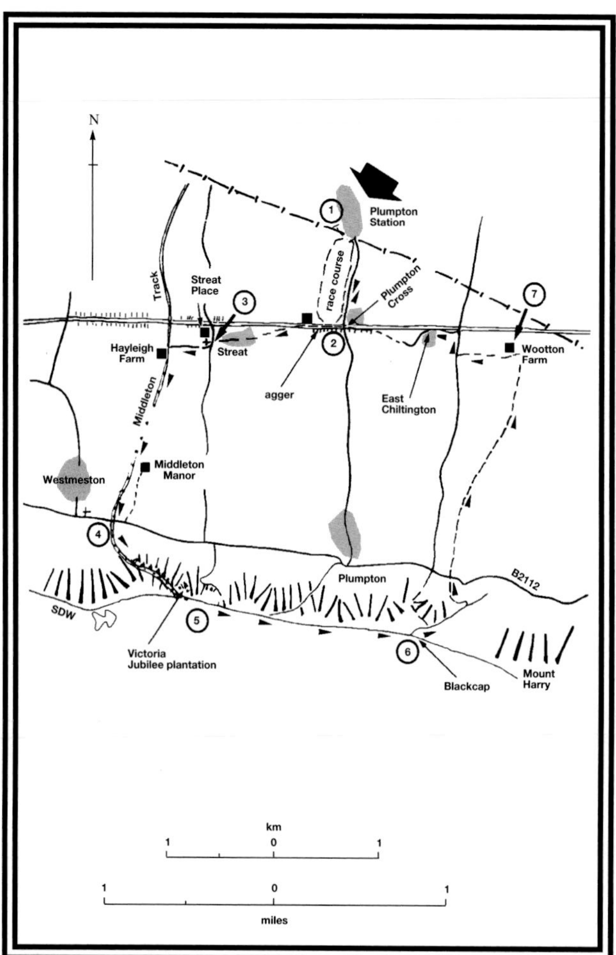

set, heading through Bedlam Street and along the lane over Oreham Common to Woods Mill, south of Henfield. Here it crossed the River Adur at Streatham Farm. The road turned west again to pass close to a villa at Buncton under the shadow of Chanctonbury Ring, with its Iron Age hillfort and Roman temple, before turning more to the north-west, to arrive at West Chiltington Common. It crossed the little River Stor and then, raised on a causeway, ran across the Arun marshes and over the tidal river to join Stane Street at Hardham.

This is a secretive, slumbering road, but well rewards exploration. The best walk starts at Plumpton, and links the surviving stretch with the pre-Roman Middleton Track, which crosses the Sussex Greensand Way just north of Hayleigh Farm near Streat. The track heads up on to the South Downs, mounting Streat Hill as a typically Romanised terraceway, 20 feet wide to begin with and then narrowing to about 10 feet in width as it nears the top of its climb, and joining the ancient ridgeway. From here, you can look down across the Weald and the line of the Roman road.

4 A CIRCULAR WALK/CYCLE RIDE AT PLUMPTON

This circular walk or cycle ride follows the main east-west route in South East England and passes along a Romanised trackway on to the South Downs, giving magnificent views over the Weald.

Instructions

1. Start at Plumpton. From the station walk south on the minor road till you come to the racecourse entrance.

2. Turn right along the trackway. This is along the line of the Sussex Greensand Way and the substantial *agger* lies on your left. Continue along the trackway, which bears away from the Roman road although still following its general line.

3. Arrive at Streat and turn left. Cross the minor road and bear right along the trackway past the church, parallel to the Roman road, which lies to the north. When you arrive at the little lane turn left on to it past Hayleigh Farm. This is the Middleton Track. Keep going along the Middleton Track past Middleton Manor till you reach the B2112.

4. Cross the B-road to the bridleway opposite. This is the continuation of the Middleton Track. Follow the bridleway as it climbs the downs, becoming a most pronounced Romanised terraceway as it passes above the Victoria Jubilee Plantation.

OS maps:
1:50,000 Landranger sheet 198

1:25,000 Pathfinder sheet 1288 [Burgess Hill]

Distance: 8 miles

Pubs/hostelries:
On the walk: East Chiltington
Nearby: Plumpton, Ditchling

Roman engineering works:
agger visible in places
terraceways

Other antiquities:
tumuli

Above: *Streat Place on the Sussex Greensand Way.*

Left: *Climbing up the downs scarp on the Romanised Middleton Track.*

5. Bear left to join the South Downs Way to Blackcap.

6. Turn left to descend from the downs. Keep going downhill and then leave the trackway and bear left down to the B-road. Cross the B2112 and follow the bridleway northwards. Keep going along it for about 1½ miles till you reach Wootton Farm.

7. Turn left along the concrete farm drive to the road and then turn right. Go along the minor road for 200 yards and turn left. You are now back on the line of the Sussex Greensand Way. Continue along the Sussex Greensand Way to the pub. Here the lane bears south but the Roman road carries straight on. Follow the lane to the church, and turn right to follow a trackway which bears back to the Roman road. Follow the line of the Roman road between houses and back to the road at Plumpton.

THE ROMAN ROAD FROM SEAFORD TO RIPE

INCLUDING THE FAMOUS 'RABBIT WALK'

The Seaford-Ripe road is a purely local Roman road. It runs from the coastal hillfort and small Roman settlement at Seaford Head over the South Downs to Ripe, where there was a Roman land settlement scheme for time-expired soldiers.

Corn was the great Roman crop

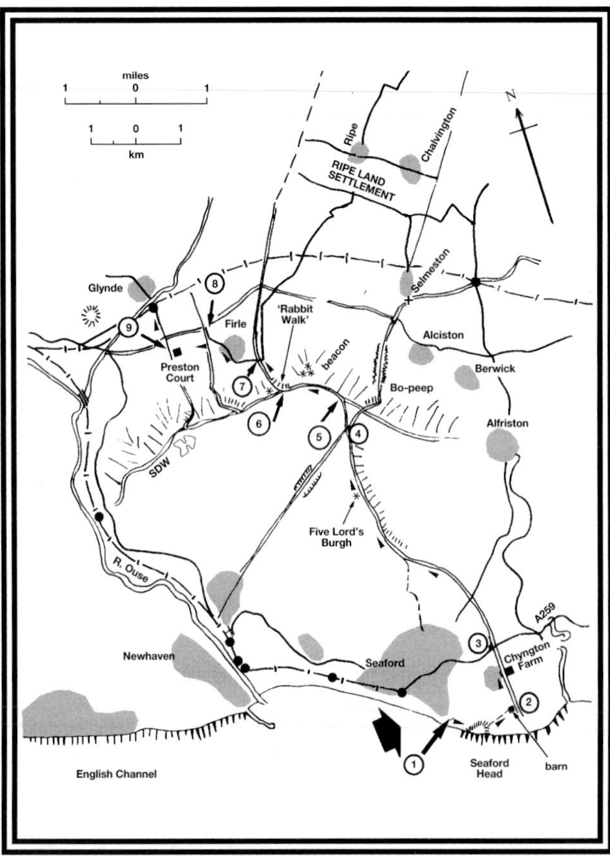

of the South Downs. From here the grain was transported to destinations as far-flung as the Imperial granaries of Rome, whose citizens were all provided with free Empire-grown corn, and the granaries of the garrison troops of the north of England. It would have travelled this local road at the start of its journey.

The Seaford-Ripe road heads inland from the windy heights of Seaford Head, where the walk begins, with magnificent views eastwards along the chalk cliffs to the Seven Sisters. It passes Chyngton Farm to reach the wide open downland on the edge of a magnificently steep, wooded coombe. Here it turns to the north-west to keep to a ridge of land above the steep valley side. Traces of its Romanisation show in the clever terracing along this stretch. It is still in use as a track, and passes the tumulus known as Five Lord's Burgh and crosses another local Roman road. It continues on to Firle Beacon, which is crowned by a superb group of tumuli commanding great misty views across the expansive Weald. It then turns westwards, used by the South Downs Way for 700 yards, and descends the steep scarp face of the downs on the 'Rabbit Walk' to the little village of Firle, tucked neatly beneath the guardian bulwark of Firle Beacon.

The Rabbit Walk is a beautifully engineered Roman terraceway, the best known of many along the South Downs, and locally called 'borstals'. As with other terraceways, it runs on a uniform gradient of about five degrees and was constructed by cutting away the hillside above, thus forming a ledge with an outward slope so that it would not be gullied on the inside.

The Rabbit Walk is a wonderful sight as it descends the hillside, though from the top you would not guess its existence. In 1930, Cecil Curwen the great Sussex archaeologist complained that it had been 'damaged by cavalry action during the war' — presumably by mock charges up and down it. Sadly, enthusiasts biking on it in recent years have hugely accelerated its erosion.

Our walk leaves the Seaford-Ripe road at the foot of the downs as it can be followed no further, but a noticeable *agger* carries on the line across Firle Park to the west of Heighton Street. The road continued beyond the A27, though nothing can be seen of it today, and it formed the

OS maps:
1:50,000 Landranger sheets
198 & 199

1:25,000 Pathfinder sheets
1324 [Eastbourne and Seaford]
1308 [Newhaven and Polegate]

Distance: 10 miles

Pubs/hostelries:
On the walk: Firle, Glynde
Nearby: Seaford, Lewes

Roman engineering works:
Rabbit walk terraceway

Other antiquities:
Seaford Head hillfort
Firle Beacon tumuli
Romano-British site on Charleston Brow

western boundary of the land settlement at Ripe.

5 A WALK FROM SEAFORD TO GLYNDE

This walk crosses on to the downs along a local road and descends along a terraceway known as the Rabbit Walk.

Instructions

1. Start on the cliffs to the east of Seaford near the Golf Club on Hawk Brow [TV490982]. Walk eastwards along the cliff-top path. Pass over the remains of the once formidable Seaford Head hill-fort, half of which has gone down the cliff face into the sea. Turn inland and go along the concrete roadway to the barn.

2. Walk inland down the hill along Chyngton Lane on the line of the Seaford-Ripe road. Carry on along the private road through the farmyard at Chyngton Farm and keep going along the lane to cross the A259.

3. Bear right into Chyngton Lane (north) and keep going along it. Cross a minor road and keep going along the trackway opposite sign-posted to Firle and Bo-Peep Borstal. Continue along the ridgeway track and the terraceway past the trig point (458ft) and Five Lord's Burgh tumulus and on to a junction of trackways.

4. Turn left on to the farm track heading for the posts at the old field boundary. Continue along the track to the old gate post at the junction with the Gardener's Hill road.

5. Turn right and follow the way-marked bridleway up the hill. Go through the gate on to the South Downs Way and turn left along it towards Firle Beacon, along the route followed by the Seaford-Ripe road.

6. Go through the kissing gate and bear right, leaving the South Downs Way, on to the more faintly marked path. This is the start of the 'Rabbit Walk', which is invisible from above so that it seems as if the path is about to plunge into a deep coombe. Follow the Rabbit Walk to the foot of the downs and go through the gate beside Firle Plantation.

7. Leave the Roman road here. Turn left along the lane into Firle, bearing round with it to the right.

Above: *The Seaford-Ripe Roman road on the top of the downs.*

Left: *The Seven Sisters chalk cliffs and the English Channel, looking to Seaford Head, start of the Roman road to Ripe.*

Left: *Starting off inland along the Roman road down Chyngton Lane.*

Above: *The Rabbit Walk Roman terraceway carries the road neatly down the steep scarp into the Weald.*

8. Turn right at the road junction and then left along the drive to Preston House. Just beyond Preston House turn left along the footpath till you come to the track at Preston Court.

9. Turn right, follow the track and cross the A27. Continue along the road opposite to Glynde.

STANE STREET

The Roman road from London to Chichester

Stane Street is one of the most famous of Britain's Roman roads and neatly demonstrates Roman surveying methods. Between London and Ewell it adheres to a course following a straight line drawn between London Bridge and Chichester. Beyond Ewell there are several other alignments which carry the road on a course designed to avoid Leith Hill and a steep tract of the South Downs, but which lead directly to its destination. It is still a line of communication, with alternating stretches of busy main road and delightful green lanes, passing through woodland and meadow and over the downs. It is such a remarkable road that two equally attractive walks follow it over the

This is no ghostly highway, sliding like a moonbeam through the countryside, but very much a road with a purpose. The road is early and military in character, for all that it passed through the friendly territory of King Cogidubnus of the Regni, and was built in AD 43-44, hot on the heels of Vespasian and the II Legion, Augusta, as they set off on their south-western campaign, which was launched from Chichester. Stane Street provided Vespasian with an efficient means of communication with his commander, Aulus Plautius, camped near London and then at Colchester. The road was provided with posting-stations, two of which are well known, though little remains to be seen, at Alfoldean and at Hardham.

Oddly, this direct link between London and Chichester is not included in the Antonine Itinerary, where Route VII, London-Chichester, goes via Silchester, Winchester and Bitterne. Its omission may reflect the nature of the itinerary, showing that it relates to official 'progresses' from place to place and not the recommended shortest route between centres. An alternative explanation is that Stane Street, the military highway, outlived its usefulness and parts of it fell into disuse early on in Roman times. We do not know the answer.

Stane Street left London by the Roman bridge at Southwark and passed through Clapham, Balham and Merton. Beyond Morden the A24 follows the line to Ewell, with some vestige of the *agger* still visible along the boundary of Nonsuch Park. At Ewell the second alignment began, rising up on to the North Downs but not visible until the start of Walk 6 at Thirty Acre Barn, near Epsom, where a line of green lanes marks its route on to Mickleham Downs and along the Mole valley, where it is terraced. It bears a little to the south, descending to the river at Burford Bridge, where walk 6 ends.

At Burford Bridge Stane Street crossed the River Mole before turning south to Dorking. The A29 runs on it through Ockley, distinctly raised on its *agger* and known in former years as Stone Street Causeway. At Oakwood Hill the modern A29 bears off to the east but Stane Street continued ahead to Rowhook and through Roman Woods to bridge the River Arun and enter the Alfoldean posting station.

The A29 rejoins Stane Street here and forges ahead along it, straight as a ruled line, through Five Oaks, Billingshurst and Adversane to Pulborough. It crosses the Arun again at Pulborough Bridge, running on a causeway over the marshes. Here a new alignment was set, to meet the Sussex Greensand Way at Hardham posting station.

Beyond this posting station Stane Street passes behind Coldwaltham and Watersfield, and carries on to Hadworth Farm at the foot of the downs near Bignor

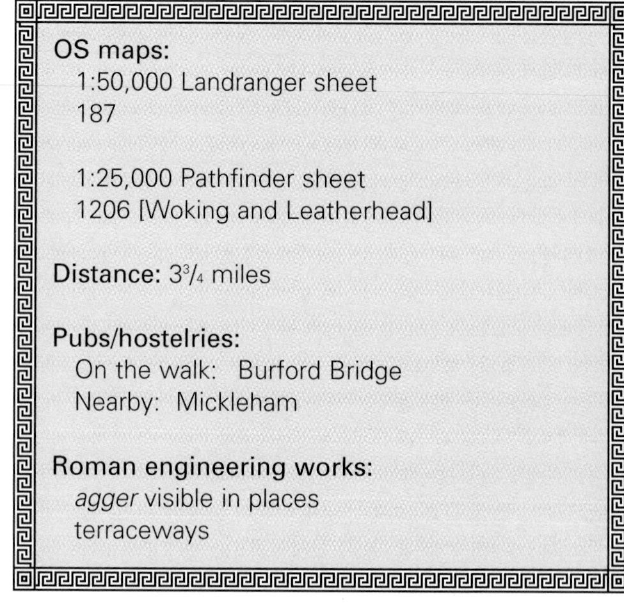

OS maps:
1:50,000 Landranger sheet 187

1:25,000 Pathfinder sheet 1206 [Woking and Leatherhead]

Distance: 3¾ miles

Pubs/hostelries:
On the walk: Burford Bridge
Nearby: Mickleham

Roman engineering works:
agger visible in places
terraceways

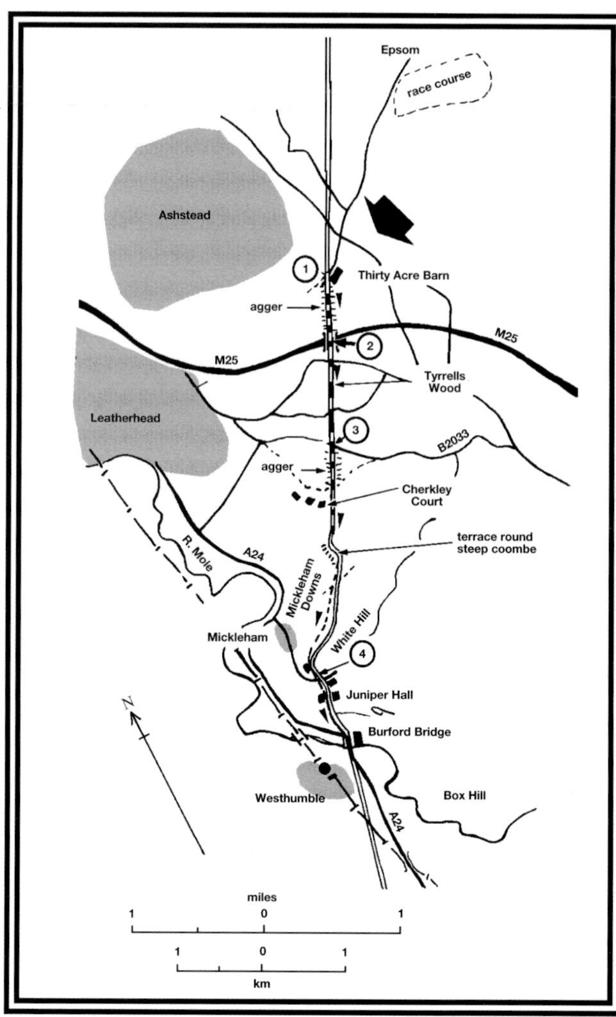

Villa. This was one of the largest villas in Roman Britain, the centre of a farming estate. It was probably owned by a wealthy Romano-British family with important connections at Chichester. The villa, which was first excavated in 1811, is famed for its beautiful 4th-century mosaics.

Here Stane Street turned southwards to climb the downs on a convenient spur, where this attractive walk begins. On reaching open downland, Stane Street becomes a tall, slender *agger*, set between ditches 84 feet apart. The shape of the *agger* here is mystifying, as it is very narrow and it seems impossible that ordinary processes of erosion should have accentuated it as a feature rather than spreading it out. Still, this narrow highway is fine to walk upon as the view unfolds ahead with the spire of Chichester Cathedral beaconing the old road to its destination against the wide backdrop of sea and sky.

This sets the traveller in exalted mood all through Eartham Wood and over Long Down, where the *agger* widens to a remarkable 60 feet. The A285 runs along the Roman line for a quarter of a mile to Seabeach, where Stane Street runs up a field and is joined by a trackway over Halnaker Hill, with a fine view ahead to the green spire of Chichester Cathedral. At Warehead Farm the A285 swings on to the line again and follows the Roman road through Halnaker, where the walk ends, and on to Westhampnett. Here the two roads diverge briefly, but the main road rejoins the Roman line and uses it right into Chichester.

6 A WALK FROM EPSOM TO BURFORD BRIDGE

This walk follows Stane Street, now a wide bridleway, over the North Downs.

Instructions

1. Start at Thirty Acre Barn [TQ197569], at the end of the lane called Shepherd Walk. Stane Street heads off south-west, along the left-hand pathway.

2. Continue over the M25. Keep going along Stane Street through the little woodland to the minor road. Cross the minor road and continue through Tyrrells Wood and over the golf course to the B2033.

3. Cross the B2033 and carry on along the Roman road past Cherkley Court on to Mickleham Downs. Turn right at the head of the coombe, keeping to Stane Street, which resumes its south-westerly alignment along White Hill, though the modern track diverges from it.

4. Follow the track down Juniper Hill with the Mole valley on your right. The Roman road runs parallel to the track as a hollow way just up the hillside. When you reach the minor road the electricity transformer is actually built in the hollow of Stane Street. Turn right here to the B-road, which soon rejoins the Roman line, and descend past Juniper Hall Field Centre to Burford Bridge.

Above: *Stane Street, now a terraceway, rounds the head of a combe on Mickleham Downs.*

Left: *The Stane Street, as a green lane near Thirty Acre Barn.*

Below: *Stane Street descending to Burford Bridge.*

Bottom: *Pines alongside Stane Street in the Mole Valley.*

OS maps:
1:50,000 Landranger sheet
197

1:25,000 Pathfinder sheets
1286 [Cocking and Sutton]
1305 [Chichester and Bognor Regis]

Distance: 6¼ miles

Pubs/hostelries:
On the walk: Halnaker
Nearby: Sutton, Eartham

Roman engineering works:
high and conspicuous *agger* with side-ditches
terraceway

Other antiquities:
Bignor Roman villa

Below right: *High agger of Stane Street between its widely spaced ditches on Bignor Down.*

Below: *Fingerpost on the downs pointing the ways to Londinium and Noviomagus.*

Right: *Looking to Chichester along Stane Street on Halnaker Hill.*

7 A WALK FROM BIGNOR TO HALNAKER

This lovely walk takes us from the Roman villa at Bignor over the South Downs to Halnaker.

Instructions

1. Start at Bignor [SU983144]. Follow the footpath in the south-west corner of the village over the stream and to the left, climbing steeply up through the woods. Turn right along the lane. Stane Street runs as a parallel terrace just beneath the lane.

2. Arrive at the Gumber Corner car park where the South Downs Way comes in from the left. Go straight through the car park following the sign to *Noviomagus*. Stane Street comes in from the right. Turn left on to it and continue through Eartham Wood.

3. Cross the minor road. Go over the stile, through the woodland and downhill. Go through the gate on to the A285.

4. Bear left along the A285 for a quarter of a mile to the lay-by near the entrance to Seabeach House, where it swings off the Roman line.

5. Follow the footpath on the line of Stane Street over the stile and up Halnaker Hill. Carry on over the hill to Warehead Farm.

6. Cross the A285, which now takes up the line of Stane Street, and go along the footpath opposite parallel to Stane Street to Halnaker. You can drive along Stane Street right into Chichester.

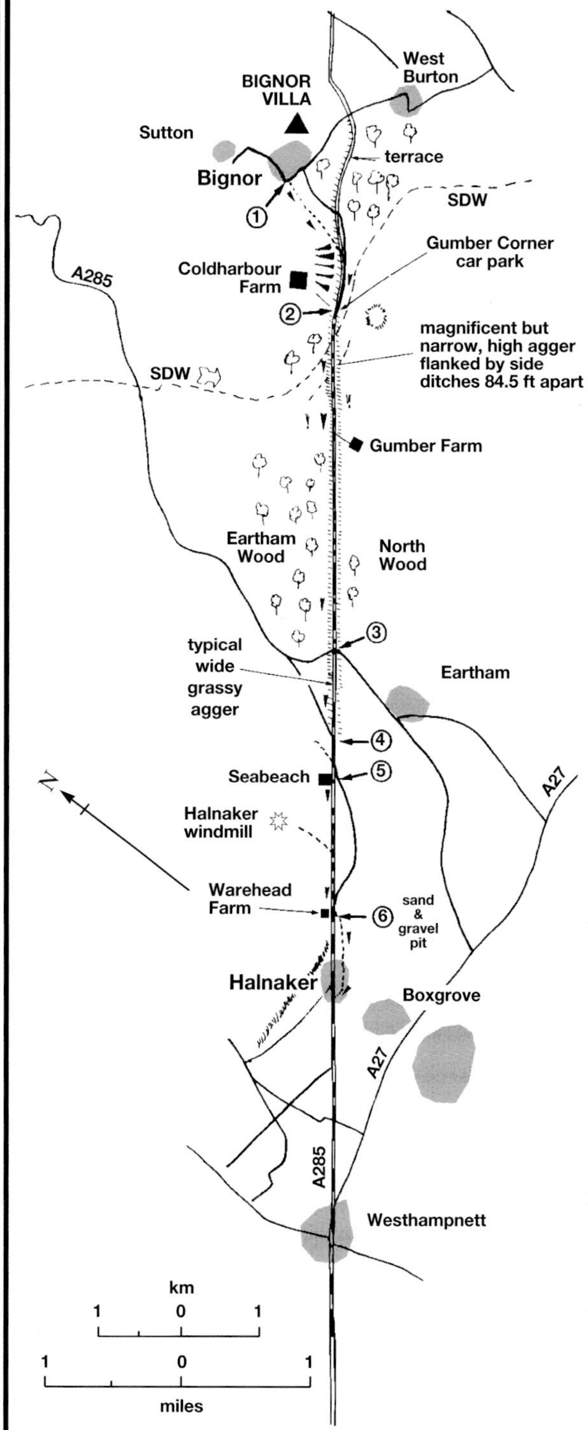

West Burton
BIGNOR VILLA
Sutton
terrace
Bignor
SDW
①
Gumber Corner car park
A285
Coldharbour Farm
②
magnificent but narrow, high agger flanked by side ditches 84.5 ft apart
SDW
Gumber Farm
Eartham Wood
North Wood
③
typical wide grassy agger
Eartham
④
Seabeach
⑤
N
A27
Halnaker windmill
Warehead Farm
⑥
sand & gravel pit
Halnaker
Boxgrove
A27
A285
Westhampnett
km
1 0 1
1 0 1
miles

— II — THE SOUTH WEST

'The Romans' says Isidore,
'made roads almost all over the world to have their marches
in a straight line and to employ the people' and criminals were frequently
condemned to work at such roads ...'

WILLIAM CAMDEN
Britannia (1789)

Above: *The formidable ramparts of Maiden Castle, a stronghold of the Durotriges, stormed by Vespasian and the IInd legion, Augusta in AD 43-44.*

The Romans in the South West

Though trading links with Rome had been established at least a hundred years before, direct Roman involvement began with the arrival in AD 43-44 of the II Legion, Augusta, under its legate the future Emperor Vespasian, a man at once determined and humane.

Vespasian and the II Augusta were probably dispatched to the South-West by Aulus Plautius while he waited for the arrival of the Emperor Claudius to march on Colchester. Vespasian, who had distinguished himself at the battle of the Medway, moved along the line that was later to be followed by Stane Street and launched his initial attack on the South West from the friendly territory of King Cogidubnus at Chichester, where the fleet that had brought the Roman army across the English Channel could find safe anchorage. Vespasian turned westwards, though the actual route he took is unknown, and, supported by his fleet and by a developing network of roads, he was able to advance swiftly into the territory of opposing tribes.

In the words of the famous Roman historian, Suetonius, Vespasian fought 30 battles, reduced 20 hillforts, conquered two warlike tribes and captured the Isle of Wight. It is certain that one of the tribes was the bitterly anti-Roman Durotriges of Dorset and southern Somerset. They fought hard, though in vain, to defend their hillforts from legionary attack. The remains of many of the defenders have been found severely mutilated, testimony to the

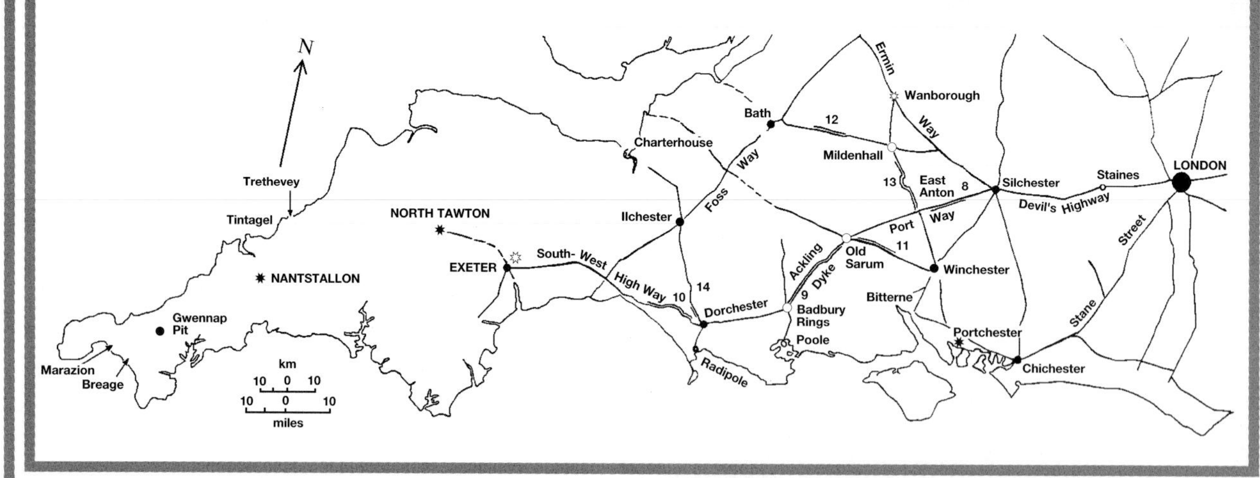

ferocity of the Romans once inside the hillforts. In storming Maiden Castle, near Dorchester, Vespasian's troops bombarded the defenders using ballista, engines of seige which fired specially manufactured iron-headed bolts, and had an effective range of about 400 yards. Excavations in the associated war cemetery have brought to light the remains of some of the slain, one of whom had a Roman ballista bolt lodged in his spine.

The Romans were victorious and pushed westwards. It is probable that the second 'warlike tribe' overcome by Vespasian was the Dumnonii of Devon and Cornwall. Certainly, by AD 55-57 a legionary fortress had been established at Exeter, though by this time, of course, Vespasian was no longer legionary legate. By AD 55-64 a permanent fort had been established as far west as Nanstallon, near Bodmin.

By the end of the first century the army had moved away from Exeter, testimony to the peaceful state of affairs in the area, and Exeter became a Roman town built on the normal grid-iron pattern. The natural resources of the region were exploited even sooner. Lead from the Mendips found its way to Pompeii, where it was used to make a cistern since found buried in volcanic ash from the great eruption of AD 79. The Mendip lead mined early on in the Roman occupation contained a high percentage of silver, so the ore was mined under military supervision for use in the imperial mint. Later on the silver-bearing ores were worked out and, as was usual Roman practice, the working of the lead mines passed into the hands of private contractors.

Cornish tin was first mined in the first century BC, before the Roman conquest, but the British mines closed when Rome overran Spain and exploited the tin mines there. The Cornish tin was not mined again, so far as we know, until the third and fourth centuries, when the Spanish mines became exhausted. Sadly for archaeology, later mining has more or less destroyed the Roman workings.

During the centuries of Roman rule the South West became a highly populated and civilised part of the province. Towns flourished and there were many villas.

Wool was another valuable product of the South West, and wool combs of Roman age have been found on the Wessex chalklands. Significantly, a specific article of woollen clothing, a heavy-duty hooded cloak, was known as the *byrrus britannicus*. It is not known, however, whether this meant that British wool was used for such clothes or merely that you would need it to protect you from British weather. Winchester (*Venta Belgarum*) is likely to have been the *Venta* referred to in a late Roman text as a centre of wool production. It is possible that during Roman times British wool was as highly regarded and as much of a money spinner as it was to become in the Middle Ages when the wealth made from wool went to build so many magnificent churches.

Above: *Sheep were probably an essential part of the economy of the South West in Roman times.*

The Roman Road System in the South West

The road system of South West England shows mastery of design and a grasp of the geography of the area. It is basically simple: one trunk route, known here as the South Western Highway, which runs westwards from London to Silchester and then south-westwards through Old Sarum and Badbury Rings hillfort, before turning west again to Dorchester and Exeter. It is likely that this road was planned, if not constructed, during Vespasian's campaign, creating a direct link with the developing route centre and port of London. Certainly, the heroic stretch known as Ackling Dyke, which crosses the Dorset Downs, has all the hallmarks of a road of conquerors. It is arguably the most magnificent piece of Roman road in Britain, a huge grassy *agger*, obviously designed to impress and intimidate the warlike Durotriges through whose territory it runs and across whose burial mounds and temples it slashes as ruthlessly as the II Legion, Augusta slashed the defenders of Maiden Castle.

Along the South Western Highway there were a number of centres from which roads radiated: Silchester, Old Sarum, Dorchester and Exeter. Winchester was a further centre of radial routes. In this way the South West was covered by a complex network of roads, some of which still await discovery. In addition, that most enigmatic of Roman roads, the Foss Way, runs across the West Country from Axminster in a north-easterly direction through Ilchester and Shepton Mallet to Bath.

It was at one time doubted whether true Roman roads were ever built west of Exeter, but Roman milestones found in Cornwall now testify to the existence there of Roman roads, though no trace of the roads themselves has been found. There must have been a Roman road on the north coast of Cornwall, for two milestones have been found close to each other at Trethevey and at Tintagel (the latter is now in Tintagel church). These milestones relate to two phases of road mending and their inscriptions allow them to be dated to AD 251-253 and AD 308-324 respectively.

The ghost of another Roman road stirs in the shadows further west where a milestone was found at Gwennap Pit in 1942. This has been resited in the garden of Mynheer Farm and dates from AD 238-244. Did this stone stand beside a road heading north-south and connecting the two tin-mining areas, or was it sited beside a road running lengthwise along the spine of the Cornish peninsula? We do not know. Two more Cornish milestones exist, both on the south coast, strongly suggesting a road in their vicinity. One is at Breage, north-west of Helston and was erected in the reign of Postumus (AD 258-268), the other, the most famous Roman milestone in Cornwall, is now cemented into the floor of the church at St Hilary near Marazion, but was set up originally in AD 306-307 'to the Emperor Caesar Flavius Valerius Constantinus Pius ...'

Above: *Litchfield church.* **Left:** *At Clap Gate on the Port Way.*

THE SOUTH WESTERN HIGHWAY

The Roman road from London to Exeter

This road was first of all a military highway built as a consolidating route which enabled the Romans to hold on to territory annexed by Vespasian and the II Legion, Augusta. It is likely that west of Badbury Rings (*Vindocladia*) it follows Vespasian's actual campaign route.

Vespasian subdued the South West very quickly, pushing at least as far west as Exeter (*Isca*), which had become an important military base, in fact a legionary fortress, by AD 55-57. It is likely that road-building commenced as soon as territory had been overrun.

Later, this Roman road served the peaceful purposes of commerce and administration, and the Antonine Itinerary follows it all the way from Old Sarum to Exeter. In yet later days, when Roman times were forgotten, it was given evocative names: 'The Devil's Highway', the 'Port Way' and 'Ackling Dyke'.

The South Western Highway headed west from London and bridged the River Thames at Staines or, as old records spell it, 'Stanes' — betraying its Roman origin. It then crossed the lonely forested heaths between Bagshot and Bracknell, known today as the Devil's Highway, to arrive at Silchester (*Calleva Atrebatum*), the tribal capital of the Atrebates.

At Silchester, this road turns south-west to continue straight to Old Sarum (*Sorviodunum*), known today as the Port Way, a name likely to derive from the Dark Age usage of the word 'port' to mean a market town. This is a masterly route, one straight alignment that runs for 36 miles whilst crossing the Hampshire Downs and several rivers. For the first 7½ miles it cannot now be seen, but up on the Hampshire Downs it becomes visible and heads resolutely south-west where a good walk follows it. It runs as a lane past Walkeridge Farm and then as a pathway alongside the three-mile-long wood known as Caesar's Belt, where snowdrops grow and larks wing heavenwards from the fields, scattering their songs on those trekking the Roman road below.

At Bradley Wood, where the walk ends, the 27-foot-wide *agger* is very well preserved, though no longer in use as a roadway. A lane joins the line and runs on it, in a very straight line, for some 2½ miles to East Anton (*Levicomagus*), near Andover, where it crossed the Winchester-Wanborough Roman road.

Beyond Andover the Roman line is picked up again by the minor road through Monxton and past the prominent Iron Age earthwork, Quarley Hill Camp. Here it turns a little more towards the south and heads straight for Old Sarum, 9½ miles distant, alongside the railway, with its *agger* in use as a trackway. It entered Old Sarum by the eastern gate.

Old Sarum is an ancient site: Stone Age, Bronze Age and Iron Age people were here; to the Romans it was *Sorviodunum*, to the Saxons it was *Searisbyrig*; it was refortified by Alfred the Great, burned down by the Danes and reinhabited. The Normans, to whom it was *Sarisberie*, built a fortress and a cathedral here and a town grew up around them, clustering around the foot of the hill. By 1220 it had become overcrowded and the water supply uncertain, and was abandoned. The tale is told of how a leading churchman realising that something had to be done, roused the citizens with the cry:

'In the Name of God, let us descend into the Meads ...' and thus modern Salisbury was founded two miles away in the 'meads', the flat, fertile land by the river.

Beyond Old Sarum, where our second walk on the South Western Highway begins, the road is set out on two basic alignments which take it the 25 miles to Badbury Rings. The first runs from Old Sarum on to the downs. Here the Roman road is crossed by the formidable, overgrown earthwork known as the Bokerley Dyke, a great bank and ditch, constructed in the twilight of Roman times to try to hold back the rapacious invaders who were rapidly reducing the province. It is perhaps the most striking example in Britain of an earthwork deliberately thrown across a Roman road to break the line of communication in the face of Saxon invaders, and neatly demonstrates that from being the great communicators of civilisation the roads could rapidly become the means whereby civilisation perished.

The road carries on over the Dorset Downs, deviating very little from the set alignment. The awe-inspiring length of the road on the downs is known as Ackling Dyke, and is certainly one of the outstanding Roman roads in Britain. It is a truly magnificent feat of engineering on a heroic scale, and the walker is dwarfed and overawed by its presence. This mighty road must have been built to convince the British that the Romans were in control, for across the dry downlands what other purpose can be ascribed to the huge *agger*, 40 feet wide and 6 feet high? Indeed, on Oakley Down Ackling Dyke clearly slices through the prominent group of tumuli. This must have been a deliberate act: the conqueror slighting the monuments of the conquered.

Ackling Dyke strides onward to Badbury Rings and seems originally to have been designed to pass to the east of this hillfort to Poole harbour. Possibly, this early line of the road was Vespasian's first connecting link between his fleet and the newly surveyed road to London. The main South Western Highway now turns more to the west and passes to the north of Badbury Rings as a magnificent *agger*, its line made the more imposing by three tall Roman tumuli that stand in a row beside it. The lane follows it to Shapwick, where the walk ends.

Beyond Shapwick, across the River Stour, the South Western Highway is not followed by any modern roads till it reaches Stinsford, a mile from Dorchester (*Durnovaria*). Here, standing on the north-facing verge of the B3150 is a slender, cylindrical Roman milestone, not quite *in situ*, since it was moved in the 19th century, but very near its original position. Sadly, any inscription it possessed has not survived the ravages of time.

From Stinsford, a branch-road leads off to the northwest through Charminster to join the Dorchester-Ilchester road while the South Western Highway runs straight through Dorchester to pass well to the north of the old stronghold of Maiden Castle. It then covers the 52½ miles to Exeter in three separate stages, cleverly adapted to the terrain over which it had to pass.

First, it keeps to the ridge of the downs in a series of straight alignments, followed today by lanes as far as Spyway. Beyond this it had to adapt its course to the difficult country of steep, irregular hills which prevented the building of an aligned road. Instead it runs along the hillsides through Loders to Bridport. This stretch of the road from just beyond Dorchester to Loders, with superb views to the south coast, is followed here as a cycle ride/drive.

OS maps:
1:50,000 Landranger sheet
185 [& 174 for circular walk]

1:25,000 Pathfinder sheet
1203 [Kingsclere and Ashmansworth]

Distance:
Walk 8a — 5 miles
Walk 8b — 12 miles

Pubs/hostelries:
Nearby: Hannington
Kingsclere

Roman engineering works:
agger visible in places

Other antiquities:
Ladle Hillfort

Below: *The huge agger of Acking Dyke on Oakley Down, clearly slicing through a group of earlier burial mounds.*

Above: *Three tall Roman-style tumuli stand beside the Roman road at Badbury Rings. Roman tombs were always found in stately procession alongside important roads.*

The road continues beyond Bridport through Chideock to Charmouth where it turns away from the coast over Fern Hill to Symonds Down, near Axminster. Once beyond Symonds Down the country becomes easier and the Romans were able to set out their road on long, straight alignments for the final 26 miles to Exeter.

8a A WALK ALONG THE PORT WAY

This walk follows the Port Way from White Hill to Clap Gate over the gently rolling Berkshire Downs.

8b A CIRCULAR WALK TAKING IN THE PORT WAY

This walk follows the Port Way over the downs to Clap Gate and returns to White Hill via Ladle Hillfort and Watership Down.

Instructions

1. Both walks start at the car-park on White Hill [SU518564] and take the byway towards Walkeridge Farm.

2. Turn right along the lane, which is on the Port Way, and follow it to the B3051. Cross the B-road and keep going along the short stretch of green lane. Emerge on to the road which comes in from the right and turns along the line of the Port Way. Continue along this road.

3. Where the road turns off to the left carry straight on along the Port Way, a permissive bridleway through the copse, and cross the track. Go through the gate and continue along the Port Way.

4. Cross the minor road with the woodland covered *agger* on your left and continue along to Clap Gate, on the old A34 [SU463522]. Walk 8a finishes here.

Walk 8b

5. To follow the circular walk leave the Port Way at Clap Gate and turn right along the old A34 to Litchfield.

6. Turn right opposite the farm and follow the track on to the downs.

7. Turn left just beyond the hill crest and follow the trackway on to Great Litchfield Down. Follow the Wayfarer's Walk past Ladle Hill-Fort [SU478568] along the crest of the scarp, along Watership Down and back to White Hill.

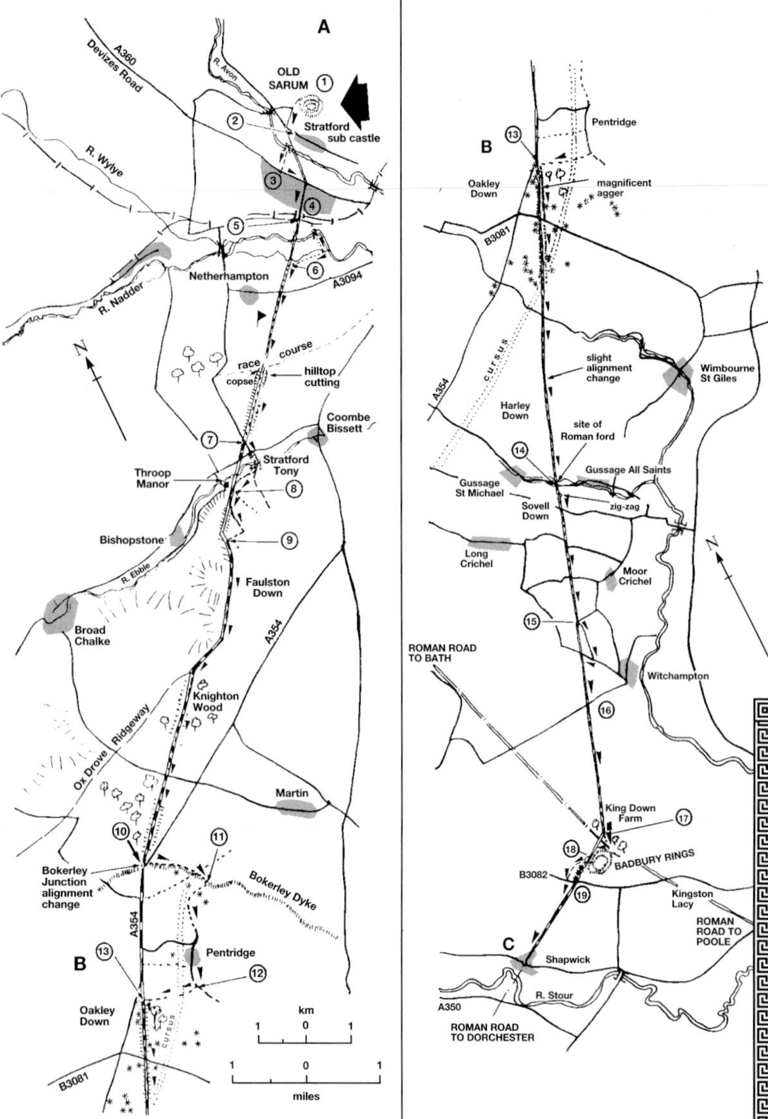

9 ACKLING DYKE

This is a long walk from Old Sarum to Shapwick and includes one of the most exciting stretches of Roman road in Britain.

Instructions

1. Start at Old Sarum. The Roman road cannot be followed for the first mile or so but it can be seen running round the earthworks at Old Sarum and then descending to the river. Go down the minor road to Stratford-sub-Castle. Turn right along Mill Lane to cross the River Avon by the footbridge and then turn left.

2. Follow the footpath uphill from the river to the Devizes road (A360).

3. Turn left along it to rejoin the Roman road just past the pub.

4. Turn right into Roman Road beside the cemetery. Turn right over the railway and left down Church Lane to Lower Bemerton.

5. Turn left along Lower Road, briefly leaving the Roman alignment. Turn right to follow the footpath over the two streams of the River Nadder and bear right back to the Roman road.

6. Turn on to the footpath along the Roman line to the A3094 between West Harnham and Netherhampton. Cross the main road and go up the approach road to the golf course, continuing up to the racecourse. Go through the copse and into the Roman cutting through the hilltop. Continue along the prominent *agger* on the other side to the minor road junction near Stratford Tony.

OS maps:
1:50,000 Landranger sheets
184 & 195

1:25,000 Pathfinder sheets
1241 [Salisbury (north)]
1262 [Salisbury (south) & Broad Chalke]
1281 [Shillingstone & Tollard Royal]
1282 [Fordingbridge]
1300 [Blandford Forum]

Distance: 25 miles

Pubs/hostelries:
On the walk: Stratford-sub-Castle
Shapwick
Nearby: Gussage All Saints

Roman engineering works:
great *agger* visible on the downs
cutting through hilltop
terracing
zig-zags

Other antiquities:
Bokerley Dyke
Old Sarum
Badbury Rings
tumuli
Dorset Cursus

Above: *Shapwick Cross, where the walk ends.*

change of alignment takes place, setting the Roman road fairly and squarely for the eastern side of Badbury Rings. Follow Ackling Dyke downhill and across the stream, site of a Roman ford, to the lane between Gussage St Michael and Gussage All Saints.

14. Cross the lane and follow the Roman road zig-zag up Sovell Down, beside a later chalk pit and continue across three more minor roads to the cross-roads by the old bus shelter [ST984080].

7. Turn left and go across the crossroads at Stratford Tony, continuing over the River Ebble. Turn right along the track past the church to Throope Manor House. Bear left here back on to the Roman road.

8. Carry straight on where a track turns to the left to follow the Roman road up Faulston Down.

9. Rejoin the Roman road. Continue along the Roman line. Cross over the Ox Drove back on to the straight alignment and keep going through Knighton Wood. Cross the minor road and continue to Bokerley Junction. At the high point of Bokerley Junction Ackling Dyke makes a change of alignment to the south, and is followed for the next 1½ miles by the main A354 and a walker's diversion must be followed.

10. Cross the road and head back along it for 200 yards. Turn right (east) along Bokerley Dyke. Cross another bridleway.

11. Turn right along the trackway through a large group of barrows. Follow the track through Pentridge.

12. Turn right where the track forks.

13. Turn left on to Ackling Dyke on its most famous stretch on Oakley Down, passing through the group of barrows and across the B3081. Keep going along this Roman road on its magnificent, prominent *agger*, across a lane and up on to Harley Down, where another slight

15. Here the Ackling Dyke carries on, but for the next half mile the right of way no longer follows it, necessitating a final short detour. Go straight over the lane on to the trackway which bears to the left. Continue along the trackway to the minor road. Turn right along the road for 300 yards and then left into the lane which follows Ackling Dyke for a mile.

16. Turn right on to the trackway which follows Ackling Dyke for the final 1½ miles to Badbury Rings. Clearly it was intended to continue south-east to Poole Harbour. The branch to Dorchester turns to the south-west just beyond King Down Farm.

17. Turn right along the bridleway with the woodland on your right and go over the stile. Bear right away from the hillfort to join the continuation of the South Western Highway, here a prominent *agger*, as it passes to the north of Badbury Rings.

18. Go through the car park and carry on down the modern track which passes to the right of the prominent Roman tumuli. The Roman road, visible as a faint swelling, passes to the left of them. Cross the B3082 into the lane opposite, which is on the Roman line, and follow it to Shapwick.

10 THE SOUTH-WESTERN HIGHWAY

This magnificent ride along the South-Western Highway from Winterbourne Abbas to Loders follows a line of lanes and gives wide views inland and along the coast.

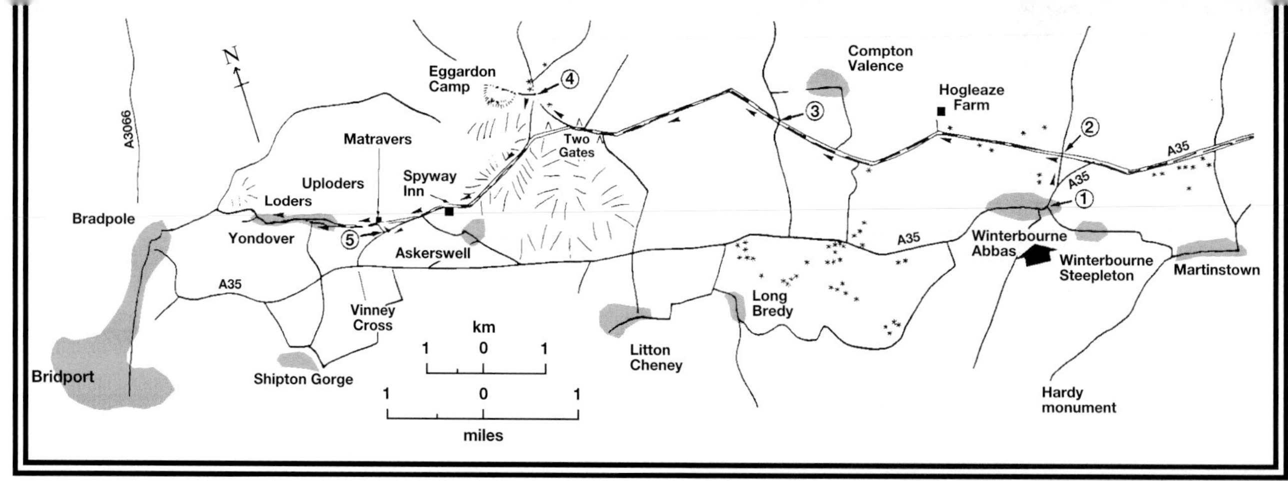

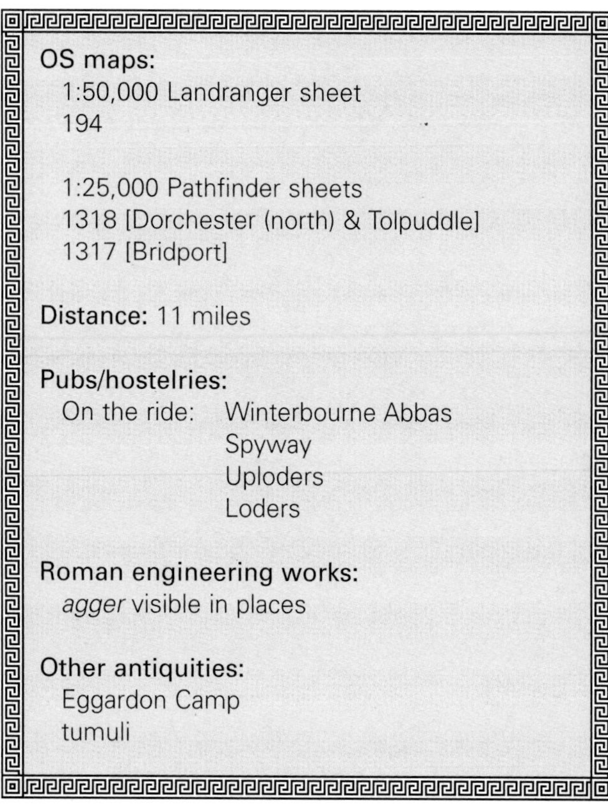

OS maps:
1:50,000 Landranger sheet
194

1:25,000 Pathfinder sheets
1318 [Dorchester (north) & Tolpuddle]
1317 [Bridport]

Distance: 11 miles

Pubs/hostelries:
On the ride: Winterbourne Abbas
Spyway
Uploders
Loders

Roman engineering works:
agger visible in places

Other antiquities:
Eggardon Camp
tumuli

Instructions

1. Start at Winterbourne Abbas. Follow the A35 briefly back towards Dorchester and then turn left along the minor road.

2. When you reach the crossroads at SY627911 turn left on to the Roman road. Continue along the Roman road, climbing ever higher along the ridge with two changes of alignment and wide views both to the north and the south.

3. Go straight across where the road bears to the right, and continue along the Roman road. Keep straight on past the masts to Two Gates. Here the Roman road carried straight on through the farm gate along a now broken-up track.

Left: *Walking the South Western Highway west of Dorchester.*

Below: *Ford. The Roman crossing has given its name to the hamlet.*

Leave the Roman line and follow the modern road to the crossroads at the trig point (820ft) opposite spectacular Eggardon Camp.

4. Turn left and follow the modern road downhill. It rejoins the Roman line and continues through Spyway.

5. Turn right and then left through Uploders, roughly along the Roman line, and continue through Yondover to Loders. From here it is easy to get to the coast at Bridport.

THE ROMAN ROAD FROM CHARTERHOUSE TO WINCHESTER

This was a commercial road built to transport silver-lead mined in the Mendips to Winchester and thence via Southampton Water to the Imperial Mint at Lyons. It was a route of great importance because the prosperity of the Roman Empire was underpinned by silver coinage and the Romans obtained their silver from lead by desilverisation.

This road must have been built early on after the initial pacification, since the highly argentiferous Mendip ores were mined just as soon as the Romans could get to them, which was within six years of the landing at Richborough. An ingot of Mendip lead, dated to AD 49 and countermarked by the II Legion was found near Southampton. Moreover, Mendip lead, identified by chemical tests, was found in a cistern at Pompeii, which was buried under the ashes of Vesuvius in AD 79. Indeed, the elder Pliny, who perished in the Vesuvian eruption, commented in his 'Natural History' that British argentiferous lead was so easily mined that a production limit had to be fixed to protect the existing silver-lead mines of Spain!

The Mendip mines, centred around Town Field, about 4 miles east of Priddy, near Charterhouse, were initially controlled by the army since mineral rights were vested in the Emperor. Increasingly, though, as the higher grade ores were worked out, the mining passed into the hands of commercial lessees. The small fort which guarded the workings spawned a rough little town which later developed its own brooch-making industry.

This road can be traced from Ubley Warren, half a mile south-east of the Roman lead mining community, and runs south-eastwards along the spine of the Mendips past the Castle of Comfort Inn and through Green Ore and Whitnell Corner. Shortly beyond this the line becomes obscure, but certainly passed north of Maesbury Castle hillfort and over a golf course. It crosses Foss Way at Beacon Hill and carries straight on to Long Cross, East Cranmore and Old Sarum.

It leaves Old Sarum, where the walk starts, to follow a remarkably direct route virtually due east along a delightful line of lanes and paths. Castle Road carries it to the River Bourne and the site of a Roman ford at Ford, whence it climbs up to Bracknell Croft. Here on the hilltop, beyond the A30, the Roman alignment turns slightly to the east and the road continues as a prominent, grassy *agger* down into Stock Bottom and, as a well engineered terrace, to Middle Winterslow — arriving there along 'Roman Road' — a reassuring name!

Here the Roman alignment changed again and is followed by a line of lanes to Buckholt Farm, where the walk leaves the Roman line, which descends to the site of the Roman station at *Brige*. A lane comes in on to the line past Hildon House, before the road descends to Bossington near Horsebridge in the Test valley.

The Roman road crossed the River Test at Bossington originally, it is thought, by a ford, but later by a bridge, the piles of which were reputedly unearthed in the 1780s when the Andover Canal was being dug at Horsebridge Lock. At the same time a lead ingot was found, dated to AD 60, presumably lost in crossing the river. The Roman road climbs out of the Test valley and, turning back to a more easterly course, becomes a conspicuous terrace on the side of a steep coombe beneath Ashley Down. It crosses Farley Mount Country Park and runs along Romsey Road for the final 1½ miles to Winchester, entering by the west gate.

The road fell out of use in Saxon times, for the Germanic invaders tended to eschew Roman lines. The Normans, though, revived the length between Old Sarum and Winchester as a royal road which passed close to the palace at Clarendon and through the excellent hunting grounds of Clarendon and Buckholt forests. We know for certain that King John used the old Roman highway during his hunting expeditions of the early 1200s. Yet for all this, the direct Roman road is now the forgotten route

OS maps:
1:50,000 Landranger sheets
184 & 185

1:25,000 Pathfinder sheets
1241 [Salisbury (north)]
1242 [The Wallops]

Distance: 11½ miles

Pubs/hostelries:
On the walk: Middle Winterslow
Broughton
Nearby: Stratford-sub-Castle
Salisbury

Roman engineering works:
prominent *agger*
terraceway

Other antiquities:
Old Sarum
site of Brige, Roman station near Buckholt Farm

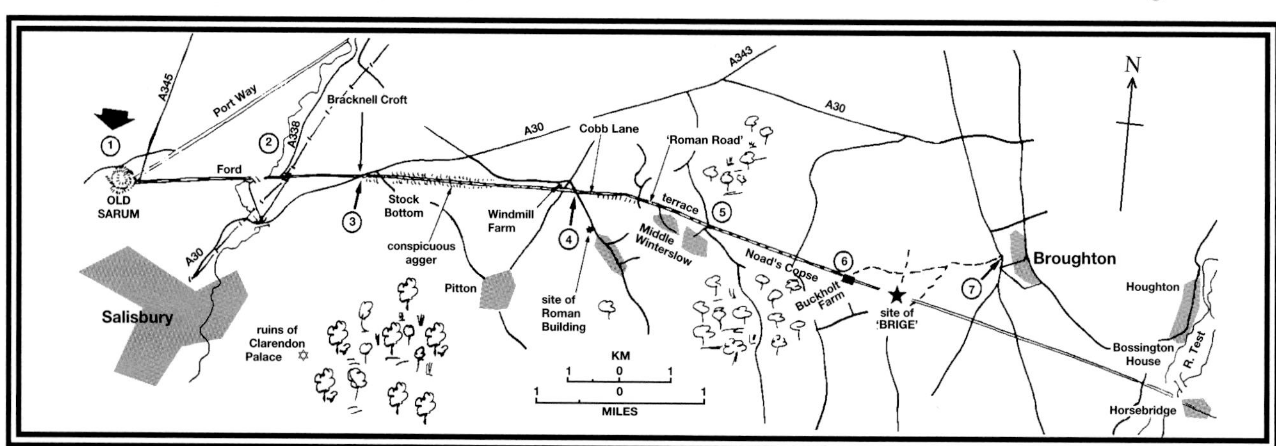

and the main road today detours to the north through Stockbridge. This must be partly because the old bridge over the River Test fell into disrepair and from the 1300s onward the historic line was once again abandoned.

11 A WALK FROM OLD SARUM TO BROUGHTON

This rural ramble follows an important commercial Roman route that later became a royal highway for Norman kings.

Instructions

1. Start at Old Sarum. Cross the A345 and follow the lane opposite, which is on the Roman road and cross the River Bourne at Ford. Bear left on the opposite bank and carry on along the lane.

2. Cross over the railway on the road bridge used by the A338 and turn left into Old Malthouse Lane which follows the Roman line up the hill to Bracknell Croft. Look back to Old Sarum from here. See how the road points directly to it.

Below: *Looking ahead from the ramparts of Old Sarum along the Roman road from Charterhouse to Winchester.*

3. Cross the A30 at Bracknell Croft to continue along the Roman road, which is on a most conspicuous *agger* and in use as a path. Cross the minor road and continue into Stock Bottom. Carry on along the Roman road and turn left at the road by Windmill Farm and then right at the crossroads, briefly leaving the Roman line.

4. Turn left into Cobb Lane back on to the Roman road to Middle Winterslow along a distinct terrace. Go straight into Middle Winterslow along 'Roman Road' and continue along 'The Causeway'. The next stretch of this Roman road is followed by the Clarendon Way, a modern long distance footpath between Salisbury and Winchester.

5. Turn left and then right at the little green and keep going through Noad's Copse. Go straight across at the junction and continue along the lane to Buckholt Farm. The Roman road carries straight on downhill to *Brige*, a Roman station between Old Sarum and Winchester.

6. Leave the Roman road and follow the official diversion through the farmyard. Follow the trackway over Broughton Down, continuing downhill to cross the B3084.

7. Turn right along the road and then left into Broughton.

THE ROMAN ROAD FROM SPEEN TO BATH

This was the Romans' main road to the west. For most of its 40-mile course, during which it crosses the Marlborough Downs, it runs high up on the hills, passing close to the great stone circle of Avebury, under the shadow of enigmatic Silbury Hill and past countless tumuli. The direct and uncompromising course across the downs suggests an original military use for the road, though this is not known for certain. It became the road to Bath which was then, as in the 18th century, a noted spa town. The spa was flourishing as early as the end of the first century AD and continued to attract visitors, taking advantage of the hot mineral springs, until the Saxons wrecked the place early on in the fifth century and it reverted to its former marshy condition.

The Bath Road branches from the Ermin Way, the Silchester-Cirencester road, on Sole Common, near Speen. Its course can be traced as stretches of handsome *agger* all the way to Froxfield. Here it turns west along the high ground north of the A4, but few definite traces can be found today. It descends to Mildenhall (*Cunetio*), crossing the Winchester-Wanborough road. Beyond

Marlborough it lies beneath the A4, but on Overton Hill it runs north of the modern road as an *agger*, 40 feet wide and 2-3 feet high. Beyond West Kennet the Roman road is again in use as the A4 as far as that puzzling prehistoric mound, Silbury Hill, the largest ancient man-made hill in Europe.

The Romans must have used Silbury Hill as a sighting point in their road survey, for here the Roman and modern roads part company. The A4 bears round Silbury Hill and the Roman road heads due west over the downs, becoming a conspicuous *agger* where it crosses the A361 south of Beckhampton, where the walk joins it. From here it can be followed on foot, an open downland walk along a green lane over Calstone Down, the old highway keeping tryst with the sky and seemingly part of a landscape which was ancient when the Romans came. On the steep slope of Morgan's Hill, on the edge of the Marlborough Downs, it is a beautiful Roman terrace. As it descends Morgan's Hill, it is joined by the Wansdyke, an earthwork constructed in the Dark Ages.

Wansdyke follows the Roman road all the way from Morgan's Hill to the hills above Bath. It was built to define the territory of Wessex in the face of Danish settlement in the Midlands, and extended to try to curb the expansion of

Mercia under Penda. It has preserved the alignment of the Roman road, but its purpose as a defensive boundary line put paid to the use of the Roman road as a highway. From Morgan's Hill onwards, with the exception of a short length of footpath approximately on the line, the Roman road is no longer a right of way. It is interesting to see how the fate of the road has been sealed by history.

The Roman road passes through Harley Farm and on over the fields as a footpath to Sandy Lane (*Verlucio*), a Roman site mentioned in the Antonine Itinerary, where this walk ends. Here it turns west again and continues over the hilly land for 10 miles to Ashley Wood, above Bath, where it turns through Bathford to join the Foss Way at Batheaston.

Left: *Cottages at Sandy Lane, Roman Verlucio.*

12 A WALK ON THE MARLBOROUGH DOWNS

This walk on the top of the grassy downs from Beckhampton to Sandy Lane passes through a landscape printed indelibly with the human past, from Neolithic times through the Bronze Age, Iron Age, Roman, Dark Age and Medieval.

OS maps:
1:50,000 Landranger sheet 173

1:25,000 Pathfinder sheets
1184 [Melksham]
1185 [Devizes and Marlborough]

Distance: 8½ miles

Pubs/hostelries:
On the walk: Beckhampton, Sandy Lane
Nearby: Avebury, Heddington

Roman engineering works:
distinct *agger*
terracing on Morgan's Hill

Other antiquities:
Dark Age earthwork — Wansdyke
site of Roman Verlucio

Instructions

1. Start at Beckhampton. Walk along the busy A361 for three-quarters of a mile to SU075683.

2. Turn right on to the Roman road to Bath. Continue on it along the Roman line over Calstone Down to Morgan's Hill, where the Wansdyke joins the Roman road, and past Smallgrain Picnic Area. Here the Roman road carries straight on, on its westerly course downhill to Harley Farm, followed by the Wansdyke.

3. Turn right along the road for 100 yards and then left along the bridleway which parallels the Roman road. When you reach the road at Stockley, turn left and then after 200 yards, just before you reach the entrance to Harley Farm, turn right.

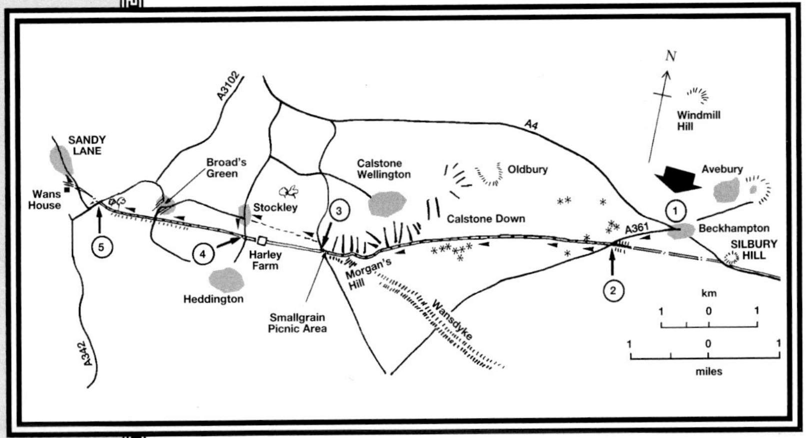

4. Follow the footpath along the line of the Roman road to Broad's Green. Cross the lane and continue along the Roman line to the corner of the wood. Here the Roman line turns to the north-west and the footpath follows it alongside the wood to the A3102.

5. Turn left along the A-road for 200 yards and then turn right at the crossroads to follow the narrow lane to Sandy Lane, site of *Verlucio*.

THE ROMAN ROAD FROM WINCHESTER TO WANBOROUGH
AND THE CHUTE CAUSEWAY

This was a purely civilian road, built to link two *civitas* capitals, Winchester (*Venta Belgarum*) and Cirencester (*Corinium*) via Wanborough, where traffic could transfer to the Ermin Way. It is probably a later road than those considered so far, but is none-the-less likely to have been built before the end of the first century AD.

The Wessex chalklands were rich pasturage for sheep and the economy was dominated by sheep ranching. In fact, Winchester was probably the site of a *gynaceum*, a government weaving centre serving the cottage industry which produced distinctive woollen cloth of a closely woven variety. Such cloth may have gone into the *byrrus britannicus*, a distinctive, heavy-duty woollen coat with a capacious hood.

This road was engineered to carry freight, for it avoids steep gradients at all costs. We can envisage the heavy goods waggons trundling along this road, creaking under the weight of precious bales of wool or rolls of British cloth, along with local pottery from Savernake and other goods.

OS maps:
1:50,000 Landranger sheets
174 & 185

1:25,000 Pathfinder sheets
1222 [Andover]
1202 [Ludgershall & Hurstbourne Tarrant]
1186 [Hungerford & Savernake Forest]

Distance: 18 miles

Pubs/hostelries:
On the walk: Charlton Down
Marten
Great Bedwyn
Nearby: Hatherden
Tangley
Wilton

Roman engineering works:
agger conspicuous in many places
Chute Causeway — nine separate alignments

Other antiquities:
Iron Age Fossbury Castle on Haydown Hill

The road runs straight from Winchester to the River Test. Once across the river, where there was probably a ford, the Roman road passes through Harewood Forest, and runs along the outskirts of Andover, followed in part by roads and lanes. At East Anton (*Levcomagus*) it crosses the Port Way, part of the great South Western Highway. Here there may have been a tile works to support many well-to-do villas nearby, and from here for the next 18 miles the Winchester-Wanborough Roman road can be followed on foot or by bike along lanes and trackways.

In Conholt Park the *agger* can be seen very clearly to the west of the modern road, passing like a shadow alongside a row of ancient Spanish chestnut trees, its silent guardians. See them with drifted snow on their noble boles in a biting east wind when the starlings chatter and a great lonely sense of the passing of time sweeps over the wintry parkland, and who knows what ghostly traffic you may see rumbling slowly along beside them? Then turn to look to your right to Conholt House in its dignified splendour: mellowing yellow stone with a red brick garden wall and glasshouses showing above it, the true descendant of a wealthy villa!

Beyond Conholt House, the Roman road runs along its most famous stretch, the 'Chute Causeway'. It has arrived on the verge of the deep Hippenscombe valley, and had it been a military road some way would have been found to cross this natural barrier more or less along the surveyed alignment. Instead, keeping to typically Roman short, straight lengths and abrupt, angular turns, the road describes a great semicircle to the west around the head of the deep coombe to rejoin the surveyed alignment on the farther side. In all, nine separate alignment changes are made in this manoeuvre, and the length of the road is twice as long as the direct route along the survey line. Obviously all the time taken up in following this detour was considered worthwhile. The initial east-west stretch of the route is raised on a wonderful *agger*, from which you can look down on the backs of hovering kestrels hunting in the valley below. Then the road bears back on itself to rejoin the survey line near Tidcombe and is still followed by a minor road on to Marten.

At Marten the Roman road continues over fields on the same north-westerly alignment and crosses the A338. Lanes carry on the line over the Kennet and Avon Canal, where it can be followed no more, and the walk ends.

The road continues past Savernake Forest to the east of the Grand Avenue and descends through Black Field to cross the river Kennet to the Roman town of Mildenhall (*Cunetio*), where a new alignment was set taking the road through Ogbourne St George and Chiseldon, where it crosses the M4. A final alignment, heading north-east,

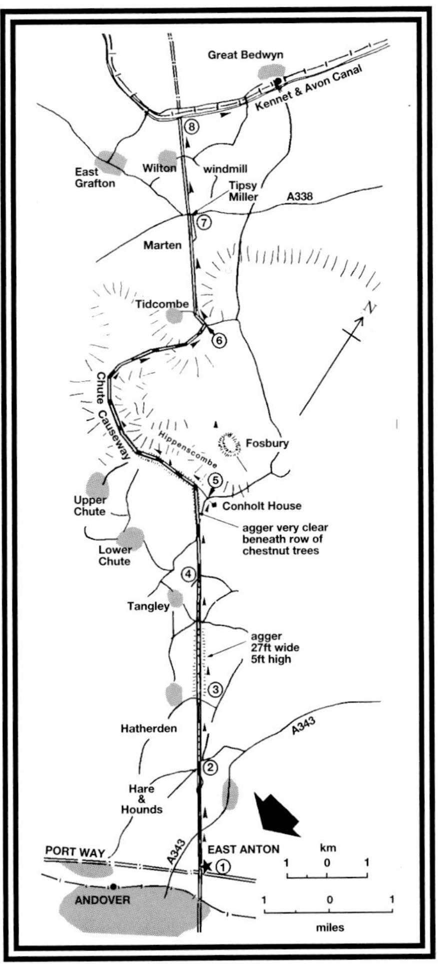

Above: *The agger and Spanish chestnut trees under snow in Conholt Park.*

takes the Roman road to its junction with Ermin Way near Wanborough House.

13 A WALK/CYCLE RIDE FROM EAST ANTON TO GREAT BEDWYN

This walk/cycle ride follows peaceful green lanes and minor roads that run along a great commercial highway of Roman times, including the extraordinary Chute Causeway. The walk/cycle ride ends on the banks of the Kennet and Avon Canal.

Instructions

1. Start at East Anton (Andover station is about 2 miles from the start of the walk). Head north-west along 'Icknield Way', on the line of the Roman road. Cross the A343 and carry on along the green lane which follows the Roman road to the 'Hare & Hounds'.

2. Bear right past the pub and turn left along the Roman road, now a lane, opposite.

3. Go straight over at the crossroads and follow the little lane. Cross over the road near Tangley and continue along the green lane for just over half a mile.

4. Carry straight on along the Roman line where a road comes in from the left. Follow this road into Conholt Park on a fine *agger*.

5. Turn left at the entrance to Conholt Park and follow the Chute Causeway, in use as a minor road raised on a high *agger*, for five miles round the deep Hippenscombe valley to the T-junction near Tidcombe.

6. Turn left and follow the minor road, leaving the Roman alignment briefly at Marten and reach the A338.

7. Turn left opposite the 'Tipsy Miller' and then right on to the lane signposted to Wilton Windmill. Keep going till you reach the Kennet and Avon Canal.

8. Leave the Roman road here and turn right alongside the canal and follow the towpath into Great Bedwyn, where there is a railway station.

THE ROMAN ROAD FROM DORCHESTER TO ILCHESTER

Dorchester (*Durnovaria*) was founded by the Romans as a new town to replace the British hillfort of Maiden Castle, scene of Vespasian's best known battle for the South West. It is certain that Dorchester started as a Roman fort, but remains of this have not yet been found. In any event, the fort was soon replaced by a town, for Maiden Castle seems not to have been occupied after AD 70 and it is reasonable to assume that the inhabitants moved or were moved at that time to the new town in the valley. Becoming the tribal capital of the Durotriges, Dorchester flourished and attained its greatest prosperity during the fourth century.

Dorchester was a route centre: the South Western Highway passed through it coming from Badbury Rings and heading on to Exeter; another road ran southwards to the Roman port at Radipole near Weymouth, and this road ran north-west to Ilchester (*Lindinis*) on the Foss Way.

Left: *The Roman line north of East Anton.* **Below:** *The Chute Causeway.*

Above right: *The new Roman town of Dorchester seen from the ramparts of Maiden Castle, the old Iron Age stronghold which it replaced.*

Right: *The road invites us onward ...*

OS maps:
1:50,000 Landranger sheet
194

1:25,000 Pathfinder sheets
1318 [Dorchester (north) & Tolpuddle]
1332 [Weymouth (north) & Dorchester (south)]

Distance: 4 miles

Pubs/hostelries:
On the walk: Dorchester
Grimstone

Roman engineering works:
agger visible in places

Other antiquities:
Roman aqueduct
Poundbury prehistoric camp

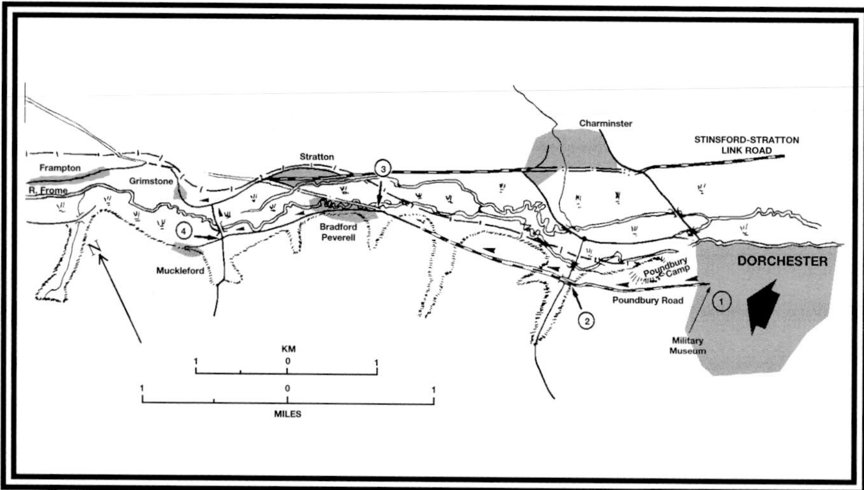

The Roman road from Dorchester to Ilchester has to a large extent remained in use as a main routeway and is followed along much of its course by the A37. Its survival as a major road is due in part to the way it was cleverly engineered with easy gradients for civilian rather than military uses. The route is designed to run on two alignments, a short north-westerly one out of Dorchester and then a longer north-north-westerly one for the rest of its course. For the first 2½ miles, the road offers two alternative routes. The more important, direct route which is followed by this cycle ride/drive, left Dorchester by the west gate to run as a lane to Bradford Peverell, where it crosses the River Frome to Stratton. This stretch of the road is particularly interesting as it is crossed and recrossed by the aqueduct which carried *Durnovaria*'s water supply from the River Frome over the hill to the town. The other route ran from Stinsford, a mile to the east of Dorchester, through Charminster to Stratton and the junction with the shorter route. This was probably the later of the two roads and could have functioned as a Roman bypass for Dorchester.

From Stratton the combined route heads up on to the downs, gradually closing with the modern A37, which it meets at the top of the hill. From here the road is cleverly aligned so that it can run in straight lengths but does not have to climb or descend any steep slopes. It carried on through Yeovil, but has been obliterated by development till beyond the A3088. Here Larkhill Road continues on the line which is resumed by the A37 into Ilchester.

The Roman aqueduct was constructed at the end of the first century AD to carry water 12 miles from the River Frome at Frampton to the new Romano-British town at Dorchester. This aqueduct is not the grand stone feature that the name would seem to imply, but an ingenious open channel some 6 feet deep and 4 feet wide, that follows the contours of the hills, appearing today as an earth shelf. It is cut several times by the Roman road and some have said that they could not have been in use together. However, it would have been easy for the water channel to have been carried over or under the road at the points where the two intersect. The mere existence of this aqueduct shows to what extent and how quickly 'Romanisation' took place in the South West, for what apart from burgeoning pride in their Roman town could have induced the citizens of *Durnovaria* to engineer this feature when they could far more easily have dug wells to supply them with water?

14 A CYCLE RIDE/DRIVE OR WALK FROM DORCHESTER TO GRIMSTONE

This is an easy ride/walk along a line of lanes on the Roman road north-west of Dorchester, passing close to the Roman aqueduct.

Instructions

1. Start in Dorchester. Turn north-west along Poundbury Road beside the Military Museum. Pass Poundbury Camp [SY682911] and continue along the lane over the bypass.

2. Continue along the Roman road. The Roman aqueduct is visible on the left as it curls around the hillside. Carry on into Bradford Peverell.

3. Leave the Roman road here and carry straight on to the crossroads at Muckleford.

4. Turn right, crossing over the River Frome. Turn left along the A37 to Grimstone.

Below: *Bradford Peverell, where the Dorchester-Ilchester Roman road crossed the river Frome.*

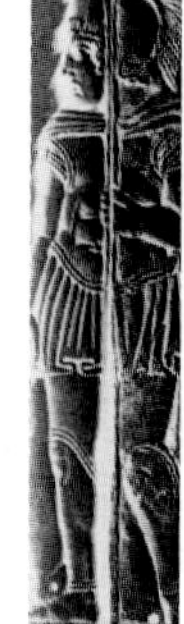

— III —
EASTERN ENGLAND

'Go and announce to the Romans ...
that the gods desire my city of Rome shall
be the capital of all the countries of the world ...'

LIVY

The Romans in Eastern England

In immediately pre-conquest times Hertfordshire and Essex were the main power-base of the Catuvellauni, under their princes Togodumnus and Caratacus, sons of Cunobelinus (the Cymbeline of Shakespeare), whose capital was at Colchester. Other eastern tribes included the Trinovantes, now absorbed by the Catuvellauni, and the Iceni of Norfolk, under their king, Prasutagus. Togodumnus and Caratacus had far-ranging influence, so it is hardly surprising that Aulus Plautius regarded Colchester as the capital of Britain and sped towards it with his invasionary force in AD 43. The Emperor Claudius himself came over from Rome to sack Colchester, receive the submission of the British and install Plautius as the first governor of the new province, Britannia, issuing him with orders to subdue 'the rest'.

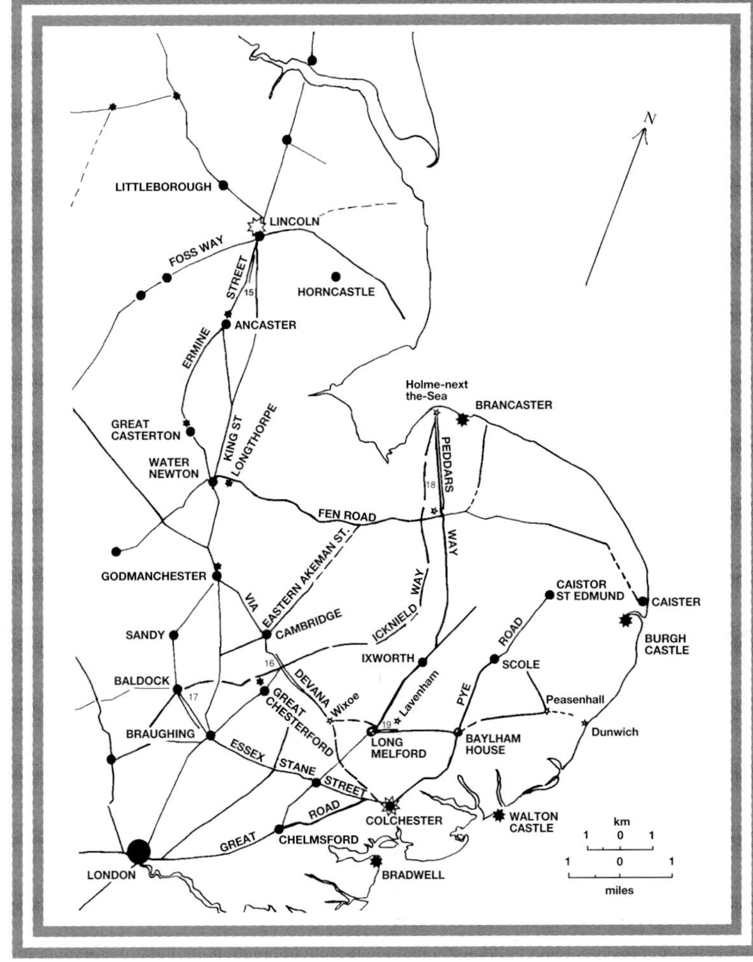

The army had reached Colchester from London along the route that was later to become the Great Road and which now lies, for most of its length, beneath the modern A12. Colchester became the capital of the new province and the Roman roads in the area radiate from it along the routes followed by the army. A legionary fortress was built and, in AD 49-50, a Roman town, Camulodunum, was founded there as a colonia, a land settlement for time-expired soldiers. On the east of the new town was built a large and imposing temple to the deified emperor, Claudius. The Roman peace came to this part of eastern England and spread up Ermine Street behind the IX Legion which, by AD 60-61, had moved its permanent base to Lincoln. This was valuable land to the Romans, who set about farming the uplands, embanking and draining the Fens and growing corn and other crops.

By AD 60, the client king of the Iceni had died. The heavy-handed behaviour of Roman officials, coupled with the extortionate demands of the unpopular Catus Decianus, the Roman financial administrator, incited the Iceni to open revolt under their queen, Prasutagus' widow, Boudicca. The insensitivity to wounded British pride of building a *colonia* and temple on the site

of the historic tribal capital at Colchester ensured that the Trinovantes and Catuvellauni also rose against their Roman overlords. Tacitus' description of the burning of *Camulodunum*, *Londinium* and *Verulamium*, and the butchering of their inhabitants still has power to horrify:

'Unguarded, unprepared, as if in the midst of peace, they were surrounded by a host of the Barbarians. Everything else in the colony was reduced to ruins in their fury, or was consumed by fire ... whoever stayed behind, whether from the weakness of sex, or the infirmities of age, or the attraction of the place, fell beneath the rage of the enemy. The municipal town of Verulamium experienced the same disastrous fortune .... In the several places which I have mentioned, it appeared that 70,000 souls had perished, of Romans and the allies. For the enemy neither made nor sold prisoners, nor transacted anything else pertaining to the commerce of war; but they hastened to butcher, hang, burn, crucify ...'

The Boudiccan revolt was the single most important uprising to occur in Britain under the Romans, and it was touch and go at the time as to whether the then governor, the brutal Suetonius Paulinus, would be able to contain it. The revolt spread, quite literally, like wildfire, and soon much of the south and east was ablaze. Suetonius Paulinus, campaigning against the Ordovices of North

Wales, rushed southward, but not before heavy losses had been inflicted upon the IX Legion, which had attempted to relieve Colchester. With difficulty he put down the uprising, but great was his vengeance. In the confusion, Boudicca died. Some say she committed suicide, others that she was poisoned.

Decianus, the hated procurator, had fled in horror to the continent and Nero's replacement was an inspired choice. The new procurator was Julius Classicanus, a man of wide understanding into the motives for rebellions and how to prevent them. Due to his influence, Suetonius was replaced by a more conciliatory governor, Petronius Turpilianus, who with Classicanus as his right-hand man calmed the south of the province, which never again rose in rebellion.

The Roman Road Network in Eastern England

Two trunk roads forge into Eastern England from London. Ermine Street heads north via Godmanchester to Lincoln, while the Great Road drives relentlessly eastwards to Colchester, before turning north as the Pye Road to Caistor St Edmund, tribal capital of the Iceni.

These two roads represent the routes followed by the conquering army. The Great Road to Colchester is the route taken by Claudius in AD 43, while Ermine Street north of Godmanchester lies on the campaign route of the IX Legion, which arrived at Godmanchester from Colchester along the *Via Devana*. Later, Ermine Street was carried south through Braughing to the new Roman town of London.

A road ran northwards from Chelmsford to Ixworth and continued to the coast of the Wash at Holme-next-the-Sea, its northern part later known as the Peddars Way. From Holme there was probably a ferry connection to Lincolnshire. North of Ixworth this road is paralleled by the Icknield Way, an ancient trackway straightened and Romanised. It ran along the dry chalklands through Baldock and Worsted Lodge towards the coast on the Wash.

Bottom: *Eastern England was densely populated in Roman times and rose to be a very civilized part of the province. Here we look across north Norfolk to the 700 year old tower of Aylmerton church.*

Opposite left: *The Fens: large areas were reclaimed by the Romans to whom it was valuable agricultural land. This picture shows the fen landscape near the Romano-British settlement at Cottenham.*

Below: *One of the Bartlow Hills, a spectacular group of tall Roman burial mounds which date from the late 1st to the middle 2nd century A.D. They contained very elaborate grave goods, including glass perfume bottles and an enamelled bowl. Clearly the people buried here were important and civilized.*

There were three major cross-country roads: the Fen Road, which ran on a causeway across the Fens, although modern roads tend to ignore it altogether; the Wixoe-Peasenhall road, which now runs, in part, on minor lanes and paths; and the Essex Stane Street, which is a main road along virtually its entire length.

Eastern England was heavily settled and the road system is complex and complete with numerous interconnecting roads, lanes and trackways — many roads here must unknowingly possess Roman ancestors.

ERMINE STREET

The Roman Road from London to Lincoln

Ermine Street was the Romans' great road to the north, the forerunner of the Great North Road and the modern A1, though it does not follow either of these roads for any considerable length. It led from the civilian south into the military north and the legionary fortresses, first at Lincoln and then at York.

In AD 44 the IX Legion advanced from Colchester along the *Via Devana* to Godmanchester, where they turned north up Ermine Street. Later, Ermine Street was extended southwards to the new hub of the road system at London and the route became the main highway to the north. The Antonine Itinerary follows it from Godmanchester to Lincoln.

Ermine Street leaves London via Bishopsgate and heads due north to Ware, keeping to a direct but rather hilly route. The A10 takes up the Roman line beyond Ware and continues to Braughing, now a small village, but in Roman times an important route centre. From here Roman roads radiate in several directions.

Ermine Street carries on northwards and crosses the ancient Icknield Way. Then it turns a little to the north-west and continues on to Godmanchester, where it was joined by the *Via Devana*. Beyond Godmanchester it changes alignment and is joined by the A1. It forges ahead, to reach the important Roman industrial area around the village of Water Newton, site of the Roman town of *Durobrivae*.

Water Newton was the centre of one of the largest pottery industries in Roman Britain. All manner of pots, bowls and dishes were made here, numerous everyday items of distinctive colour-coated pottery now known as 'Nene Valley Ware'. This pottery was distributed across the country and was probably transported along the River Nene by barge. A branch road heads down to the site of a quay on the river from the industrial area, and King Street heads off to the north.

Beyond Water Newton, Ermine Street runs across fields to rejoin the A1 near Stamford and continues through

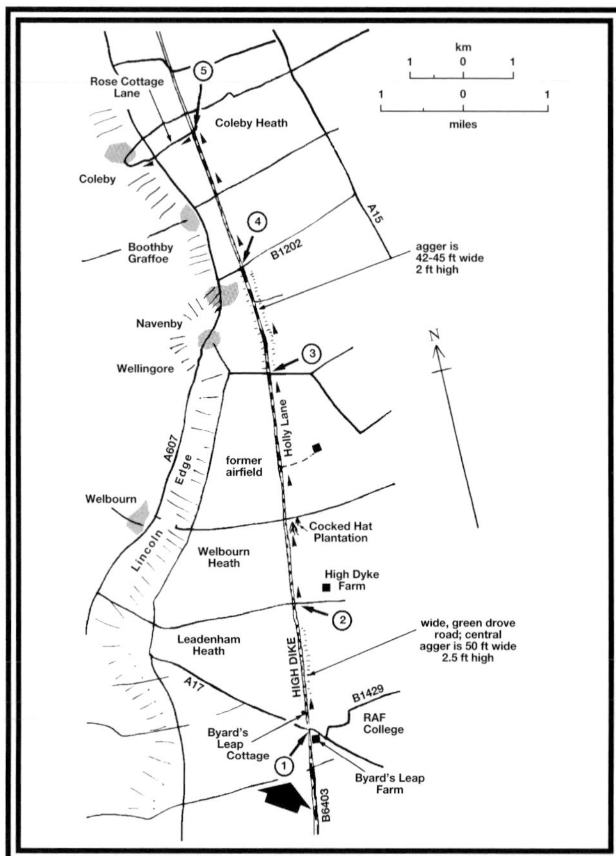

OS maps:
1:50,000 Landranger sheets
130 & 121

1:25,000 Pathfinder sheets
781 [Lincoln (south)]
797 [Newark-on-Trent (east) & Navenby]
814 [Long Bennington & Caythorpe]

Distance: 8 miles

Pubs/hostelries:
On the walk: Coleby
Nearby: Harmston
Navenby
Wellingore
Welbourn
Leadenham

Roman engineering works:
agger visible

Above: *Newport Arch, Lincoln. The only Roman archway still standing in Britain.* **Above right:** *On the Lincoln Edge looking across the Vale of Trent.*

Greetham to Colsterworth. From Colsterworth to Byard's Leap the B6043 follows Ermine Street, a dangerously straight road heading up hill and down dale as it forges relentlessly onward. Beyond Byard's Leap, where this walk starts, the green lanes continue this indomitable push northwards, making for a superb walk or ride on the Lincoln Edge, passing above a string of villages that cluster along the spring line below. The walk ends by heading downhill to the village of Coleby.

From Lincoln, where it crosses Foss Way, Ermine Street carries on straight to the Humber estuary and the ferry crossing to Yorkshire, followed by a line of lanes and tracks, their course cut by airfields. A branch road, which also heads for York but avoids the Humber crossing by going via Doncaster and Tadcaster, heads north-west from just north of Lincoln.

Ermine Street is an epic road. Along the high ground of the Lincoln Edge it is raised on a great *agger*, over 40 feet wide, dominating the landscape and striding onward towards the north, full of energy and zest for conquest: a road on the roof of the world watched over only by the hurrying skies of history.

15 A WALK/CYCLE RIDE FROM BYARD'S LEAP TO COLEBY

This is an open, windswept walk/cycle ride along Ermine Street on the top of the Lincoln Edge.

Instructions

1. Start at the junction of the A17 and the B6403, just west of RAF Cranwell and near Byard's Leap Farm. Head north past Byard's Leap Cottage along Ermine Street — the High Dyke — marked on OS maps as the Viking Way. Continue over Leadenham Heath.

2. Cross over the minor road and carry on along Ermine Street over Welbourn Heath. Cross over the road by Cocked Hat Plantation and keep going along Holly Lane past the former Wellingore Airfield to the junction.

3. Go straight ahead along the lane, noting the slight change of alignment from east of north to west of north made just above Wellingore, to the T-junction.

4. Go straight across on to the trackway that follows Ermine Street onwards. Cross the B1202 on to the little metalled lane that now follows Ermine Street.

5. Leave Ermine Street where Rose Cottage Lane makes a sharp turn to the left to go down the Lincoln Edge to Coleby. Follow the modern lane down the steep hill, cross the A607 and follow Dovecote Lane into the village.

VIA DEVANA

The Roman Road from Colchester to Godmanchester

We do not know what name the Romans gave this road. The name *Via Devana* is not ancient, dating only from the 18th century, bestowed in the belief that it led to Chester (*Deva*). Previously the name for the road was 'Wool Street' or 'Worsted Street', harking back to the prosperous days of the medieval wool merchants.

It is an early Roman road, dating from AD 43-44, and built in the footsteps of soldiers of the IX Legion, Hispana, who marched this way on campaign after the emperor Claudius, had received the submission of 12 British Kings. The *Via Devana* started at Colchester and passed north-westwards through Cambridge to Godmanchester. The IX Legion built forts at both Cambridge and Godmanchester, though neither fort is visible today. By AD 60 part of the IX Legion was stationed at Longthorpe, and it was probably from there that about half the Legion and their commander, Petillius Cerialis, set out in a headstrong attempt to relieve *Camulodunum* when news broke of the great rebellion. They must have hurried down this road to be cut to pieces by the Boudiccan rebels, with Cerialis lucky to escape with his life. Where the disastrous ambush occurred remains unknown.

The road seems to have passed through a mainly rural area and it is likely that sheep were raised here. This was prosperous countryside, where the *Pax Romana* brought a civilised way of life.

The *Via Devana* branched north-west from the Great Road at Lexden Heath, Colchester, and, although its course is not known in detail, it would have followed the Colne valley through Great Yeldham, possibly along the A604. From Great Yeldham the Roman road runs along the line of the dismantled railway, and close to Ridgewell, a Roman villa. Haverhill High Street lies along it and then

it forms the wide, green bank in Hare Wood.

From the Streetly End-Horseheath road to the Gog-Magog hills it is followed for about 10 miles by a green lane showing considerable remains of the *agger*. This is the best stretch to walk — a length of the road that does not go through any villages, but passes straight and purposefully across the farmland, a raised causeway, open and lonely. Nearby, though, are attractive Cambridgeshire villages: Horseheath, where a few old houses keep company with the inn; West Wickham, on the high ground looking into Suffolk, with nearby Yen Hall Farm, which is named in a Saxon land charter of AD 974; Balsham, with its rich church carvings; thatched Streetly

End with its disused windmill and Linton with its quaint grouping of old houses by the church and in its main street, now designated an Outstanding Conservation Area. It crosses the Romanised Icknield Way at Worsted Lodge, an important crossroads in Roman times, and continues in a north-westerly direction to the Gog-Magog hills south of Cambridge, where the walk ends.

The road then turns west to avoid the fenland along an ancient, pre-Roman earthwork called Worts' Causeway, following it for about a mile, today along a minor road. The *Via Devana* then turns through Cambridge, followed by the modern main road. A Roman town was founded at Cambridge, *Duroliponte*, which was sited by the bridge which carried the *Via Devana* over the River Cam. In the Dark Ages the town was deserted and during the sixth century the monks of Ely, searching amid the fallen masonry for a stone coffin to entomb their foundress, St Ethelreda, described the site as 'a waste chester'.

Beyond Cambridge the Roman road is still in use as the A604 as it heads straight for Godmanchester, where the *Via Devana* ends. The Gartree Road takes up the north-westerly orientation for Leicester.

Far left: *The East Gate, Lincoln.*

Left: *The delightful green lane which follows the Via Devana.*

Above: *Early 18th century milestone near Cambridge. Tradition suggests that the fine set of milestones of which this is an example are in fact re-used Roman stones. Did they originally stand along the Via Devana?*

16 A WALK FROM HORSEHEATH TO CAMBRIDGE.

This delightful walk follows the Roman road, now a green lane, to the Gog-Magog Hills via the important crossroads with the Icknield Way (the A11) at Worsted Lodge.

Instructions

1. Start at Horseheath. Walk north towards Streetly End.

2. Turn left along the *Via Devana* [TL614477], following it over the hill to the south of Streetly Hall.

3. Cross the West Wratting-Bartlow road at Musgrave and continue to the B1052 (signposted 'Roman road walk').

4. Cross the B-road and continue over a lane to Worsted Lodge on the A11 — the Icknield Way.

5. Cross the A11 and follow the *Via Devana* along the green lane.

6. Finish at the car park on the Gog-Magog Hills.

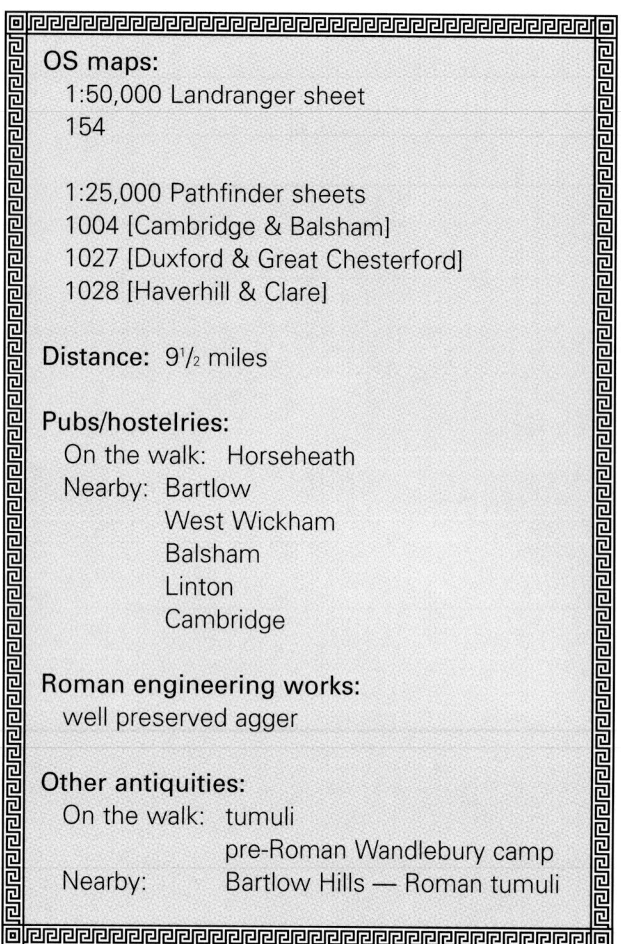

OS maps:
1:50,000 Landranger sheet 154

1:25,000 Pathfinder sheets
1004 [Cambridge & Balsham]
1027 [Duxford & Great Chesterford]
1028 [Haverhill & Clare]

Distance: 9½ miles

Pubs/hostelries:
On the walk: Horseheath
Nearby: Bartlow
West Wickham
Balsham
Linton
Cambridge

Roman engineering works:
well preserved agger

Other antiquities:
On the walk: tumuli
pre-Roman Wandlebury camp
Nearby: Bartlow Hills — Roman tumuli

THE ROMAN ROAD FROM BRAUGHING TO GODMANCHESTER

This Roman road runs more or less parallel with Ermine Street, which it leaves at Braughing and rejoins at Godmanchester, having swung westwards in a wide loop through Baldock, Biggleswade and Sandy. It is a rewarding road to follow today, since little of it is used by main roads and along much of its length it consists of lines of green lanes, bridleways and footpaths.

Between Braughing and Baldock it was built along the line of a pre-existing track, straightened, aligned and engineered to Roman standards. At one time it was known as 'Stane Street', a name associated with Roman roads elsewhere.

For the first 2½ miles of its course from Braughing, an important route centre even before the Roman conquest, the road cannot be traced. It passed across Hamels Park to Cherry Green, where the walk joins it. Here it becomes visible, an *agger* some 24 feet wide, at first hidden in the woodland beneath the bluebells and then followed by a green lane known as Back Lane all the way to Hare Street. In Old English the name 'Hare Street' means a military or army road. This Hare Street was referred to in 1498 as *Harestrete*. The Saxon villages of Cottered and Ardeley are situated not on this old highway but a little way off, as was normal Saxon practice.

At Hare Street the B1037 runs along the Roman road for a quarter of a mile, after which the Ordnance Survey shows the Roman line carrying straight on, crossing the fields in the same rigid alignment. However, evidence suggests that the Roman road did not follow the direct survey line here, and an alternative course has been proposed along which traces of the Roman road can be seen.

This course heads downhill in a more westerly direction, approximately along the line of a footpath and lane to pass beneath Cromer's great white windmill to Luffenhall. It bears back on to a north-westerly course along a lane known for centuries as the 'Roman Road' or the 'Highway' and bears back to the true alignment for the final 1½ miles into Baldock, joined by the A507 at Windmill Hill, though a parallel footpath serves for the walk.

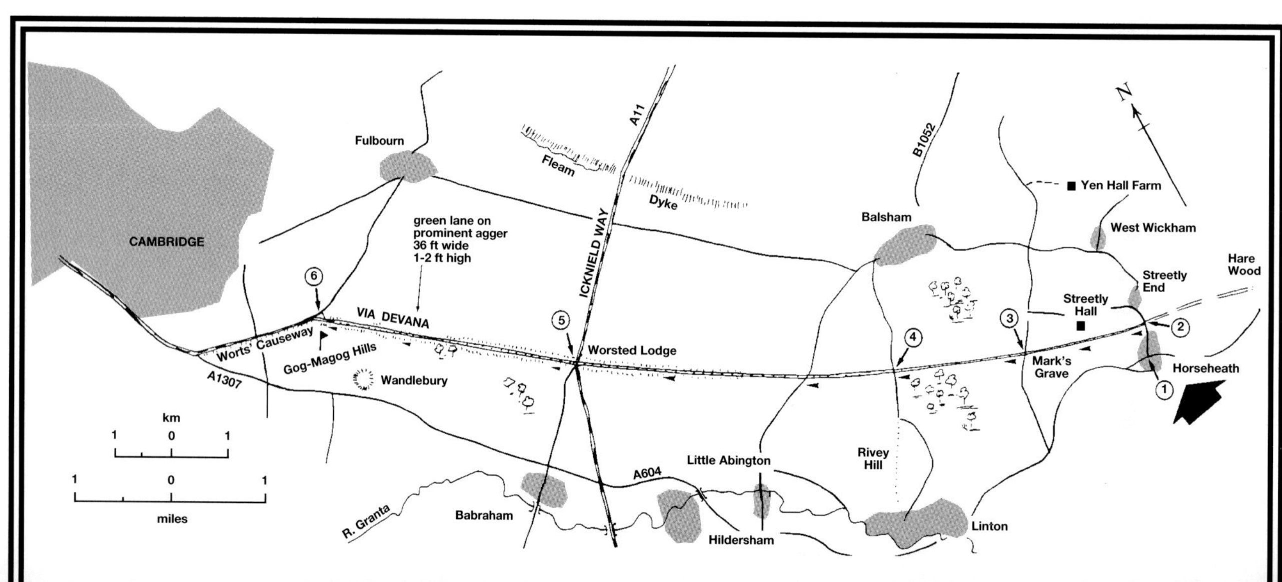

Baldock, where the walk ends, is a gracious old town, and was an important Roman settlement which grew from an earlier British site on the ancient Icknield Way. From Baldock the Roman road continues straight through Biggleswade to Sandy, where a little lane takes up the line. In the 13th century the Roman road from Baldock to Sandy was known as *Brunstrate* or *Brunnestrate*. In Old English *brun* means brown, so that it is likely that the name of the road referred to the colour of its gravel metalling.

At Sandy, where there was a minor Roman settlement, the road changes alignment, and is marked today by a line of green lanes across the fields to Godmanchester. Roman Godmanchester was dominated by the main roads that met here, particularly Ermine Street. As can well be imagined, the earliest activity at the site was military, but a town soon grew up. The present name comes from Godman, a Danish chieftain with whom Alfred the Great concluded a treaty of peace.

17. A WALK FROM WESTMILL TO BALDOCK

This walk follows a Romanised British trackway.

Far left: *Back Lane heads west along the Roman road.*

Below: *Coin showing the head of Antoninus Pius. National Museum of Wales.*

Left: *Tomb of Facilis, a Roman centurion. Colchester Museum.*

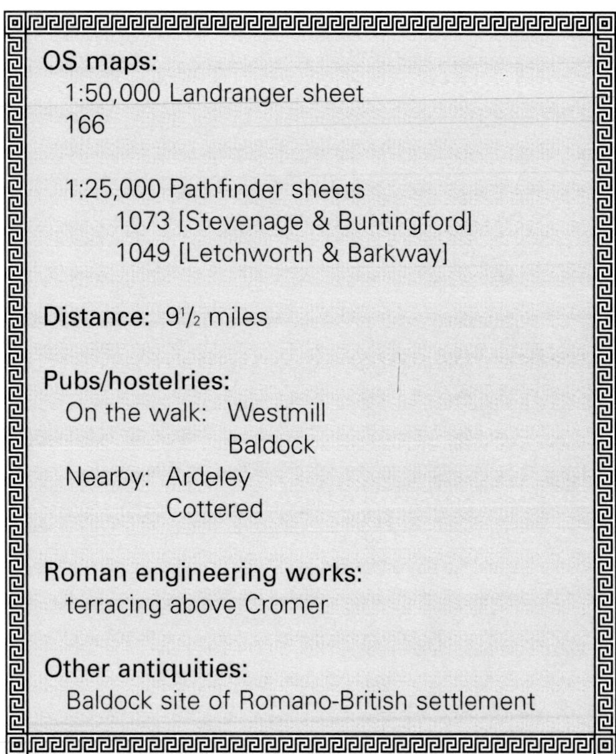

OS maps:
1:50,000 Landranger sheet
166

1:25,000 Pathfinder sheets
1073 [Stevenage & Buntingford]
1049 [Letchworth & Barkway]

Distance: 9½ miles

Pubs/hostelries:
On the walk: Westmill
Baldock
Nearby: Ardeley
Cottered

Roman engineering works:
terracing above Cromer

Other antiquities:
Baldock site of Romano-British settlement

Instructions

1. Start at Westmill, which is just off Ermine Street. To get to the Braughing-Baldock road follow the road westwards past Gaylors Farm and Cherry Green Farm, where the road turns abruptly to the left to the point where the Roman road crosses the modern road [TL356256].

2. Turn right on to the Roman road, Back Lane, which heads north-west past Peasefield. Keep going along Back Lane to Hare Street. At Hare Street the B1037 comes in from the right and runs along the Roman alignment for a quarter of a mile.

3. Carry straight on downhill along the footpath. Cross the Cromer-Cumberlow Green road and follow the lane opposite along the 'alternative Roman road'.

4. Here the Roman road goes straight over, but the right of way does not. Turn left and then immediately right on to the road used as a public path. Keep straight on where this bears left and follow the track to rejoin the Roman road.

5. Go on along the minor road for a few yards and continue along the Roman road over Hickman's Hill towards Windmill Hill.

Top: *Rustic Arderley* **Above:** *Elegant Baldock*

6. Before you reach Windmill Hill, in order to avoid walking on the busy A507, turn left on to a footpath which continues as a bridleway into Baldock.

THE ROMAN ROAD FROM CHELMSFORD TO THE WASH
INCLUDING THE PEDDARS WAY

This road leaves Chelmsford (*Caesaromagus*) along New Street and Rectory Lane, where the A130 joins it and follows it to Little Waltham. Here it turns north-east, through Braintree, crosses the Essex Stane Street and continues to Long Melford and the crossroads with the Wixoe-Peasenhall road. It is followed by the rather winding A134 and then by lanes and hedgerows to Ixworth, where there was a fort and a major civil settlement. It continues to the Roman villa at Stanton Chare. This southern part of the route is insubstantial, with little *agger* to be seen, so that across fields the course is lost. This is typical of East Anglian Roman roads, which tended to be only very lightly constructed.

It is probable that the southern part of the road was built in the AD 40s or 50s and was heading for Caistor St Edmund (*Venta Icenorum*), tribal capital of the Iceni, while the northern part was built after the Boudiccan rebellion. This turns north-east at Stanton Chare to head to the Wash and a ferry crossing linking it with Lincoln (*Lindum*), allowing for the speedy deployment of troops should there be further unrest. This road ran straight through the lands of the Iceni, a rebuke and a reminder that Rome would not tolerate insurrection.

From Stanton Chare onwards the road bears the later name of the Peddars Way, which may relate to its use in the Middle Ages by pedlars and merchants. Certainly the road construction becomes far more impressive. From here to its destination it follows long, straight alignments, expertly surveyed, with engineered terraces down to river crossings and changes of alignment on high points. This part of the road was obviously built by the Roman army with immediate military needs in mind. A fine *agger* crosses the fields from Stanton Chare towards Knettishall Heath Country Park, where begins the long distance path, the Peddars Way, and the Norfolk Coast Path.

The Roman road zig-zags downhill to cross the Little Ouse. It crosses the Thetford-Diss road and the River Thet and continues in a north-north-westerly direction to cross the A11 and go on to Galley Hill [TF924929]. Here a new alignment was set, followed for the next 34 miles all the way to the north Norfolk coast.

At Castle Acre, where the walk begins, there was a Roman camp, but today the place speaks of the Norman, not the Roman, past. Lands here were granted to William de Warenne, who married William the Conqueror's daughter and built both the castle which gives this place its name and the priory, now a magnificently thoughtful ruin beside the River Nar.

This is a superb long walk. From Castle Acre onwards the Peddars Way shows a well preserved *agger* for the entire 20 miles to the coast at Holme-next-the-Sea. At Holme, the Peddars Way loses itself among the coastal sandhills, its original destination unknown. Probably the point to which it ran has been destroyed by the sea, a common occurrence on these treacherous shores. One thing seems certain, though, that there was a ferry connection across the Wash to Lincolnshire, with a now-lost tidal inlet providing a safe haven. Maybe there was even a Roman land-settlement scheme for retired soldiers here, similar to those noted in Sussex near Ripe and on the Yorkshire Wolds. The Peddars Way would have formed its western boundary.

18 A WALK FROM CASTLE ACRE TO HOLME-NEXT-THE-SEA

This is an enjoyable walk along the Peddars Way.

Instructions

1. Start in Castle Acre. Follow the lane north-west on the alignment of the Peddars Way and keep straight ahead on to the track at the trig point to reach the B1145.

2. Cross the B-road into the lane opposite. Continue along the rough lane. Keep going all the way to Harpley Dams on the A148.

3. Cross the A148 and continue straight along the waymarked Roman road. Go straight across at the crossroads near Anmer Minque.

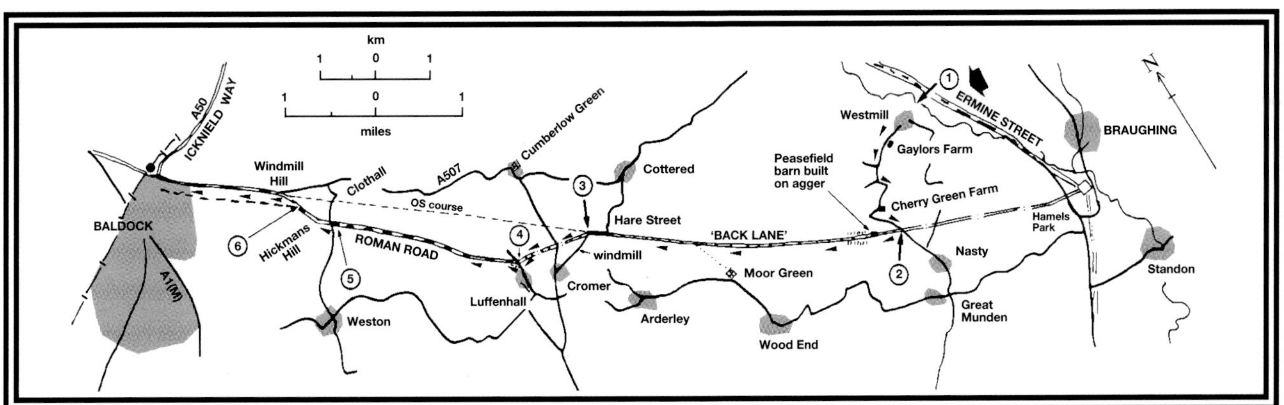

OS maps:
1:50,000 Landranger sheet 132

1:25,000 Pathfinder sheets
881 [East Dereham & Castle Acre]
880 [King's Lynn (south)]
859 [King's Lynn (north) & Sandringham]
839 [Snettisham]
818 [Hunstanton]

Distance: 20 miles

Pubs/hostelries:
On the walk: Castle Acre
Ringstead
Holme-next-the-Sea
Nearby: Great Massingham
Sedgeford

Roman engineering works:
agger conspicuous in places

Other antiquities:
tumuli on Harpley Common

4. Cross over the B1153 and keep going, crossing over several more roads and passing close to the village of Fring. Cross the stream on the site of a Roman ford at Fring Cross.

5. Cross the road and follow the Peddars Way, which is marked here only by a footpath. Follow the path to the other side of the hedge and then, leaving the Roman alignment briefly, turn to the left and then the right, past some cottages to the B1454.

6. Turn right and then left to rejoin the Peddars Way along the lane at Sedgeford Magazine. Cross the disused railway line. The path soon joins a lane and leads into Ringstead.

7. The Peddars Way goes straight ahead here, but the way is impassable. Turn left into Ringstead and then right, going past the church. Turn right again at the T-junction and then left back on to the Roman road.

8. Continue along the minor road, which is more or less on the Roman line, but veers away from it past the windmill.

9. Turn left on to the waymarked footpath (opposite a bungalow) which bears to the right on to the Roman alignment followed by a hedgerow.

10. Cross the main road and follow the Peddars Way to its present conclusion in Holme-next-the-Sea.

Below left: *Ford (and elegant 'footbridge') at site of Roman ford at Fring Cross.*

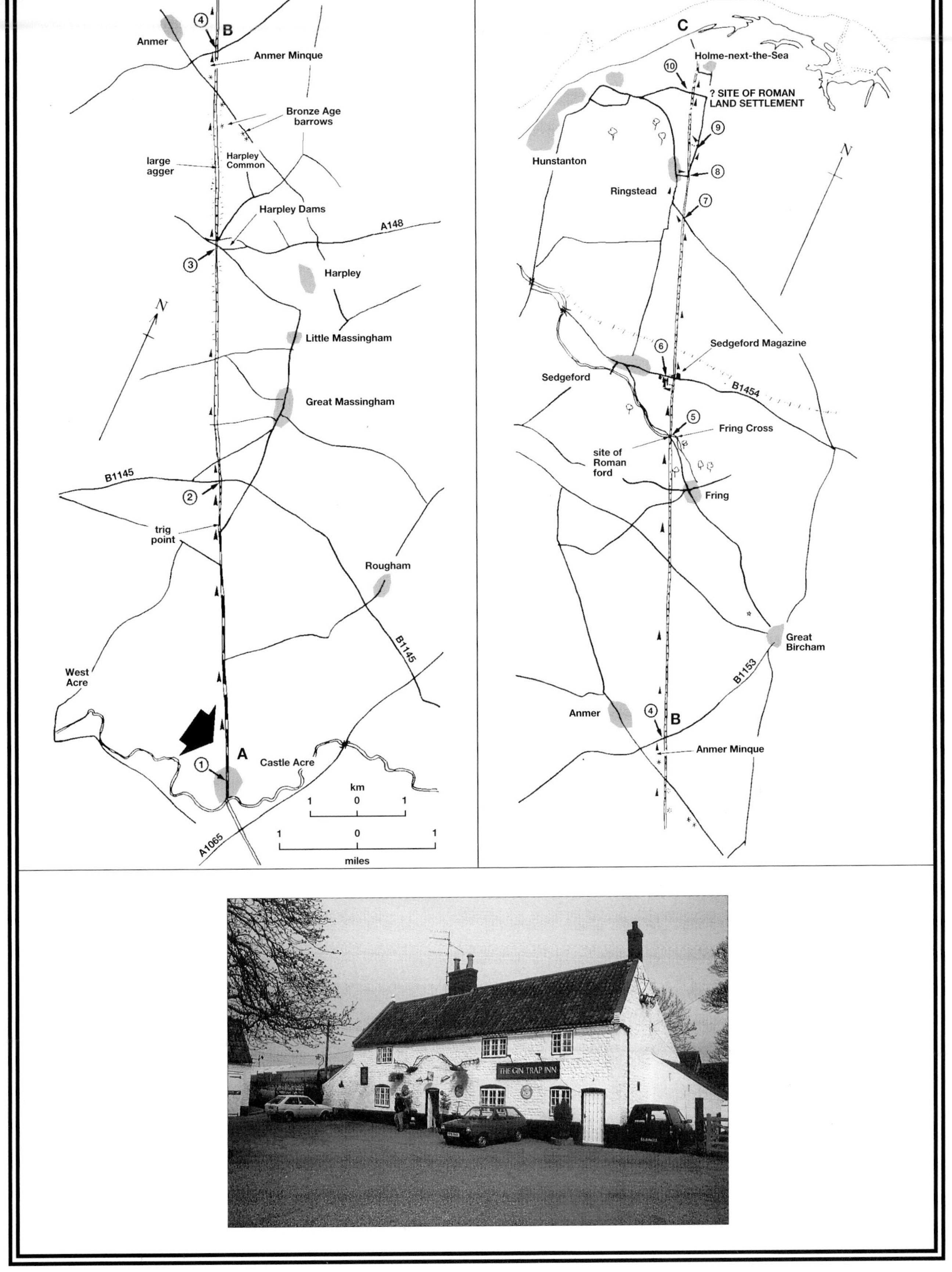

Left: *Priory ruins at Castle Acre.* **Inset:** *Ringstead. A welcome halt.*

THE ROMAN ROAD FROM WIXOE TO PEASENHALL

This road was probably heading for a Roman port now vanished into the North Sea in the vicinity of sea-sunk Dunwich, and branched from the *Via Devana* near Wixoe. The course is uncertain for the first four miles or so, but after this it is a terraced, valley-side road, running in short, straight lengths above the River Stour via Cavendish to Long Melford and in use today as the A1092. There was a small Roman settlement at Long Melford, where this road crosses the Chelmsford-Holme road just south of the magnificent 'wool' church.

Above: *Long Melford. The 'Wool Church' beside the Roman cross roads.*

The best surviving stretch of the road for walkers starts at Long Melford, where the walk begins, and crosses the Chad Brook where the Roman surveyors set a rigid alignment, aiming for Barking Tye above the Gipping valley, nearly 15 miles off. It passes through Washmere Green, now followed by lanes and footpaths, and continues over fields paralleled by a track to cross the River Brett at Brent Eleigh. Here an old coaching road heads over the hill to Lavenham and the walk turns off along it. The Roman road continues to Monks Eleigh Tye and on over fields to beyond Bildeston, where its line is taken up by lanes. From Barking Tye its exact course is not known, but we can trace it again where it crossed the River Gipping at Baylham House, where there was a Roman fort and a small civil settlement (*Combvretovium*). Here in the Gipping valley it also crossed the main road from Colchester to Caistor St Edmund, known as the Pye Road.

The road continued through Petthaugh to Peasenhall, beyond which it has not been traced. It is likely that it carried on to the coast near Dunwich, the once-flourishing town which has vanished entirely beneath the waves. Certainly there was Roman activity in the Dunwich area. It's easy to imagine that the tidal inlet enclosed by a shingle bar on which the fortunes of medieval Dunwich depended had an earlier precursor, making it a safe haven along a treacherous, crumbling coast. Perhaps this was a naval base, though positive evidence one way or another would require the sea to give up her dead. There were reputedly Roman artefacts found at Dunwich, and the two 40-foot-high hillocks, the Cock and Hen Hills, features of the medieval city destroyed by massive coastal flooding in December 1740, were almost certainly Roman tumuli.

Throughout its length the Wixoe-Peasenhall Roman road is only lightly constructed, lacking heavy foundations or a prominent *agger*. This is fairly common among the Roman roads in East Anglia and means that when the fields are ploughed the roads are completely destroyed. It also suggests a non-military origin for the road, which ran through increasingly Romanised countryside organised into large estates centred on villas, such as the one unearthed at Long Melford in 1958. It was, none the less, important, and the Antonine Itinerary follows it. We can envisage Roman dignitaries and officials, businessmen, merchants, travellers of all kinds from the mighty to the lowly, travelling this road through the rolling landscape, a region of mixed farmland.

In the centuries since the close of Roman times, when this road was severed by the fierce bloodshed and destruction of the Saxon and Danish wars, the places through which it passes have played their own small parts in history. At Brent Eleigh, where a 600-year-old church hides among the tall trees, a unique manuscript was found, written in the 12th century by Thomas of Monmouth, a Norwich monk, and recounting the life and miracles of St William of Norwich. Nearby, at Long Melford, Sir William Cordell entertained Queen Elizabeth I in the placid red-brick Hall, which faces the wide street of the little town.

19. A WALK FROM LONG MELFORD TO LAVENHAM

This delightful pastoral stroll follows one of the lesser-known Roman roads of Eastern England, from the lovely Suffolk village of Long Melford to Brent Eleigh, and then along a disused coaching road to famous Lavenham.

Instructions

1. Start at Long Melford, south of the famous church. The Roman road can be seen faintly crossing the green as a terrace. Turn left along the main road (the old A134) on the line of the Peddars Way.

2. Turn right through the garden centre opposite the entrance to Kentwell Hall. Follow the green lane and cross over the Long Melford bypass. Bear to the right along the

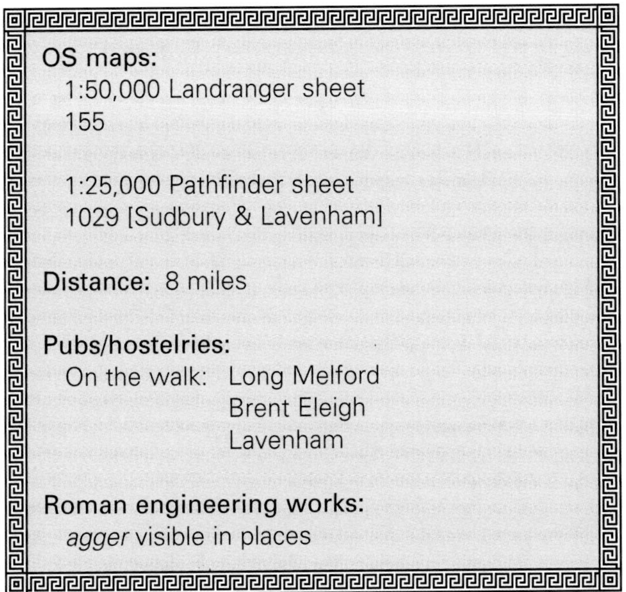

OS maps:
1:50,000 Landranger sheet 155

1:25,000 Pathfinder sheet 1029 [Sudbury & Lavenham]

Distance: 8 miles

Pubs/hostelries:
On the walk: Long Melford
Brent Eleigh
Lavenham

Roman engineering works:
agger visible in places

bridleway down to Chad Brook. Cross the stream and go uphill to the lane.

3. Turn left along the lane, which comes on to the Roman line. Pass the old sand pit on the right and the entrance to Bassett's Farm on the left.

4. Carry straight on along the byway where the lane turns off to the left. The byway follows the Roman road for about a quarter of a mile and then swings to the right. Follow it round to the right and back on to the Roman alignment at Slough Farm.

5. Go straight through the farmyard on to the footpath to the road junction at School Farm. The Roman road carries on straight ahead as the little lane to Washmere Green.

Above: *Destination of the Wixoe-Peasenhall Road? The foreshore at Dunwich.*

6. Cross the B1071 and continue along the lane for a further quarter of a mile. Here, where the lane turns abruptly to the right, the Roman road carried on across the field, though its course cannot now be seen. Leave the Roman road here and turn right along the lane, and in about 200 yards follow it round to the left.

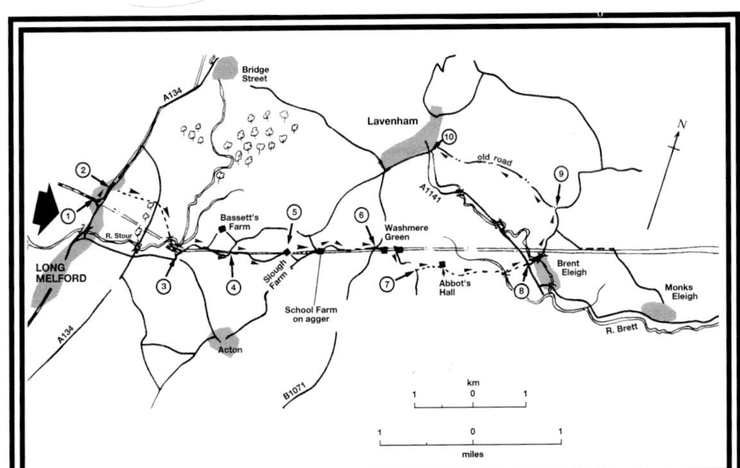

7. Turn left along the bridleway which runs parallel to the Roman road to Abbot's Hall. Continue along the lane, crossing over a small stream and reach the A1141 at Brent Eleigh.

8. Cross the main road into Brent Eleigh. Follow the lane over the bridge and uphill past the entrance to the Hall. Ignore the turning to your right.

9. Turn left along the bridleway on the line of the old road along the ridge and past Clayhill Farm.

10. Bear right into Lavenham.

— IV —
LONDON

'All these cities were connected with each other, and with the capital, by the public highways, which, issuing from the forum of Rome, traversed Italy, pervaded the provinces, and were terminated only by the frontiers of the Empire ...'

EDWARD GIBBON
Decline and Fall of the Roman Empire (1776-1788)

Following Roman roads in London is quite a different game to following them in the open countryside and through villages and market towns. Hence no specific walks have been included in this chapter. And yet, the Roman roads of London are in many ways the most fascinating in Britain. Here we have the point of departure and arrival of the great radial routes. Almost without exception, the major Roman roads of the London area fan out to far-flung destinations and point back to the Roman town, and in that lies their fascination and romance. All roads led to *Londinium*. The invitation is to go and explore: you won't be disappointed!

Above: *Watling Street: the Roman road runs along Tabard Street.*

Below: *The Silchester Road: Oxford Street lies along the Roman road to the South West.*

The Romans in London

Londinium was founded by the Romans on a gravel terrace on the north bank of the River Thames, just east of the

Above: *Watling Street: the old trackway joins the through-London Roman road at its junction with the Silchester road at Marble Arch.*

Below: *The river Thames at London.*

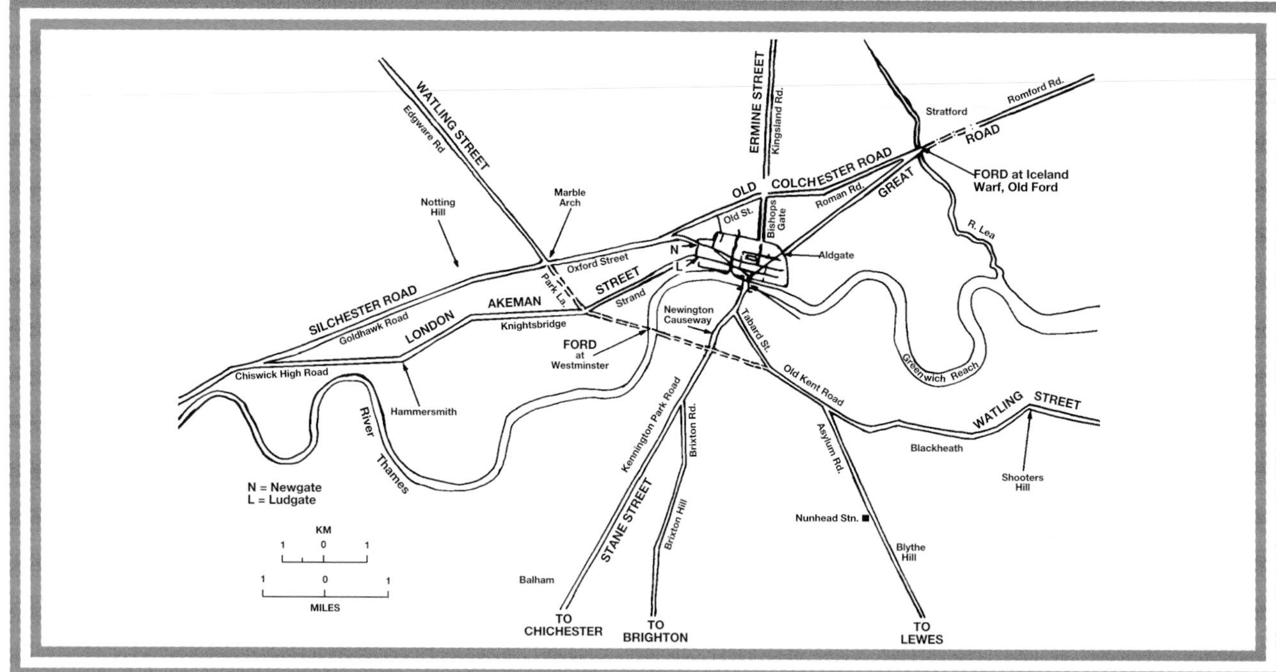

confluence with the Walbrook, after the successful invasion of AD 43. The date generally accepted is AD 50, but this leaves an awkward gap of some seven years during which even a military presence here has not been proved. A recent theory is that in AD 43 Aulus Plautius built a fort to house the invasionary force in the Mayfair area, but as yet there is no hard evidence for this.

Roman London, even at its greatest extent during the 4th century AD, covered but a very small area of what is now Greater London. The remains of the Roman city lie buried some 20 feet (6 metres) below the modern surface due to the accumulation of the debris and rubbish of nearly 2,000 years of occupation.

Its site at once proved advantageous and London developed fast, ousting Colchester from its pre-eminent position. It became the hub of the road system. In the AD 50s a bridge was built between London and what is now Southwark, and this became a focus for roads needing to cross the river. The roads converging on the site, and the open Thames ensured that London soon became a thriving international port, with wooden wharves built along the river.

In AD 60, when he heard that Colchester had fallen to the Boudiccan rebels, Suetonius Paulinus made for London, already a growing town, and the townsmen and women shouted with joy, thinking that their deliverance

Above: *Watling Street: the Roman road heads resolutely along the Edgeware Road.* **Above right:** *The London Akeman Street. Fleet Street is built on top of the Roman road.*

had arrived. But Suetonius Paulinus, once he had been apprised of the size of the rebellion, knew that he could not meet the rebels in London, for his small force would be annihilated. He decided to sacrifice the town and wait for reinforcements to arrive before giving battle to the rebels. He left London to its fate, deaf to the cries of the townspeople, whose fears for their safety were wholly justified, as the town was burnt to the ground and its inhabitants, men, women and children, butchered.

Following the suppression of the Boudiccan rebellion London was rebuilt and became more important than it had previously been, replacing Colchester as the capital of the province. Julius Classicanus, the wise and understanding procurator dispatched by Rome to sort out the financial troubles of the province, set up his base in London, where he also died. His ashes were interred in one of the out-of-town cemeteries along the roads now converging on the growing town. His grieving widow, Julia, set up a handsome monument to him.

By AD 70 London had become a city, and an important one at that. Its first forum and basilica had been built, along with a small temple and, as if to show just how Roman it could be, two public baths. When their city was declared the official capital of the province in the early second century, the inhabitants set about an ambitious building programme, importing Kentish ragstone up the Thames for the purpose. A palace was built for the governor in AD 80-100, while a new forum and basilica were constructed. Moreover, a fort was built on the north-west of the city in about AD 120.

The city was unwalled for its first hundred years or so, but in about AD 200 a city wall with gateways through which the roads entered was constructed on the northern side. Later, in the fourth century, when prosperous cities were seen as rich pickings by the marauding Saxon tribes, a further wall was built along the Thames. The decline of Roman London reflects the decline of Roman Britain. It fell into disrepair, threatened by the raiders and frightened for its life.

Roman Roads in London

The London area in immediately pre-Roman times was dominated by the river. The Thames, which today is tamed, embanked and dredged, is a far narrower, deeper, swifter stream than its Roman ancestor. The Roman *Tamesis* was a wide, muddy river with numerous bars and islets, and bordered by extensive marshes. It is likely that the Thames was not tidal much above Westminster and Chelsea, though this has not yet been shown conclusively. What has been demonstrated, though, is that the army of invasion of AD 43 most likely forded the shallow Thames at Westminster. The Westminster ford was the crossing point of that ancient trackway which became the Roman Watling Street, so it is probable that the ford was a long-established route over the river.

From the Westminster ford the 'Watling track' had to cross an expanse of mudflat and marsh, beyond which it continued via Park Lane to Marble Arch. For some reason the site chosen for the Roman town and focus of routes on the Thames was downstream of the old ford of Westminster. Perhaps the tides were unreliable at Westminster; perhaps, as some think, a pontoon bridge had already been thrown across the Thames from Southwark to London — somewhat nearer to important *Camulodunum*; or perhaps it was just realised that the gravel terraces by the Walbrook were a better place to build a town. For whatever reason, London soon became the hub of the road system, displacing Colchester, which after the initial phase of the invasion lay some way to the east of the theatre of operations. The roads which radiated from London are still in use today.

WATLING STREET

The pre-Roman 'Watling track' and the Roman Watling Street, both of which underlie the modern A2, arrive from Canterbury along Shooters Hill above Greenwich, aiming directly for the Westminster ford. The road was forced to swing southwards from Shooters Hill to avoid running into the sweeping loop of the River Thames as it rounds Greenwich Reach, and may well have followed the line now taken by Blackheath Hill, Blackheath Road and New Cross Road; certainly it continues along the line, but slightly to the south of, the Old Kent Road.

The original, pre-Roman, route to the ford of Westminster must have veered to the south of the Old Kent Road and it is possible that part of this roadway to the ford was discovered in Lambeth Palace gardens, where a gravelled trackway was unearthed. Moreover, the old ferry steps north of Lambeth Palace went by the name of Stangate, an appellation which suggests a connection with a paved ford. Stukeley makes the exciting comment that a Roman road 'went from Stangate ferry ... to Deptford and Blackheath ...' and remarked upon the fact that the 'ancient way' was 'pointing to Westminster Abbey'.

Beyond the ford the trackway is known to have continued approximately to the site of Buckingham Palace and to have run along Park Lane to Marble Arch and Edgware Road. Remains of the trackway have not been found along Park Lane but this is hardly surprising since after the construction of London Bridge the main road would have crossed the river there. The Park Lane track probably remained a track throughout Roman times, used only by light traffic. The ford may well have become impassable at high tide by the late second century, due in part to improved navigation downstream, though it had probably always been a hazardous crossing.

The Roman Watling Street, which crossed the Thames by bridge at Southwark rather than brave the Westminster ford, is known to have run along the Old Kent Road and continued along Tabard Street to reach Stane Street at Borough High Street in Southwark. Here the traveller would turn north along Stane Street to cross London Bridge.

Once over the river, the Roman travelling Watling Street would have to turn to the west through *Londinium* to rejoin his road outside the western limits of the city. Watling Street seems to have had no route of its own through Roman London, but picked up the Romanised trackway again at Marble Arch. Today it can be traced easily up Edgware Road, along which parish boundaries follow it all the way from Marble Arch to Edgware. Pipe-laying along Edgware Road revealed the construction of its Roman predecessor: very solid, with kerbs of concrete fixing the edges of the road. The foundations were of gravel and were overlain by flints mixed with lime.

ERMINE STREET

Ermine Street, the Roman road for Lincoln and the north, leaves London along Bishopsgate following a single alignment to Edmonton, which shows up very clearly on modern maps and is just as clear on the ground. This being so, it at first seems odd that tracing the road back from Bishopsgate to London Bridge is far from an easy task, and the course of Ermine Street within *Londinium* remains unknown. It is true that from the bridge Fish Street and Gracechurch Street do lie on a direct line to Bishopsgate, but by AD 75 London's first forum and basilica had been constructed right across the northern part of Gracechurch Street. This prevents any link being drawn between it and Ermine Street since the Roman town planners are unlikely to have set themselves on such a collision course with the Roman road engineers as to block a main road! We are left to consider whether there ever was a direct link from London Bridge to Bishopsgate.

Left: *The Silchester Road. Bath Road, Turnham Green, lies on the line.*

Above: *Roman London's massive defences: the great surrounding wall — with the Tower in the background.*

Top: *London's Mithratic temple repositioned incongrously beside a modern tower-block. Londoners — men only! — worshipped here and the doorstep has been worn away by the passage of countless Roman feet.*

Inset: *Bronze statue of the Emperor, Trajan.*

This state of affairs suggests that Ermine Street was not planned from *Londinium*, but reached it from Godmanchester when the Roman city was already in existence. This is highly plausible, since it is known that the stretch of Ermine Street between Godmanchester and London was not an invasionary campaign route. Ermine Street thus stops (or starts) not at the bridge-head but at the city limit where later the city walls and the handsome gate itself were built.

Modern Bishopsgate directly overlies the Roman road and it is certain that out-of-town Roman cemeteries bordered it on either side, for many burials have been found. Beyond Bishopsgate, Ermine Street lies beneath Shoreditch High Street, Kingsland Road, Stoke Newington Road, Stoke Newington High Street, Stamford Hill, High Road and Tottenham High Road on its way to Edmonton.

THE GREAT ROAD

The Great Road between London and Colchester was a particularly important road in the early years of Roman occupation when Colchester was the capital of the expanding province and London was fast developing as its major route centre and port. Like Ermine Street, this road seems to have started from the edge of the city rather than from the bridgehead which leads one to conclude that it was built after Roman London had been laid out. This is probably true of the stretch of the road from Aldgate, where it left *Londinium*, as far as the Lea crossing at Old Ford where it is joined by the Old Colchester Road.

From Aldgate it ran along Aldgate High Street and was seen 10 feet below the present surface during work on Aldgate East underground station in 1938. Beyond Whitechapel High Street the modern road veers to the south but the Roman line kept straight on to cross the River Lea near Iceland Wharf at Old Ford where a Roman pavement has been found. Burials were found along the Roman road at Old Ford.

The course is lost across Stratford Marshes, but can be picked up again on the Romford Road. It was seen in section in 1963, 4 feet below the modern road in front of the Passmore Edwards Museum. It then runs through

Above: *The Silchester Road: The change of alignment on Notting Hill.*

Forest Gate and Manor Park to Ilford, where it crossed the River Roding. Beyond this the modern road follows it to Chadwell Heath and on to Romford.

THE OLD COLCHESTER ROAD

Sometimes regarded as Roman London's northern bypass, this road in fact runs along the line of a pre-Roman trackway to Colchester from Silchester which remained in use throughout Roman times. It is now followed by Bloomsbury Way (which branches from New Oxford Street) and continues through Red Lion Square, Portpool Lane (south of Clerkenwell Road) and Hatton Wall to Old Street. It crosses Ermine Street in Shoreditch and runs beneath Bethnal Green Road and Roman Road, now paved and glorying in its Roman past, to reach the former ford across the River Lea at Iceland Wharf, Old Ford, near the present Iceland pub. Here the later Roman road from London joined it and continued to Colchester.

THE SILCHESTER ROAD

This was the start of the great South Western Highway and within *Londinium* it formed the main east-west street (*Via Principalis*) of the road grid, part of which is still in use today, overlain by Lombard Street. It left London through Newgate which, despite its name, was Roman, and after the building of city walls was provided with an imposing double gateway. This and the Silchester Road are buried beneath Newgate Street.

Beyond Newgate, once outside the limits of the Roman city, it crossed the River Fleet. Roman burials took place along the road here. It ran along the line of modern Oxford Street to Marble Arch and the junction with Watling Street. At this road junction a gravel road was found in 1961-2, buried 25 feet below the present surface and just to the south of the modern road. This may be the remains of the Roman highway but could, possibly, be part of the forecourt of a Roman inn situated at this important crossroads.

The Roman road runs straight beneath Bayswater Road to the high ground of Notting Hill, which was Nutting Hill in the not-so-distant past, on account of the good hazel bushes that grew thereabouts. On the hill top it made a subtle change of alignment to head directly to Staines and the bridge over the Thames. This alignment change carries it down the present Holland Park Avenue, across Shepherds Bush and straight on down Goldhawk Road, Stamford Brook Road and Bath Road, to cross Chiswick Common and Acton Green. It was visible on these two open spaces in the days before the railways erased it. It falls into Chiswick Road and continues along Chiswick High Road to Brentford where the London Akeman Street joined it.

THE LONDON AKEMAN STREET

The Strand, Knightsbridge and Kensington High Street run along the line of this Roman road, confusingly referred to in a charter of AD 1000 as Akeman Street, the name usually applied to the St Albans-Cirencester Roman road. The use of this name — which is thought to mean 'the road to Bath' — suggests that the Anglo-Saxons regarded it as the highway to the west.

It left London through Ludgate and crossed the River Fleet at the present site of Ludgate Circus, still in a noticeable dip in the urban landscape. Then it ran along Fleet Street and the Strand, where Roman burials have been found beside the road on its north side, continuing down the Mall towards Buckingham Palace and a junction with the Watling track to continue along Knightsbridge, Kensington High Street, Hammersmith Road, King Street and Chiswick High Road, where it joined the Silchester road.

West of the junction with the Watling track it was a pre-Roman route, a line of trackways on the dry ground north of the Thames, and was Romanised at a late date. It was never a military highway, running as it does on a series of short alignments.

STANE STREET

Stane Street was the Romans' road to Chichester, built very early on in the pacification of Britain, probably shortly after the invasion, and begins at the southern end of London Bridge, one of the two end-points fixed by the road surveyors. The road heads south along the east side of Borough High Street, where a Roman roadside settlement developed. The land along the south bank of the River Thames was very marshy and, to carry the road safely across, it was laid on a causeway constructed of wooden piles.

The Roman road then seems to have curved to the west from Borough High Street along Newington Causeway (the name is suggestive) to the Elephant and Castle, followed all the way by parish boundaries which confirm its age. This curve would have avoided soft, boggy ground near the Elephant and Castle, where a considerable depth of peat has accumulated.

From Newington Causeway, where the Roman road was proved 5 feet below the modern surface in 1961, Stane Street bore to the south-east, followed today by Kennington Park Road. This road runs along the straight alignment between the southern end of London Bridge and Chichester on the Sussex coast and the Roman road carried straight on along this same alignment east of Clapham High Street and along the modern Balham High Road, Upper Tooting Road and Tooting High Street to cross the River Wandle — in Roman days a fair-sized river — near the present A24 crossing.

THE LONDON-BRIGHTON WAY

This important Roman road led south through the iron-producing Weald to the corn-producing South Downs to a harbour somewhere near Brighton which has since vanished into the sea. It branched from Stane Street at Kennington to run along the line followed today by Brixton Road. It continued up Brixton Hill (which used to be known as Brixton Causeway, indicative of its Roman origin) to Streatham, which was named for the road. At the eastern end of Telford Avenue, opposite the bus station, a trench showed the gravel metalling of this famous road.

From Streatham Hill a straight alignment ran along Streatham High Road and London Road, where, in 1961, the Roman surface was found at the eastern end of Hepworth Road, a 32-foot-wide highway with a cambered surface made of stones and iron cinders and showing rutting from vehicle wheels.

Further south, at Hermitage Bridge over the River Graveney, the remains of a Roman ford were found. Beyond the ford the London-Brighton Way ran beneath London Road as far as Broad Green Avenue, beyond which Handcroft Road and Pitlake take up the line as far as the railway. Beyond the railway the Roman road slides like a shadow through Croydon and Purley towards Caterham, where it again becomes substantial.

THE LONDON-LEWES WAY

This important 'iron route' branched from Watling Street to head south along the east side of Asylum Road in Peckham, where it has been proved to lie 27 inches beneath the surface in the gardens of numbers 85 and 115. It then ran parallel to St Mary's Road to Nunhead station and on along the east side of Ivydale Road opposite the cemetery. Shortly beyond this it was proved buried, but intact, 20 feet wide with a slight camber and surfaced by tightly packed flints.

The London-Lewes Way crossed Brockley Rise beneath St Hilda's Church and ran straight to Blythe Hill. It then turned more to the south and crossed the Pool River, continuing on this alignment across the railway to the east of Beckenham station.

— V —
THE MIDLANDS

Being now got upon the Watling-street, I made this remark of it, that it is the direct road to Rome: for take a ruler, and lay it on a map of Europe from Chester through London and Dover, and it makes a straight line with Rome; so the great founders had this satisfaction when they travelled upon it, that they were ever going upon the line that led to the imperial Capitol.'

WILLIAM STUKELEY
Itinerarium Curiosum (1776)

Right: *Wall — the Roman site at the cross roads of Watling Street and Ryknild Street.*

Inset: *Wroxeter. Reused Roman columns from Viriconium, used as gateposts for Wroxeter church*

The Romans in the Midlands

The XIV Legion entered the Midlands in AD 43 along the ancient British trackway later to be Romanised as Watling Street. This passes through St Albans and Towcester to High Cross (Venonis), where the legion established a temporary fort. By the AD 50s the XIV, divided into two parts, was stationed at Wall, near Lichfield, and at Kinvaston near Penkridge. In AD 58 the whole legion moved west to a new base at Wroxeter.

One of the most striking features on the map of Roman Britain is the Foss Way, that great road which slices across the Midlands from the south-west to the north-east, passing through Bath, Cirencester and Leicester on its way to Lincoln. For long regarded as the first 'frontier' of the Roman province, dating from AD 47, the Foss Way is now seen more as a connecting road behind the front line and linked the main legionary contingents of the conquering

army: the IX at Lincoln, the XIV at High Cross and the II, who advanced up the Foss Way from their victorious campaign in the South West. Certainly the building of the Foss Way, which was done in separate sections, was part of Aulus Plautius' scheme for the pacification of Britain. It was not a frontier and was never defended by a line of forts.

The Boudiccan rebellion of AD 60 found the governor, Suetonius Paulinus, in North Wales. He hurried back to the south through the Midlands along Watling Street to meet Boudicca in pitched battle, though not before Colchester, St Albans and London had been sacked by the Boudiccan rebels and their inhabitants massacred.

Following the quelling of Boudicca's rebellion the Midlands slowly took shape as part of the province of Britain and the south part of the region was thickly settled. That peculiarly Roman institution, the town, was introduced, and many were founded. Cirencester (*Corinium*), one of the largest Roman towns in Britain, is particularly rich in Roman remains. There was considerable wealth in parts of the Midlands, particularly in the Cotswolds and in the Oxfordshire area, and many villas have been found near Cirencester (e.g. Chedworth) and near Akeman Street (e.g. North Leigh), demonstrating the quality of the Roman way of life in these parts. There were a large number of potteries in the region, particularly in Warwickshire, and lead mining took place in Derbyshire.

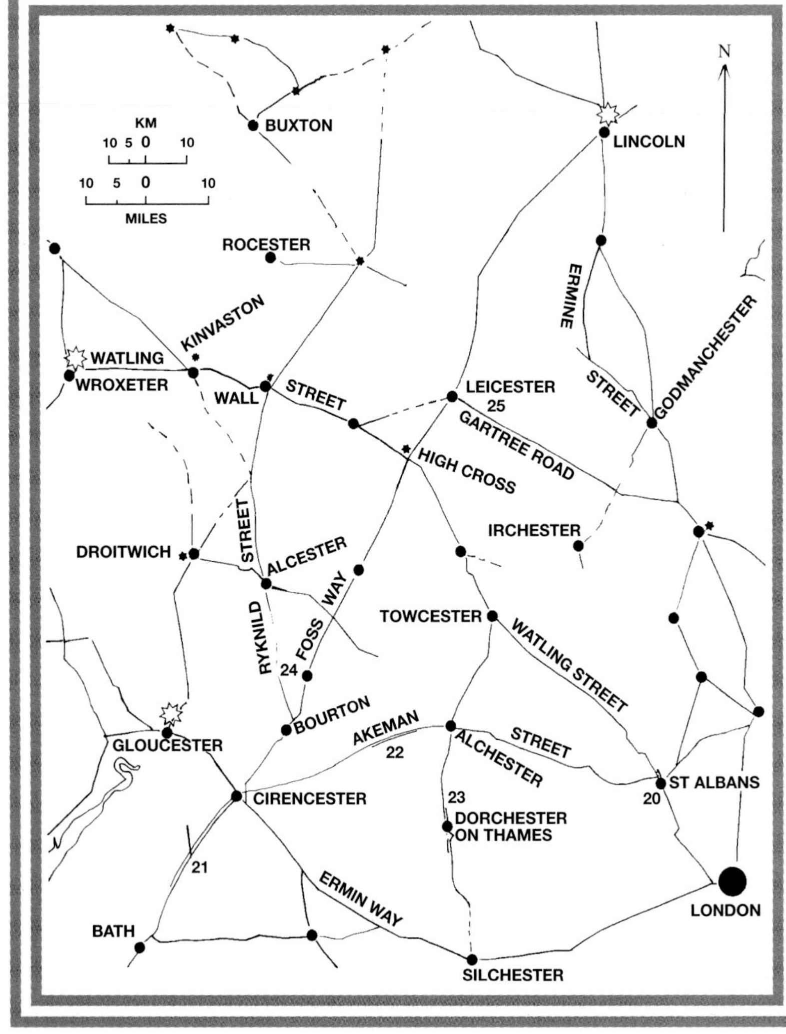

The Roman Road Network in the Midlands

The Roman roads of the Midlands fan out from four main routes, Watling Street, the Foss Way, Akeman Street (St Albans-Cirencester) and Ryknild Street (Slaughter Bridge-Chesterfield). The most important is Watling Street, the road from London through St Albans, Towcester, High Cross and Wall to Wroxeter.

There are three important route centres from which roads radiate: St Albans on Watling Street, Cirencester on the Foss Way and Derby on Ryknild Street. There were very important crossroads at High Cross (the Foss Way and Watling Street) and at Wall (Ryknild Street and Watling Street). In addition, a road heads due south from Towcester towards Silchester.

This framework of main highways was filled out by purely local roads, running between farms and hamlets, villas and towns, binding the area together.

WATLING STREET

The Roman road from London to Wroxeter

Watling Street, the Roman road which runs from the Kentish Channel ports through London and across the Midlands to the Welsh border, is probably the most famous Roman road in Britain. It is also unusual for, with the exception of one or two short lengths which run across fields, it remains in use along its entire length. In fact, it is hard to over-emphasise the importance throughout history of this line of communication. The Roman Watling Street north of London was the road upgraded by Thomas Telford in the 1820s as the Holyhead Road, designed for the Irish Mail, and extended beyond Wellington across Wales and Anglesey. The route is known to us as the A5, and, save the alignment, there is very little original Roman work left to see and admire; the coaching era and dualling of the route have obliterated it.

The Romans, however, do not deserve all the credit for this superb and lasting routeway, for it follows, in part, an ancient British track developed through the millennia preceding the Roman invasion, though the Romans had both the wit and the skill to upgrade it to a truly first class highway, straightening the road, surveying and engineering it in the true Roman fashion. Only in its passage through hilly country, such as the Chilterns, did they retain some of the prehistoric curves, altering them only by laying out the bends in a number of short, straight lengths.

Watling Street, as a Roman road, dates from early on in the pacification of Britain. It was the route used by part of the XIV Legion in AD 43-44 as they campaigned into the Midlands, and it was the road down which Suetonius Paulinus hurried to quash the Boudiccan rebellion in AD 60. The Antonine Itinerary follows the road.

Today there is only one place where Watling Street can be walked in safety and enjoyment, and that is a short mile at St Albans where the road passed through the Roman town of *Verulamium*. Walk 20 explores this stretch and the site of the Roman town.

Watling Street arrived at *Verulamium* from London. It entered the town through the massive London Gate and left through the equally massive Chester Gate. Within the town it met the roads from Braughing, Colchester, Cirencester and Silchester.

Verulamium was founded in AD 49-50 on the site of an early Roman fort on the River Ver and replaced the pre-Roman settlement in nearby Prae Wood. The early Roman town was sacked by Boudicca and her warriors, who utterly destroyed it and butchered the inhabitants. Slowly *Verulamium* rose from the ashes to become the third largest Roman city in Britain, covering 200 acres. By the end of the 2nd century the town houses were built of stone, with elaborate and beautiful mosaics. A theatre was built, the only true theatre known in Roman Britain. The massive gates at the points where Watling Street entered the city were also built at this time, while the surviving town walls are early-third-century work, built in the

Below: *Looking over the Midland Plain: Central England was an important industrial area even in Roman times.*

knowledge of the Saxon threat. *Verulamium* continued as a prosperous town right into the fifth century, but the populace slowly drifted to the new site of St Albans around the shrine of St Alban, on the opposite bank of the River Ver.

Leaving *Verulamium* by the north-west or Chester Gate Watling Street heads through Towcester (*Lactodorum*) to High Cross (*Venonis*), forward base of the XIV Legion, and junction with the Foss Way. Here, where heavy traffic now thunders along the dual-carriageway of the A5, was a notable Roman crossroads, all the more so because it was positioned so near the centre of Britain. Today five parishes and six roads meet at this isolated high-point, the only buildings being those of High Cross Hotel. In 1712 the Earl of Denbigh and other historically minded gentlemen set up a large stone monument here in recognition of its importance as a Roman crossroads. Sadly, it was wrecked by lightning in 1791, but its stump remains, incongruously positioned in the hotel garden.

From High Cross Watling Street bears west and crosses Ryknild Street at Wall. It forges ahead, straight as an arrow, through Oakengates, through the industrial area of Telford to Wellington, and then follows short, straight alignments over the hilly ground to Overley Hill. A little sunken lane follows Watling Street to the Roman city of *Viroconium* (Wroxeter) on the banks of the River Severn.

20 A WALK AT ST ALBANS

This easy circular walk includes a length of Watling Street at Roman Verulamium and passes the site of the massive London Gate.

Instructions

1. Start at the *Verulamium* car park [TL136074]. Walk north, leaving St Michael's Church on your left (which covers the site of the Roman basilica and forum) and the museum on your right. Bear left and cross the A4147 to continue up the drive of the Gorhambury Estate. This is approximately on the line of Watling Street. Pass the only known Roman theatre in Britain and carry on along the drive through the gate and across the northern half of the site of *Verulamium* that now lies under the plough. Pass out of the Roman town between the crumbling and overgrown Roman walls.

2. Continue along the drive which bears away to the left, leaving Watling Street behind. Pass Maynes Farm and bear right past 18th-century Gorhambury House. Follow the lane round to the left. Bear right with the lane through the gate and uphill to Hill End Farm.

3. Go under the M10 and cross the A4147.

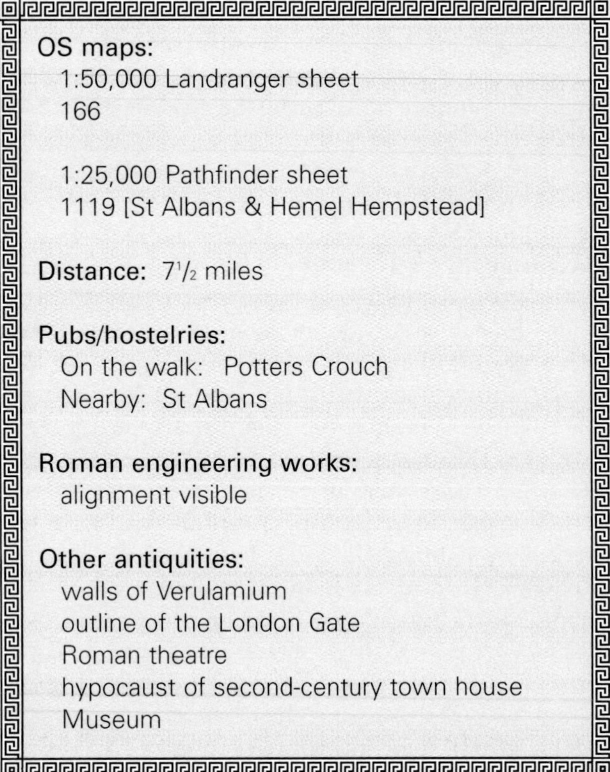

OS maps:
1:50,000 Landranger sheet
166

1:25,000 Pathfinder sheet
1119 [St Albans & Hemel Hempstead]

Distance: 7½ miles

Pubs/hostelries:
On the walk: Potters Crouch
Nearby: St Albans

Roman engineering works:
alignment visible

Other antiquities:
walls of Verulamium
outline of the London Gate
Roman theatre
hypocaust of second-century town house
Museum

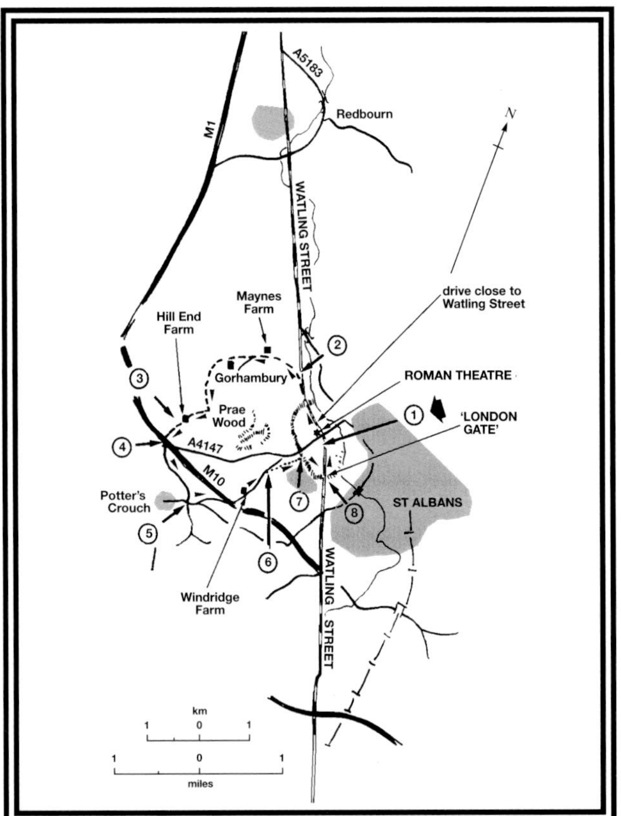

4. Continue to Potters Crouch.

5. Turn left and then bear left along Potters Crouch Lane and under the M10. Pass Windridge Farm.

6. Turn right along the footpath with houses on your right. This footpath roughly follows the line of a Roman road which ran from St Albans to Silchester.

7. Cross the road and go through the gap in the Roman town walls at approximately the site of the South West (or Silchester) Gate into that part of *Verulamium* now under playing fields. Bear right along the footpath to the site of the South or London Gate.

8. Turn left and then right across the playing fields back to the starting point.

THE FOSS WAY

The Roman road from Axminster to Lincoln

The Foss Way is intriguing: on maps it seems to cut Britain in two and its course stands out as a cross-country route totally different from other Roman roads, running diagonally through Axminster, Ilchester, Bath, Cirencester and Leicester to Lincoln. Moreover, along most of its

Above: *The Theatre at Verulamium.* **Above right:** *Looking thorough the tumbledown 3rd century town walls and across the river Ver to St Albans Abbey.*

Below: *'Lion mosaic,' on its hypocaust pillars. St Albans Museum*

length it still exists as a long string of major roads, lanes, green lanes and tracks that invite us to try to explore its whole length! One of the best walkable stretches is given in Walk 21.

For a long while it was thought that the Foss Way had been a frontier — the first frontier of Roman Britain — and it was even claimed that originally Rome did not intend to conquer the whole island, but to limit the conquest to the lowlands of the south and east. This is unlikely since the Romans needed metals and must have known of the silver-lead in the Mendips, the copper and lead in the North and the gold and copper in Wales. In fact the existence in Britain of these metals in quantity must have been one of the reasons for Rome's invasion since, once the areas concerned had been overrun, the mining started post-haste! Moreover, the Foss Way does not run along a defensible line, it is extremely long for a frontier, and even if we envisage a broad frontier zone (a concept that the Romans themselves did not develop for another fifty years at least), we have no evidence for a band of forts and military installations running along it. In fact, the Romans advanced beyond the Foss Way very shortly after it was completed and were campaigning deep into Wales by the early AD 50s.

We now know that the Foss Way was built piecemeal, with different sections completed at different times, rather than in one continuous process. This suggests that it formed a consolidating route to link the then forward bases of the legions at High Cross and Lincoln, bases from which they advanced rapidly into the west and north, with the legion based at Exeter arriving later. The Foss Way's glorious slash across the map of Britain may relate to its being conceived originally as a surveyor's base line, the important base line from which the Romans surveyed the whole country and divided it up, and for which as long a line as possible would be needed. In support of this recent suggestion it is noted that Stane Street, connecting London and Chichester, runs parallel to it, while other roads, for example the Gartree Road, run at right angles to it.

Cirencester (*Corinium*), the second largest town in Roman Britain, grew on the site of a Roman fort. The earliest fort, dating from the mid-AD 40s, was built on marshy ground and a better site was located and built on in AD 49. The army had vacated the site by the AD 70s and the thriving civil settlement that had grown up around the fort became the *civitas* capital of the Dobunni and their new administrative centre, replacing the hillfort at Trewsbury just to the south-west. Ambitious from the start, with a large forum and basilica, *Corinium* continued to prosper throughout Roman times. During the 4th century an extremely gifted school of mosaicists was centred here, and their surviving work is full of charm and assurance. In the surrounding countryside were many splendid villas, including Chedworth.

21 A WALK FROM CASTLE COMBE TO CIRENCESTER

This 23-mile walk follows the Foss Way across the Midlands. From Culkerton major A-roads now run along the Foss Way and the walk into Cirencester leaves it to follow paths close to the hillfort stronghold of the Dobunni tribe at Trewsbury Fort and the Roman fort at Trewsbury Castle. Buses run along the Foss Way into Cirencester, home of the renowned Corinium Museum.

Instructions

1. Start at Castle Combe, by the church [ST843773] and follow the footpath signposted to Nettleton Shrub through the parkland and across the stream. Continue along the track between the farm buildings and turn right to the Foss Way.

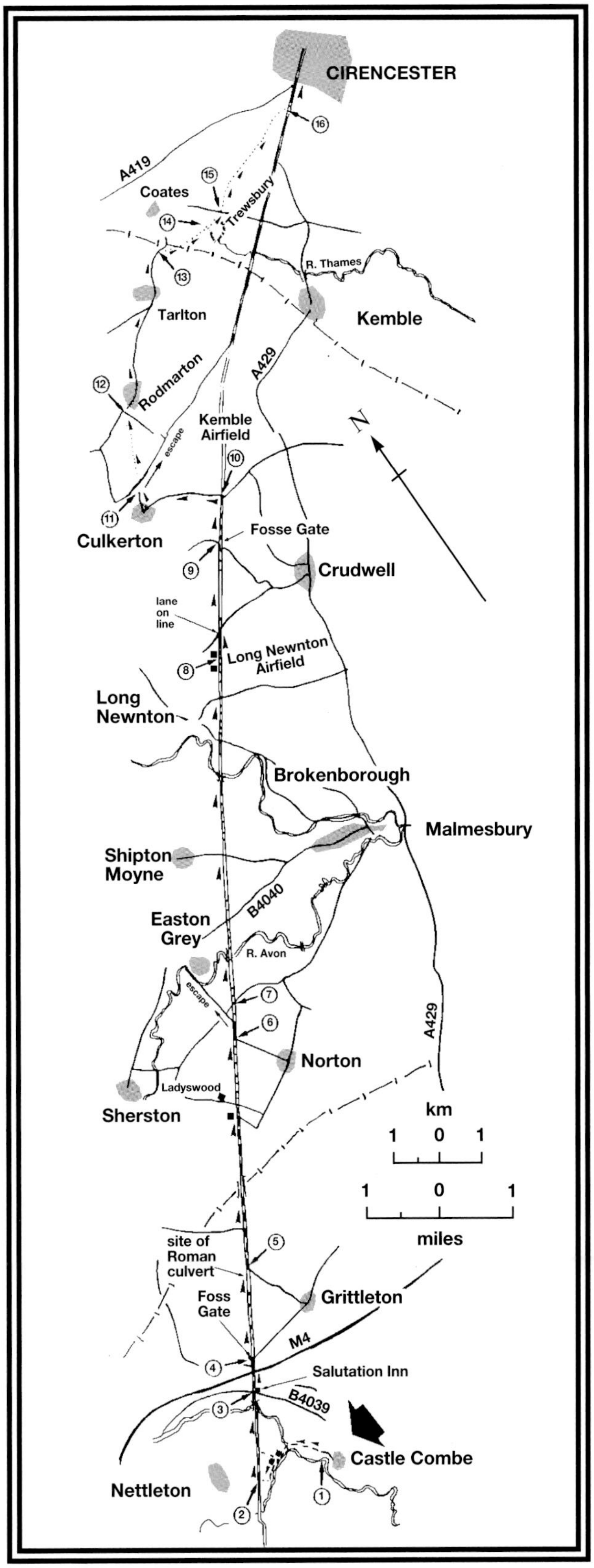

Top: *Castle Combe, where Walk 21 begins.*

Above: *Roman milestone from the Foss Way, set up in the reign of Hadrian in AD 119–120, in Leicester Museum.*

OS maps:
1:50,000 Landranger sheets
173 and 163

1:25,000 Pathfinder sheets
1168 [Chippenham & Castle Combe]
1152 [Malmesbury & Sherston]
1133 [Nailsworth & Tetbury]
1114 [Cirencester]

Distance: 23 miles

Pubs/hostelries:
On the walk: Castle Combe
Salutation Inn
Cirencester
Nearby: Grittleton
Norton
Shipton Moyne
Brokenborough

Roman engineering works:
agger visible in places

Other antiquities:
Roman Corinium at Cirencester

2. Turn right along Foss Way now a little lane.

3. Cross the B4039 and continue along the Foss Way past the Salutation Inn and under the M4.

4. At Foss Gate, turn left and then right into the green lane, on the Roman line.

5. Continue ahead where the road joins the Foss Way for a further 1¼ miles to the cross-roads near Ladyswood [ST872844]. Carry on along the green lane on the Foss Way and continue where a lane joins the Foss Way for 250 yards.

Bottom: *The Oxfordshire village of Tackley, where Walk 22 starts.*

Below: *Looking back to Tackley from Akeman Street.*

6. Either continue straight along the Foss Way or turn left to take an 'escape route' along the Roman branch road to finish the walk at Easton Grey.

7. Cross the River Avon and the B4040. Continue along the byway, which soon becomes a metalled track. Cross a minor road, the B4014, and then another minor road and keep going up the drive to Long Newnton Airfield.

8. Go through the gate in the farmyard and keep straight ahead. Keep going on the byway, which runs briefly along a lane just beyond the airfield.

9. At Foss Gate [ST942944] bear left along the minor road and turn right to continue along the Roman road.

10. When you reach the minor road between Culkerton and Chelworth, on the edge of Kemble Airfield [ST948952] the Foss Way carries straight ahead over the airfield and for this reason becomes impassable. Leave the Foss Way and turn left along the minor road into Culkerton.

11. Either take the 'escape route' and catch a bus into Cirencester, or turn right. Cross the A433 and follow the bridleway to Rodmarton.

12. Turn right along the minor road through Tarlton, continuing till just before the railway.

13. Turn right along the footpath beside the derelict Thames and Severn Canal, going under the railway and past Trewsbury hillfort just above Thames Head.

14. Cross the canal and follow the footpath past the grounds of Trewsbury House to the minor road.

15. Cross the minor road and take the footpath across the fields and over the drive of the agricultural college and so back to the Foss Way, now the A429.

16. Turn left into Cirencester.

AKEMAN STREET

The Roman road from St Albans to Cirencester

Akeman Street, the Roman road from St Albans to Cirencester, existed prior to the Roman invasion as a British track. It was Romanised very early in the pacification of Britain, forming a vital cross-country link. It left *Verulamium* through the West Gate and ran along the valley of the Bourne through the Chiltern Hills. Its course can be picked up from Berkhamsted, where it forms the present High Street, all the way to its destination at Cirencester.

From Berkhamsted it passes through the hills, approximately along the line of the A41. It changes alignment to head straight through Tring Park, where the *agger* is beautifully clear, before turning north-west again down Tring Hill, where it crosses the Upper Icknield Way. It carries straight on through Aylesbury, again used by the A41, and was set out cleverly to cross the low marshy ground of the River Ray and its tributaries. The A41 leaves the Roman alignment at the army depot on Graven Hill near the Roman town of Alchester. The Roman road was formerly traced round Graven Hill and may have approached Alchester along Langford Lane. However, it does not seem to have passed through the town but about a quarter of a mile north of it, so Langford Lane may not represent Akeman Street, but an access road leading to the town. The area is now MOD property, and thus inaccessible.

Beyond Alchester, Akeman Street turns on to a new alignment followed by a lane over the M40, across the A43 and through Kirtlington Park, where a branch road, the Oxfordshire Port Way, turned off. Akeman Street turned slightly more to the south to cross the River Cherwell by a well engineered crossing now partly obscured by the Oxford Canal. At the marshy approach to the crossing it was surfaced in broken limestone set in clay, laid upon a foundation of limestone slabs placed on brushwood. Another branch road, Ash Bank, joined Akeman Street here.

Akeman Street continued through Tackley Park, where there is a fine *agger*, and the walk joins it to follow green lanes, footpaths and minor roads. It passes through Blenheim Great Park to the site of the Roman quarries at Stonesfield overlooking the River Evenlode.

This stretch of Akeman Street is followed by the long distance path, the Oxfordshire Way, which leaves it at the Stonesfield quarries. This walk, too, leaves it here to visit the Roman villa at North Leigh. Akeman Street is terraced down to the Evenlode crossing opposite Wilcote, and continues through Ramsden to the River Windrush at Asthall and on to the River Leach to which it descends by a lovely terraceway, some 10 feet wide. In the valley bottom are the remains of the stone abutments of a bridge which carried Akeman Street over the river. From here it forges ahead to join the Foss Way at Cirencester.

Akeman Street passed through a region of pottery-making, centred on Oxford, which rose to its height in the fourth century, when it was one of the main production centres in Britain. This was a civilised part of the province where there were many villas. That near the crossing of the

Above: *North Leigh Villa. Stonesfield stands on the hill behind.*

Combe-Stonesfield road has vanished from sight. It was discovered in 1712, the first villa to be systematically recorded in this country. Little now remains to show that it ever existed, though it was a large house with rich 4th-century mosaics. The famous villa at North Leigh lies in a lovely rural setting, tucked in an encircling arm of the River Evenlode. In its final, 4th-century form it was a courtyard villa, but this was built on the site of a smaller 2nd-century house. A lavish lifestyle developed at the villas, while on the estates new crops were introduced, including grape vines and flax.

The famous quarries, where limestones were cut, were worked intermittently for many years from Roman times until 1909. They are now a series of hollows and low green mounds.

22 A WALK FROM TACKLEY TO NORTH LEIGH

This stately walk along Akeman Street (now part of the Oxfordshire Way) passes through Blenheim Great Park, skirting round some Roman quarries and finishing near North Leigh Roman Villa.

Instructions

1. Start at Tackley railway station (SP485206). Take the footpath past the overgrown fish ponds. Turn right over the stile onto Akeman Street, which here is followed by a footpath for 1¼ miles.

OS maps:
1:50,000 Landranger sheet 164

1:25,000 Pathfinder sheets
1069 [Bicester]
1092 [Woodstock]
1091 [Burford & Witney]

Distance: 8 miles

Pubs/hostelries:
On the walk: Tackley
East End, North Leigh
Nearby: Wootton
Combe
Stonesfield

Roman engineering works :
agger visible in places

Other antiquities:
Stonesfield Roman quarries — now a series of humps and hollows
North Leigh Roman villa
Grim's Ditch, Dark Age earthwork

Above: *Close-up of North Leigh Villa.*

2. Carry on where a minor road comes on to the line for 100 yards to Sturdy's Castle. Cross the A423 and continue along the footpath, which rejoins the line of Akeman Street almost immediately, to the B4027.

3. Cross the B4027 and continue along the lane, crossing the River Glyme at Stratford Bridge on the site of the Roman crossing. Carry on to the A44.

4. Cross the A44 and go through the door into Blenheim Great Park. Carry on through the park along the line of Akeman Street.

5. Cross the minor road just north of Akeman Street Farm and carry on past the villa site and across the Stonesfield-Combe road. Go downhill along the Roman terraceway across deserted Stonesfield Slate quarries to the River Evenlode.

6. Leave Akeman Street. Turn left over the bridge across the River Evenlode to follow the bridleway over the railway to North Leigh Roman Villa. Continue to the minor road.

7. Turn left along the road into East End, North Leigh.

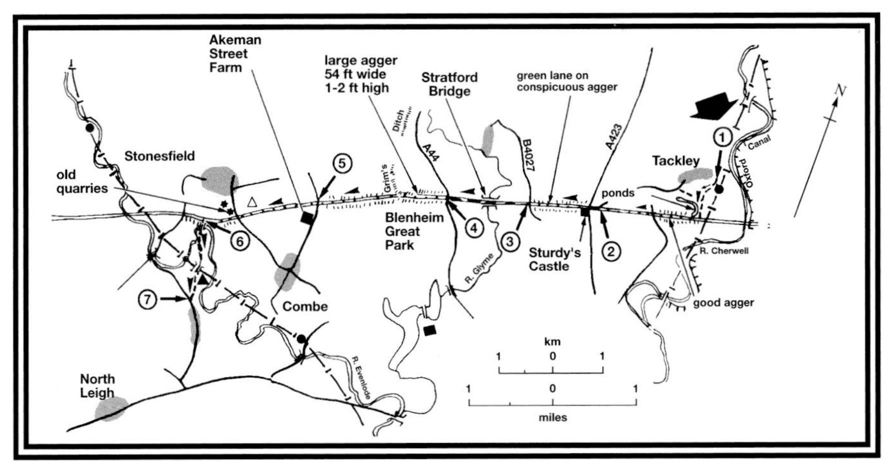

THE ROMAN ROAD FROM TOWCESTER TO SILCHESTER

This road branched south from Watling Street at Towcester. It ran in a more or less southerly direction across to Stowe Park, where it turned to the south-west, continuing over the Great Ouse at Water Stratford to Bicester. Here the Roman road turned south again, straight through the Roman town of Alchester to cross the lonely, low-lying marshlands of Ot Moor, now a patchwork of fields. In the damp and reedy centre of the moor it is followed by a raised green lane, while on the southern rim it bears more to the south-west and heads up the hillside to Beckley. Keeping to this new alignment from Beckley, the road passes over the ridge, but it is then lost in the suburbs and dual-carriageways of Oxford. Fortunately, it was traced through this area in 1840 by the Rev R. Hussey who showed that it made an important change of alignment on Shotover Hill.

This new alignment carries the road through Toot Baldon, starting point for this walk, and Marsh Baldon, whose attractive old houses are grouped indolently round its large green. It continues through Berinsfield, with wide views of the Chiltern Hills, to Dorchester-on-Thames, site of a Roman town.

Roman Dorchester was built near the confluence of the Thame and the Thames. It replaced the Catuvellaunian fort, the Dyke Hills, which lay on the flat land beside the Thames here, overshadowed by the great Atrebatean hillfort, Sinodun Camp, on the other side of the Thames.

Dorchester's Roman name is not known, but it was founded early on in the Roman occupation, possibly on the site of an early Roman fort, and was occupied throughout Roman times. It was so important that it continued to be inhabited by the Saxons. An inscription, now lost, was discovered here in 1731 and attested to the presence in Dorchester of a Roman official. The inscription probably dates from the 3rd century and it is likely that the official's duties related to tax collection. Dorchester was well placed as a tax-collection point since it was a focus of communications, not only by road but along the two rivers.

Above: *Marsh Baldon village pond.*

The only remains of the Roman town visible are parts of the earthen ramparts of its town walls, but there is plenty of reused Roman material in the abbey. Excavation has brought to light several buildings including a 3rd-century house displaying fragments of painted and decorated wall plaster, but has failed to locate the main public buildings.

The Roman road runs through the town to cross the Thame at the site of the modern bridge and continues along the north bank of the Thames for about three-quarters of a mile before crossing by ford or ferry just upstream of modern Shillingford, at a spot called Old Street Ford in a Saxon charter.

Once safely over the Thames, the Roman road runs straight up on to the downs. Today it is marked by a trackway. On the hilltop it turns back on to the alignment set on Shotover Hill, from which the Romans had to deviate in order to cross the Thames. It passes through Brightwell-cum-Sotwell, where the walk ends, and continues through Cholsey to Moulsford, where its line is taken up by the A329 which follows it through the Chiltern Hills to Pangbourne. Here it turns south to Silchester, but its course is not known with certainty.

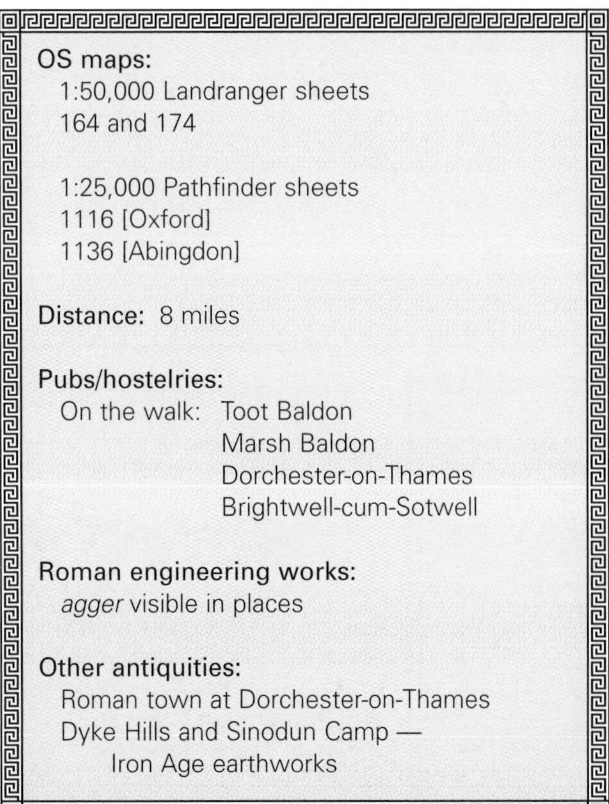

OS maps:
1:50,000 Landranger sheets
164 and 174

1:25,000 Pathfinder sheets
1116 [Oxford]
1136 [Abingdon]

Distance: 8 miles

Pubs/hostelries:
On the walk: Toot Baldon
Marsh Baldon
Dorchester-on-Thames
Brightwell-cum-Sotwell

Roman engineering works:
agger visible in places

Other antiquities:
Roman town at Dorchester-on-Thames
Dyke Hills and Sinodun Camp —
Iron Age earthworks

23 A WALK FROM TOOT BALDON TO BRIGHTWELL-CUM-SOTWELL

This walk largely follows the Roman road from Towcester to Silchester, through ancient Dorchester-on-Thames and across the river beneath the massive Iron Age hill-fort on the Sinodun Hills.

Instructions

1. Start at the bend in the lane at Toot Baldon [SP564005]. Go south along the lane on the line of the Roman road. After about 150 yards, keep straight on along 'Roman Road'.

2. Continue to Marsh Baldon.

3. Bear left and then right with the modern track, keeping to the probable alignment of the Roman road past Little Baldon Farm.

4. Cross the B4015 and continue along the track back on to the Roman alignment and through Berinsfield along 'Roman Road' and a footpath. Keep going beside a flooded gravel pit to the Dorchester bypass (A415).

5. Cross the bypass and carry on into Dorchester-on-Thames. Oxford Street is on the Roman line.

6. Leave the Roman road and turn right to take Bridge Road opposite the abbey. Turn right into Watling Lane. Keep on past the allotments and follow the footpath sign-posted 'Day's Lock'. Follow the footpath across the Dyke Hills earthwork to Day's Lock on the River Thames. Turn left alongside the river and then right over the wooden bridge spanning the Thames to Little Wittenham.

7. Turn left through the gate opposite the church. Go diagonally uphill across the field to a wood. Walk through the wood. Continue along the bridleway towards North Farm.

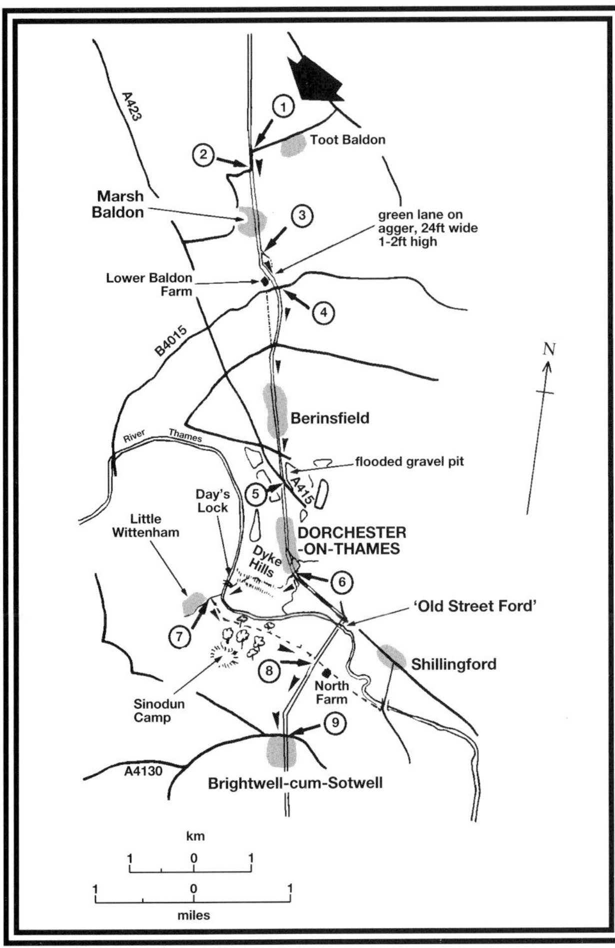

Below: *Looking to the Chiltern Hills.*

8. Before you reach North Farm turn right to rejoin the Roman road, which has ascended to this point from the former ford across the Thames. Go up the hill.

9. Cross the A4130 into Brightwell-cum-Sotwell.

RYKNILD STREET

The Roman road from Bourton-on-the-Water to Chesterfield

Ryknild Street was an important route across the Midlands, an industrial area even in Roman times. It leaves the Foss Way high on the Cotswold Hills about half a mile north-east of Bourton-on-the-Water, just to the east of Slaughter Bridge, and crosses the uplands as a low *agger* followed at first by a narrow green lane — the start of this ride/walk.

Beyond the village of Condicote Ryknild Street has to cross steep-sided and narrow valleys, but the alignment has been cleverly set so as to avoid steep gradients. At Hinchwick Manor the modern lane turns off the Roman line, which continues over the grassy and wooded uplands, where parallel routes have to be followed. The ride/walk rejoins Ryknild Street where it emerges from a private driveway known as 'the switchback'. It runs up a grassy track to its highest point, over 900 feet high, near Peter's Farm on Broadway Hill, where it turns slightly to the east to descend the spectacular Cotswold scarp at Weston-sub-Edge, where the walk ends.

A new alignment was set at the foot of the Cotswolds and Ryknild Street is followed today by a line of lanes and paths, raised in places, through Honeybourne and Bidford-on-Avon, where it crosses the river, to Alcester, site of a Roman town. It forges on through the West Midlands, where there were Roman pottery kilns at Perry Bar. On the high ground near Selly Park, Birmingham, Ryknild Street changes alignment to head for Wall, where it crosses Watling Street and continues through Burton-upon-Trent to Littlechester (*Derventio*) near Derby, where there were potteries. Here it swings to the north, passing the pottery kilns at Holbrook and Hazlewood and the lead mines at Crich to pass through Chesterfield to Templeborough on the edge of Rotherham. It is possible that it continued north to join the Lincoln-Tadcaster Roman road, but we do not know.

In Roman times the Cotswolds were a wealthy area, and

OS maps:
1:50,000 Landranger sheets
163; 151; 150

1:25,000 Pathfinder sheets
1067 [Winchcombe & Stow-on-the-Wold]
1043 [Broadway & Chipping Campden]

Distance: 14½ miles

Pubs/hostelries:
On the walk: Weston-sub-Edge
Nearby: Stow-on-the-Wold
Broadway
Chipping Campden

Roman engineering works:
agger visible in places

Below: *Dorchester-on-Thames.*

those who lived in the numerous villas led a civilised way of life. Today the Cotswold part of Ryknild Street is still inspiring, reminding us of the civilizing influence of the great Roman roads. Here, surrounded by a great sense of prosperous rural openness under the cloud-chased skies, the Roman road passes unsuspected between mottled stone villages and forges ahead with marvellous views on either side.

24 A CYCLE RIDE/WALK FROM UPPER SLAUGHTER TO WESTON-SUB-EDGE

This enchanting ride/walk along Ryknild Street, now a green lane, high on the Cotswold Hills also follows bridleways and minor lanes with good views.

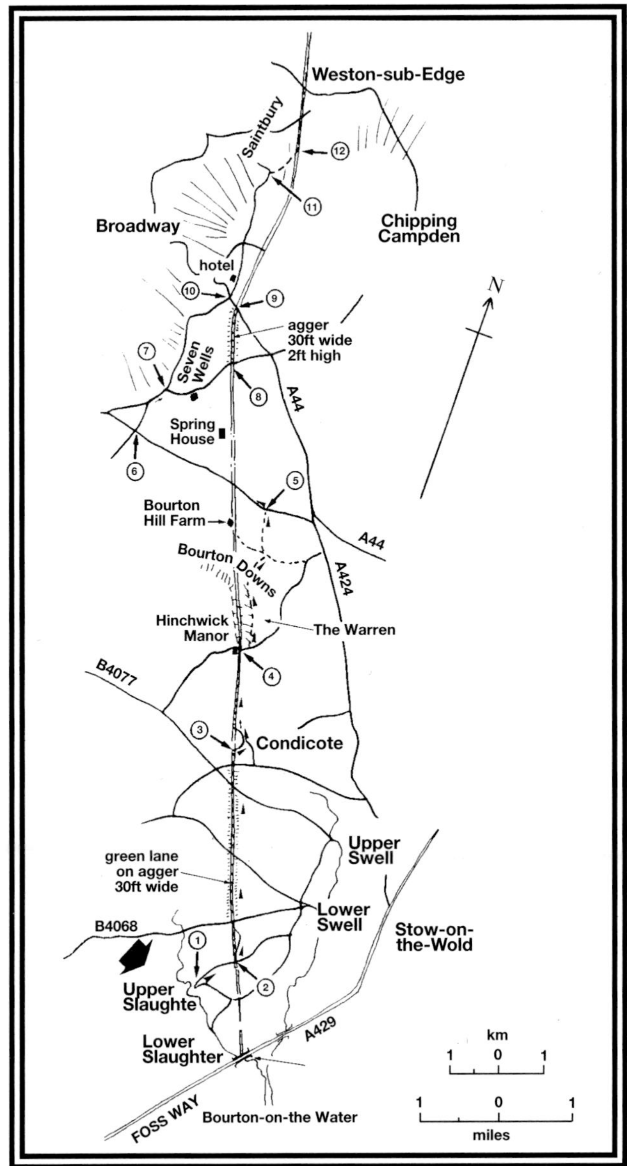

Above: *Upper Slaughter, the lovely Cotswold village where the walk starts.*

Below: *Condicote Lane treads across the Cotswolds on the raised agger of Ryknild Street.*

Instructions

1. Start at Upper Slaughter. Follow the lane uphill bearing left towards Lower Swell.

2. Turn left along the little lane that runs along the approximate line of Ryknild Street and follow it to the B4068. Cross the B-road into the green lane, Condicote Lane. Carry on along Ryknild Street which climbs up past a trig point (764 ft). Cross the B4077 and continue to the crossroads. Go straight across into the lane opposite towards Condicote.

3. Leave the line of Ryknild Street briefly to follow the modern lane round to the right through Condicote and then round to the left to rejoin Ryknild Street. Carry on along the lane on the line of Ryknild Street to Hinchwick Manor.

4. Leave Ryknild Street here — it cannot be followed again for several miles. Turn right along the minor road and then left along the bridleway. Follow the bridleway through the woodland known as The Warren and along the valley, with a steep climb up on to Bourton Downs. Turn left on to the track and, almost immediately, right again along the bridleway to the minor road.

5. Turn left and follow the minor road, crossing over the line of Ryknild Street.

6. Turn right at the crossroads and then bear right again at the T-junction.

7. Turn right along the lane and pass Seven Wells.

8. Turn left on to the track, rejoining Ryknild Street. Follow the fine grassy trackway set on the *agger* to the A44 above Broadway.

9. Leave Ryknild Street and turn left along the A44.

10. Cross over to the minor road and continue past the hotel. Go over another cross-roads.

11. Turn right on to the track to descend the Cotswold scarp with a wood on your right.

12. Bear left back on to the line of Ryknild Street, now a green lane, and follow it into Weston-sub-Edge.

THE GARTREE ROAD

The Roman road from Godmanchester to Leicester

This road was laid out early in the pacification of Britain. It was built by the engineers of the XIV Legion, Gemina, in the AD 40s, following the more easterly line of that legion's two-pronged campaign into the Midlands, and ran north-westwards from Godmanchester to Leicester (*Ratae*). It was a direct and important route and for the last 10 miles or so into Leicester has been known traditionally as the Gartree Road.

It branched from Ermine Street at Godmanchester and ran westwards to Titchmarsh, where it changed alignment slightly to descend to the River Nene, beyond which another alignment carried it through Brigstock, where remains of a Roman temple have been found, and on to Corby. Here it runs along a forest ride with clear traces of the *agger* showing alongside it, but modern Corby has destroyed most traces of the Roman road.

The road must have crossed the River Welland between Cottingham and Medbourne, but the crossing place is not known. Beyond the river, a north-westerly alignment continued the road all the way to Leicester, first followed by a lane, then running across open fields past Medbourne, Slawston and Glooston, where this walk begins. It follows lanes and tracks past Carlton Curlieu Manor, with its crocus-studded lawn and rippling pond, to Little Stretton, where the walk ends. Beyond this the road continues, somewhat distorted but still on the alignment, to the outskirts of Leicester, beyond which no trace is visible.

The countryside through which this road runs is softly pastoral, a land of folds and hollows, with unexpectedly wide views dominated by mellow church towers. Indeed, the area is particularly rich in churches and unspoilt villages. In Roman times, when the Gartree Road was an important link in the civilised landscape, it led from village to village, travelled by merchants and businessmen, by officials and farmers, by honest men and by vagabonds.

Above: *Little Stretton church.*

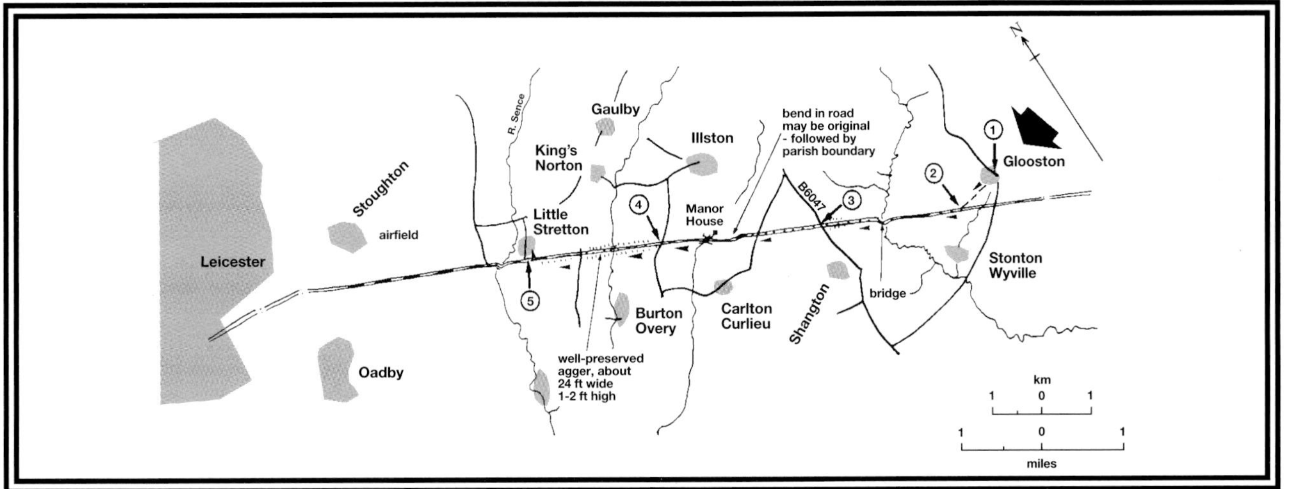

Above: *The Gartree Road slants down to cross a stream.*

Yet, as is so frequently the case with Roman roads, today's settlements turn their backs to the road, and the old highway passes between them as if it wishes to ignore them. Along the pleasant, walkable stretch of the Gartree Road, Glooston, Illston-on-the-Hill, Galby and nearby King's Norton, possessor of a handsome 18th-century church, and attractive Little Stretton, lie to the north of the road while Stonton Wyville, Shangton, Carlton Curlieu and Burton Overy lie to the south. These villages were all founded long after Roman times, showing clearly how Dark Age and later settlers rejected the past and created their own brave new world.

25. A WALK FROM GLOOSTON TO LITTLE STRETTON

This lovely pastoral walk travels over the uplands along a string of lanes and tracks which follow the Roman Gartree Road.

Instructions

1. Start at Glooston. Follow the track by the farm to the Gartree Road.

2. Bear right on to the Roman line and continue along it. Cross the bridge over the stream and go uphill with the hedge, showing traces of the *agger*, on your right. Go through the gate into Field Road to reach the B6047.

3. Cross the B6047 and continue along the little lane and over the crossroads past Carlton Curlieu Manor.

4. Go straight across down the track and over the stream. Go straight over into a lane.

5. Turn right into Little Stretton.

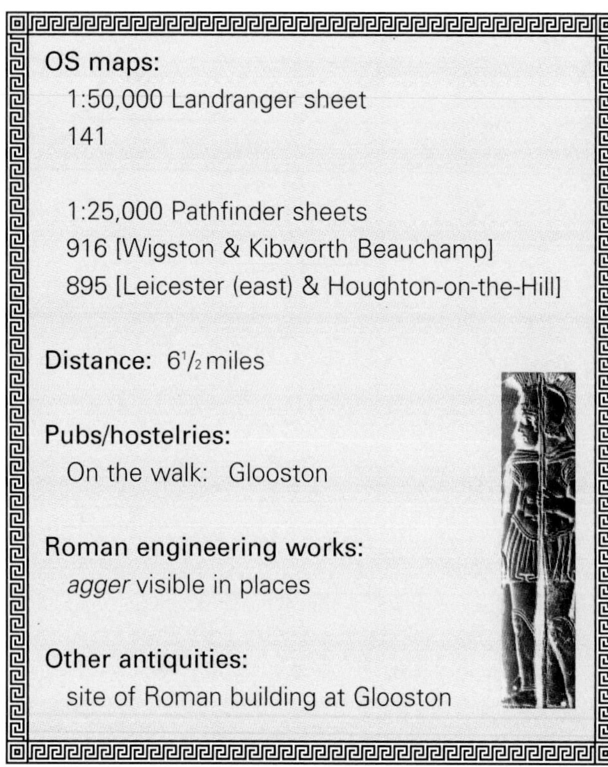

OS maps:
1:50,000 Landranger sheet
141

1:25,000 Pathfinder sheets
916 [Wigston & Kibworth Beauchamp]
895 [Leicester (east) & Houghton-on-the-Hill]

Distance: 6½ miles

Pubs/hostelries:
On the walk: Glooston

Roman engineering works:
agger visible in places

Other antiquities:
site of Roman building at Glooston

Top: *Roman stone head of a boy from Hinkley, in Leicester Museum. The excellent workmanship on the weathered head shows the height of civilization reached in the Midlands in Roman times.*

Above: *Jewellery: the native British wore much jewellery and this changed little under the Pax Romana. National Museum of Wales.*

— VI —
SOUTH WALES AND THE MARCHES

'Glory in war exceeds all other forms of success:
this is the origin of the Roman people's reputation.'

CICERO

Below: *Sarn Helen (Brecon) descends to the afon Llia along the lane used by a later coaching route.*

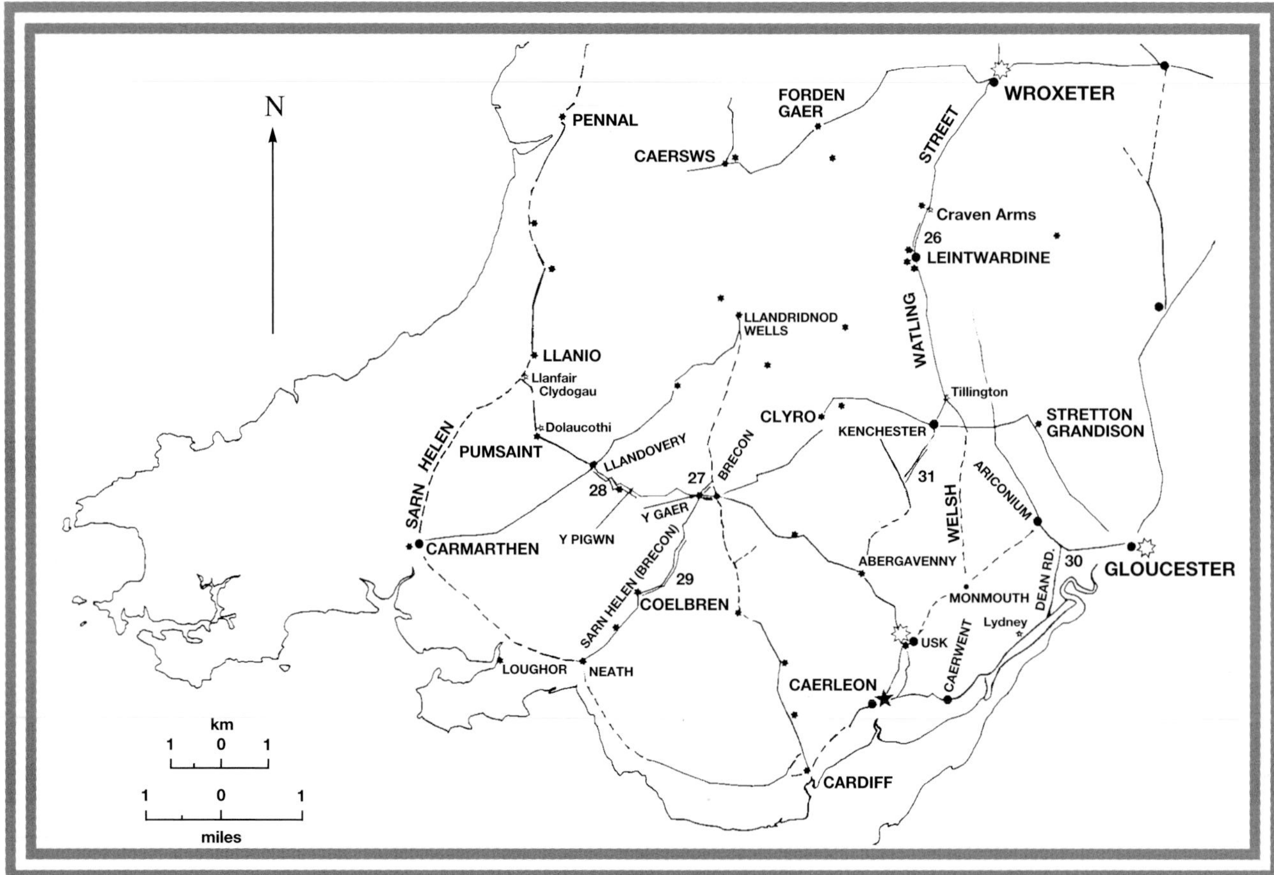

The Romans in South Wales and the Marches

The tribes of South Wales were fiercely hostile to Rome during the period of the conquest. The broken, largely mountainous terrain allowed them to wage a guerrilla war and pose a serious threat to the pacification of the province. Here in South Wales the fugitive, Caratacus, found a ready welcome. This dynamic and inspiring British prince disappeared following the battle on the Thames in AD 43, only to reappear in AD 48 as leader of the Silures, the most powerful tribe in South Wales; clearly he commanded an authority over many British tribes.

Ostorius Scapula, the governor who succeeded Aulus Plautius in AD 47, started the process of pacifying South Wales. He forced Caratacus to flee northwards and captured him, but the Silures were not totally subdued until AD 74 under the then governor, Julius Frontinus. The whole of Wales was finally brought under Roman control in AD 78 by the most famous governor of all, Julius Agricola.

Scapula moved the XX Valeria Legion to the Welsh front from Colchester in AD 49 and installed them at Kingsholm, Gloucester. In later years they moved to Chester. The main military installation in South Wales was at Caerleon (Isca) which was founded in AD 74-5 by Julius Frontinus as the base for the II Legion, Augusta, which moved forward to this spot from Exeter. Isca was a completely new foundation, replacing Usk (Burrium) as the most important military installation hereabouts. The flood-prone valley-bottom site at Burrium had been found to be unsatisfactory and, with typical Roman adroitness, was abandoned. The new fortress at Isca enclosed some 70 acres and could accommodate 5,000 men. It had good sea and river as well as road links and it continued to be garrisoned until about AD 290, when part of the Legion was transferred to the Saxon Shore fort at Richborough in Kent. Caerleon is famous for its amphitheatre, built in AD 80, about the same time as the Colosseum in Rome. It was probably used for military exercises and parades with occasional gladiatorial blood-lettings.

Wales was always a difficult land for the Romans and, except in the region along the Severn estuary, never became a totally civilian zone. A complex network of forts, fortlets and linking roads was constructed to control the area by dividing the broken terrain into manageable blocks. Remaining a garrisoned region, few towns were founded. Caerwent, Kenchester, Ariconium, and Carmarthen are here: the only ones known. There was farming along the Severn estuary lowlands, and probably some land reclamation, as shown by a series of drainage ditches on the foreshore near Cardiff. The few villas in the region are also concentrated along the south coast, including the important site and associated temple at Lydney. Generally, though, South Wales remained untouched by Roman civilisation and for many of the tribesmen life changed little under Roman rule.

South Wales was an important source of metals: iron from the Forest of Dean, lead from Glamorgan and, most important of all, gold from Dolaucothi. The gold, bound for the imperial mint, must have travelled the roads of South Wales under military escort.

Roman Roads in South Wales and the Marches

The broken landscape of South Wales and the Marches had an important effect on the Roman roads. They tend not to be built on large *aggers,* running more often along narrow terraceways; while instead of following long, straight alignments they run on short, straight lengths which ease them as directly as possible through the difficult terrain, breaking it up into patrollable blocks.

Two Roman roads run from north to south down the length of Wales. On the west, Sarn Helen runs south from Caerhun through Pennal to Carmarthen. On the east, Welsh Watling Street links Chester to its sister legionary fortress at Caerleon through Wroxeter, Leintwardine, Hereford and Monmouth.

There were several cross-country routes joining the two north-south highways. The most important ran from Caerleon via Brecon to Llanfair Clydogau on Sarn Helen. A road shadowed the south coast through Caerwent, Caerleon, Cardiff and Neath and probably continued to Carmarthen, where there was a fort and later a town.

Brecon fort (Y Gaer) was the important route centre, situated half-way between Sarn Helen and Welsh Watling Street, with six roads converging on it, including the two branches of the Caerleon-Llanfair Clydogau road, and another 'Sarn Helen' coming up from Neath.

Other route centres were at Kenchester — crossroads of the Stretton Grandison-Brecon road, and the Tillington-Abergavenny road; the Roman town of Ariconium near Weston-under-Penyard in the Forest of Dean, with roads to Gloucester, Leominster and Lydney (the Dean Road); and Llandovery — crossing of the Caerleon-Llanfair Clydogau and Llandrindod Wells-Carmarthen roads.

The network, particularly in the south-east, is remarkably complete and there is plenty to reward those in search of Roman roads: upland vistas, precipitous slopes and wild scenery in which the old road is the one tangible human artefact.

WELSH WATLING STREET

The Roman road from Wroxeter to Caerleon

This was the important trunk road by which the Romans were able to police Wales. It ran southwards from the legionary fortress at Chester through the Roman town of Wroxeter to connect by a branch road with the legionary fortress at Caerleon. Its course south of Wroxeter is explored here, while the northern part is explored in the next chapter.

The road may date from the campaigns of Suetonius Paulinus against the Silures, when the XIV Legion was at Wroxeter and there was a legionary fortress at Usk — possibly the original destination of this road.

From Wroxeter the road passes through broken terrain which makes straight alignments almost impossible to follow, yet it is remarkably well engineered to run in a series of straight lengths along the higher valley sides, while modern roads and railways wind along the valley floors.

It crosses the River Severn and runs along the deep defile of the Church Stretton valley, roughly along the line of the A49. At Marshbrook it heads up over the hillside to Bushmoor and is then followed by a little lane through Wistanstow before bearing back towards the south-west just north of Craven Arms, where this cycle ride/walk begins. From here Welsh Watling Street is followed by a line of lanes across the hilly country to Shelderton.

Beyond Shelderton the road is terraced along the hillside now a green lane and footpath to north of Leintwardine (Bravonium), through which it passes as the main street and where the cycle ride/walk ends. There was a Roman fort here, built opposite the confluence of the rivers Teme and Clun. It covered an area of about 10 acres, and on the north-west of the village some of the enclosing earthworks can still be seen. The fort was probably garrisoned by a single unit of about 500 men and acted as a supply depot for the central part of the Welsh Marches. Welsh Watling Street ran straight through the Roman fort and associated settlement, but most of the Roman earthworks are buried by the village. The church is built on two levels as it sits on a rampart! Coins, a bronze ring, roof tiles, pottery and parts of a quern have been found here.

Bravonium fort replaced the nearby fort at Buckton, and was only one of many Roman military installations in this region of intense and prolonged Roman military activity. Brandon Camp, an Iron Age hillfort, was taken over by the Romans, who built a fort of their own within its ramparts, a most unusual occurrence. Presumably this was an early site, a convenient installation along Welsh Watling Street. It stands on a knoll overlooking the confluence of the Teme and Clun to the south of

Above: *The broken frequently mountainous terrain of South Wales needed concerted Roman effort to ring them under control. The Fforest Fawr was in the lands of the bitterly anti-Roman Silures.* Below: *Intaglios. Museum of Wales.*

Leintwardine, surrounded by a bank and a ditch.

After crossing the River Teme at Leintwardine, Welsh Watling Street set out on a new alignment to pass through the hills between Aymestrey and Mortimer's Cross and on to Hereford. Just north of Hereford it was crossed by the cross-country road from Stretton Grandison through Kenchester (Magnis) to Brecon (Cicucium). The course of Welsh Watling Street is not clear between Hereford and Monmouth, though it is known that a branch road left it at Monmouth heading directly for Caerleon (Isca). Welsh Watling Street may have continued down the Wye valley to join the coast road near Caerwent.

This road is one of the surprising survivals of Roman times — passing directly across the intricate countryside of the Marches as though finding an easy alignment were a simple matter. The landscape here, celebrated in verse and music, is backed to the west by the Welsh mountains giving unexpected views.

26 A CYCLE RIDE/WALK FROM CRAVEN ARMS TO LEINTWARDINE

This enjoyable ride/walk traverses the hilly landscape of the Welsh Marches along a very important Roman road, now little lanes, a green lane and a footpath, to the Roman town of Bravonium, modern Leintwardine.

Instructions

1. Start at Craven Arms railway station [SO432831]. Head north along the main A49 and then turn left to Newington (signposted to Long Lane Industrial Estate). Go over the level crossing and continue to the crossroads.

2. Turn left on to Welsh Watling Street, cross the B4368 and go under the railway. Continue for another 3¼ miles to Shelderton. Here the Roman line leaves the modern lane.

3. Leave the Roman line briefly. Turn right to head south-west along the lane towards Leintwardine.

If you are walking, turn left after about 200 yards through the gate on to the track. Follow the track obliquely up the hill. The Roman road comes in from the left. Continue along the footpath on the Roman line. Cross over the farm track and carry on to Stormer

Above: *Selection of finds from the legionary fortress at Caerleon. National Museum of Wales.* **Above right:** *Face pot from the Roman town of Caerwent. National Museum of Wales.* **Below:** *Caerwent — a small Roman temple.*

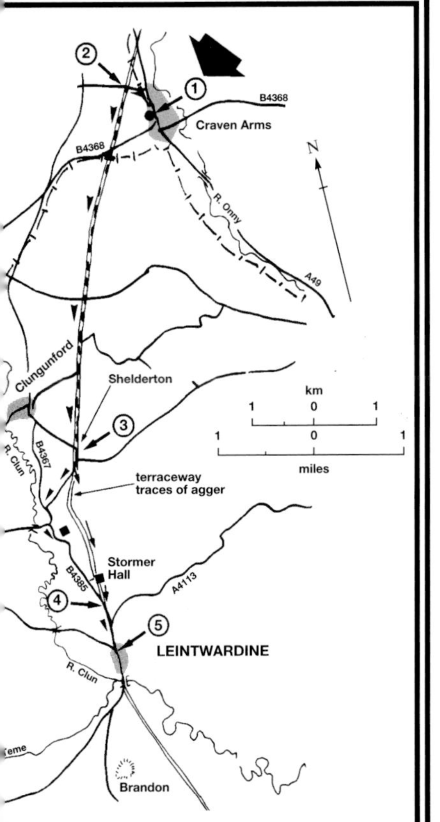

OS maps:
1:50,000 Landranger sheet 137

1:25,000 Pathfinder sheets
931 [Craven Arms]
951 [Ludlow]
950 [Knighton (Powys) & Brampton Bryan]

Distance: 6½ miles

Pubs/hostelries:
On the walk: Craven Arms
Leintwardine
Nearby: Aston on Clun
Wigmore

Roman engineering works:
agger visible in places
terraceway

Other antiquities
site of Roman town of Bravonium (Leintwardine)

Hall. Follow the yellow waymarks through the farmyard. Continue across the field and stile to the road junction at SO404751.

If you are riding, carry on along the lane and then turn left on to the B4367. In about a quarter of a mile turn left again on to the B4385 to rejoin the Roman road at SO404751.

4. Follow the B4385 and then the A4113.

5. Arrive at Leintwardine.

THE ROMAN ROAD FROM CAERLEON TO LLANFAIR CLYDOGAU

This was the major cross-country road in South Wales. It ran through Usk, Abergavenny, Brecon and Llandovery and close to the gold mines at Dolaucothi, so it was soon established as the 'gold route' of Roman Britain and is included in the Antonine Itinerary, making it an official route.

Left: *Leintwardine — site of the Roman fort, Bravonium.* **Above:** *Welsh Watling Street approaching the river Teme.*

These old mines are the only known Roman gold mines in Britain and were in operation by AD 75, the year following the subjugation of South Wales. The gold was mined under government supervision (mineral rights were vested in the Emperor) and carried under military escort along this Roman road bound for the imperial mint at Lyons and possibly Rome itself.

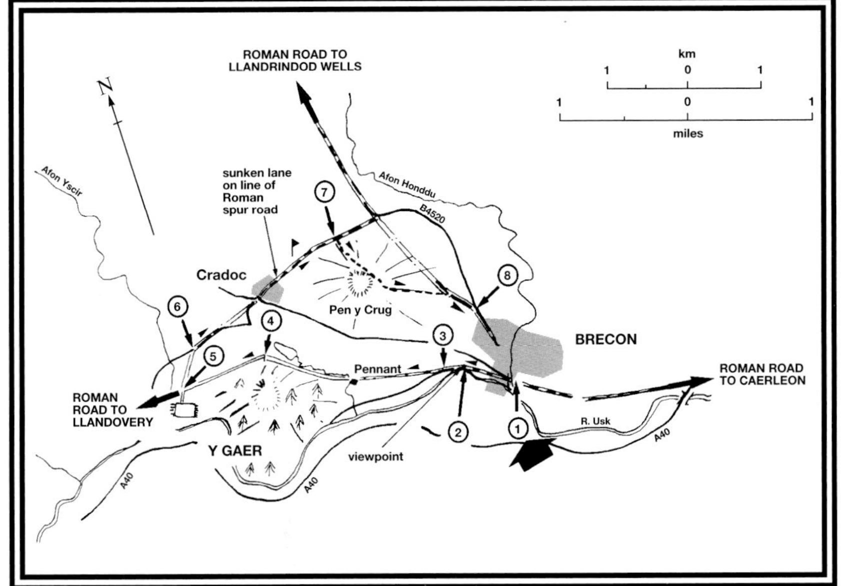

This road was probably begun early on in the pacification of Wales under the governorship of Ostorius Scapula and completed under Julius Frontinus in AD 74-75. It left Caerleon to head north-east to Llanhennock and on to Usk (Burrium). Here, it turned northwards through the hills and then west to follow the River Usk to Abergavenny (Gobannium). Beyond Abergavenny it runs in short, straight lengths to Crickhowell, where it climbs up the northern valley side, its course marked today by a little lane. It passes the Roman fort at Pen y Gaer and continues to Bwlch, where it turns along Allt yr Esgair before dropping down to Brecon, now followed by a lane and then by the A40.

Beyond Brecon, location of Walk 27, this Roman road is now a green lane as far as the major fort at Y Gaer (Cicucium). This was first built under Agricola in AD 80, and the wooden structure was replaced by stone in about AD 140. Further rebuilding took place at the end of the second century, but the fort seems to have been abandoned soon after this. It was recommissioned in the third century and the south gate repaired.

At Y Gaer, the Roman road crosses the Afon Ysgir and continues along the northern hillside above the River Usk, but its actual course is not certain for the next 6 miles to Trecastle, where Walk 28 begins. The Roman road climbs steeply out of Trecastle, still in use as a minor road, and then runs along the top of the ridge, Mynydd Bach Trecastell, which gives commanding views. The road passes the Roman marching camps and fortlet at Y Pigwn. These earthworks, set on the desolate upland, date from the early years of the Roman conquest. They are temporary marching camps, one dating from the early years of the Welsh campaign under Ostorius Scapula in AD 47, and the other from the campaign under Frontinus in AD 74-78. The later camp is smaller and lies within the ramparts of the earlier camp, at an angle to them. Both camps lie clearly visible beneath the waving grasses, though later lead workings have destroyed their southern ramparts.

The Romans replaced these camps with a permanent small fort, built to guard the road about a quarter of a mile to the west. It commands a magnificent view along the line of the road to Llandovery. Sadly, very little can be made out today, the visible earthwork being a medieval motte. In Wales, where Romans went, Normans went too!

The road passes through a shallow cutting beside the fortlet and descends the ridge as a series of zig-zags, some very waterworn. Below the zig-zags, the road changes to a more northerly course and then back to its original north-westerly alignment and arrives at Llandovery, site of a Roman fort, where Walk 28 ends.

Beyond Llandovery the road continues to the gold mines at Dolaucothi near Pumsaint, where it changes alignment to head north through Ffarmers and across the Bryn Mawr ridge before turning north-west once again to Llanfair Clydogau, where it joins Sarn Helen.

27. A CIRCULAR WALK AT BRECON

This interesting circular walk incorporates a Roman fort, an Iron Age hillfort, a riverside ramble and three Roman roads at the important route centre of Brecon.

Instructions

1. Start at Brecon on the town side of the bridge over the River Usk. Cross the tributary River Honddu and bear left to the riverside footpath to the viewpoint at SO037289.

2. Go past the boathouse and through the car park. Turn right to the minor road.

3. Bear left by the house into the lane which marks the Roman road on the last stretch of its journey from Gobannium to Cicucium. Pass Pennant and go into the woodland above the small reservoir.

4. Go through the gate and continue along the fenced track — on a last alignment for Y Gaer. Go through the gate at the end of the fenced track. The lane which crosses

OS maps:
1:50,000 Landranger sheet 160

1:25,000 Pathfinder sheets
1038 [Talgarth]
1062 [Brecon]

Distance: 6 miles

Pubs/hostelries:
On the walk: Brecon

Roman engineering works:
agger visible in places

Other antiquities:
Y Gaer, Roman camp of *Cicucium*,
Iron Age hillfort of Pen-y-Crug

here and which leads on the left to the Roman fort, is on the line of a Roman spur-road which connected the main Caerleon-Brecon-Llandovery road with the Llandrindod Wells-Cardiff Roman road. To visit the fort turn left through the farmyard. When you have visited the fort return to this point.

5. Leave this Roman road here. Turn right along the farm track.

6. Turn right on to the lane and follow it eastwards around

the sharp left-hand turn to the crossroads at Cradoc. Go straight over the staggered crossroads and past the golf course.

7. Turn right on to the bridleway. Climb up the hill past Pen-y-Crug hillfort. Bear left down the hill into the lane which bears sharply to the right taking you on to the third Roman road of this walk, the main Llandrindod Wells-Cardiff road.

8. Turn right along the B4520 back into Brecon.

28. A WALK FROM TRECASTLE TO LLANDOVERY

This upland walk gives wide views over the South Wales mountains along the 'gold route' of Roman Britain.

Instructions

1. Start at Trecastle on the A40. Turn left uphill along the minor road.

Opposite left: *Brecon town centre. The modern town lies to the east of the Roman fort, Y Gaer (Cicucium).* **Bottom:** *The 'gold route' of Roman Britain on Mynydd Bach Trecastell.* **Below:** *The south gate of the Roman fort of Y Gaer, Roman Cicucium, looking across the river Usk.*

OS maps:
1:50,000 Landranger sheet 160

1:25,000 Pathfinder sheets
1061 [Sennybridge]
1037 [Mynydd Bwlch y Groes]
1036 [Llandovery]

Distance: $8^{3}/_{4}$ miles

Equipment:
walking boots
waterproof clothing
compass
OS maps

Pubs/hostelries:
On the walk: Trecastle
Llandovery

Roman engineering works:
agger visible in places
zig-zags down Mynydd Bach Trecastell
hilltop cutting at motte near Y Pigwn camps

Other antiquities:
Roman marching camps at Y Pigwn
Site of Roman fortlet at Y Pigwn
Site of Roman fort at Llandovery

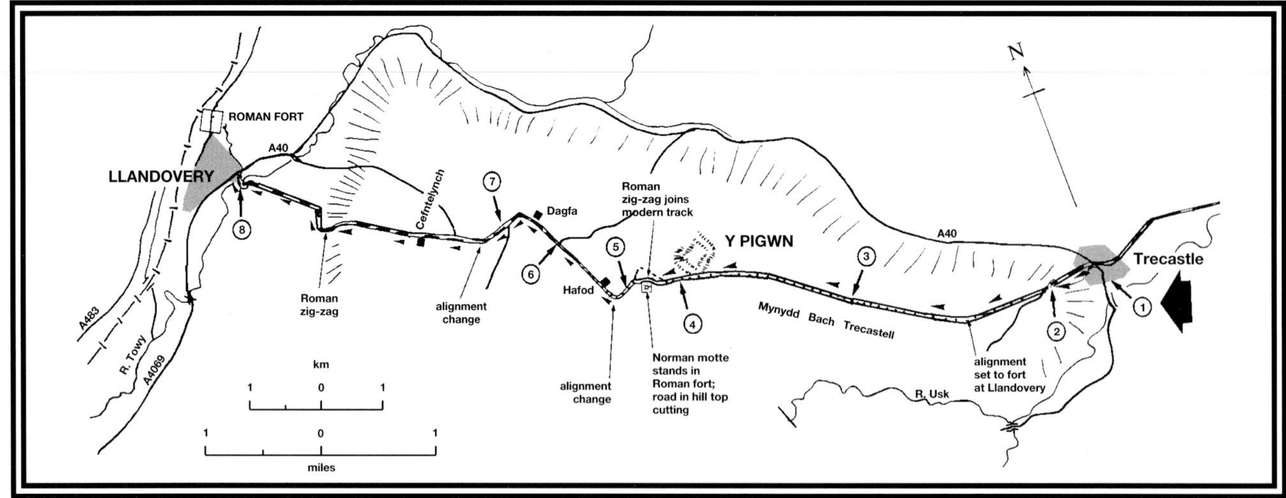

Above: *Waterworn rock-cut zig-zag descending from Mynydd bach Trecastell.*

2. Bear right at the junction and on to the lane. After three-quarters of a mile the Roman road changes alignment from west to north-west, pointing directly towards the unseen Llandovery.

3. Go through the gate and continue along the rough trackway to Y Pigwn camps, which lie on your right behind some prominent lead-mining tips.

4. Carry on along the trackway. The Roman road is the terraceway just downhill on your right. It crosses the modern track shortly before this turns abruptly to the right and carries straight on through a cutting on the east of the motte standing on the Roman fortlet. It is possible to follow the Roman line through this cutting and down the original Roman zig-zags. These rejoin the modern track about half-way down the hill before reaching the gate.

5. Go through the gate and continue past Hafod.

6. Join the lane which comes in from the right. Bear left beyond Dagfa.

7. Keep right where the lane forks and enter the plantation. Continue along the lane past Cefntelych and down another original Roman zig-zag.

8. Bear right with the road over the Afon Brân into Llandovery.

SARN HELEN (BRECON)

The Roman road from Brecon to Neath

This Roman road, which on the uplands is known as Sarn Helen, is one of the many Welsh roads of that name unconnected with the major west coast road from Caerhun to Carmarthen. Here, to avoid confusion, it is identified as the Sarn Helen associated with Brecon. This road was one of the main routes which radiated from the important fort at Y Gaer near Brecon. It is an upland road, crossing the high moorland on a course than runs south-west to Neath.

Forts and camps show that this road was part of the original military network of South Wales set up by Ostorius Scapula in about AD 47 when he launched his offensive against the Silures. The Silures and their allies, the bitterly anti-Roman Ordovices of the north, waged guerrilla warfare against Roman installations and small units. Good roads guarded by forts were imperative for the safety of the Roman soldiers. This road was an important link in the network. Later, when, under Julius Frontinus, a new forward legionary base was established at Caerleon (Isca), this road maintained its importance in policing the annexed territory.

Sarn Helen (Brecon) probably branched from the Roman road to Llandovery near Aberyscir, though this part of its course is still not known for certain. It appears as a hard, green track on the slopes of Mynydd Illtud and then passes diagonally up the hillside as a terraceway past Gelliau to be joined by an old coaching road where this road also joins it. The road then crosses the bare uplands of Fforest Fawr, skilfully engineered under the stern gaze of the Brecon Beacons through this moorland wilderness of brown, wind-driven grasses, of stinging rain and sudden outbursts of sun. First it runs as a terrace along Bryn Melyn and then as a hollow way down to the Llia valley east of the ancient standing stone, Maen Llia. Here it bears southwards along the valley floor (used for a short distance by the modern road) and then turns south-west again to strike off up the farther hillside through the site of a Roman marching camp. It continues over the hill and drops into the Nedd valley to cross the river by ford. It then bears south up the hillside as a rough terrace and, on the hilltop, turns south-west to the fort Ton-y-Castell, near Coelbren, where the walk ends.

From Ton-y-Castell the Roman road took up a more southerly alignment, but its course is lost in mounting the hillside opposite among the welter of old slag heaps. Once beyond the mining area it follows the Hirfynydd ridge and then dips down steeply via Lletyrafel to Aberdulais and Neath.

In common with most Roman roads in Wales, Sarn Helen (Brecon) does not run on an *agger* except where necessary, such as on its approach to the fort at Ton-y-Castell across a marshy hollow. On the uplands this is a level road laid direct on the rocky surface, its skilfully engineered and aligned course proclaiming its Roman origin.

29. A WALK FROM MYNYDD ILLTUD TO COELBREN

This is a testing walk in moorland terrain with superb views, clear mountain streams and an unmatched sense of vast solitude. This is a Roman road fit for the Roman eagles!

Instructions

1. Start on Mynydd Illtud at the mountain centre. Follow the trackway south-west along the hillside. Sarn Helen (Brecon) is running parallel to you uphill on your right.

2. Cross the A4215 and go along the minor road opposite towards Forest Lodge. Keep straight on along the green lane which runs along the contour to the descent to the Nant Cwm du.

3. Cross the stream and a little way on the Roman road merges from the right. Continue along the Roman road as

OS maps:
1:50,000 Landranger sheet
160

1:25,000 Outdoor Leisure sheet
11 [Brecon Beacons National Park
(central area)]

Distance: 14½ miles

Equipment:
walking boots
waterproof clothing
compass
OS maps

Pubs/hostelries:
On the walk: Coelbren
Nearby: Ystradfellte

Roman engineering works:
agger visible in places
terraceways
river crossings

Other antiquities:
Roman fort at Coelbren
Maen Llia and Maen Madoc — standing stones
Bedd Twyl Illtyd, a cromlech

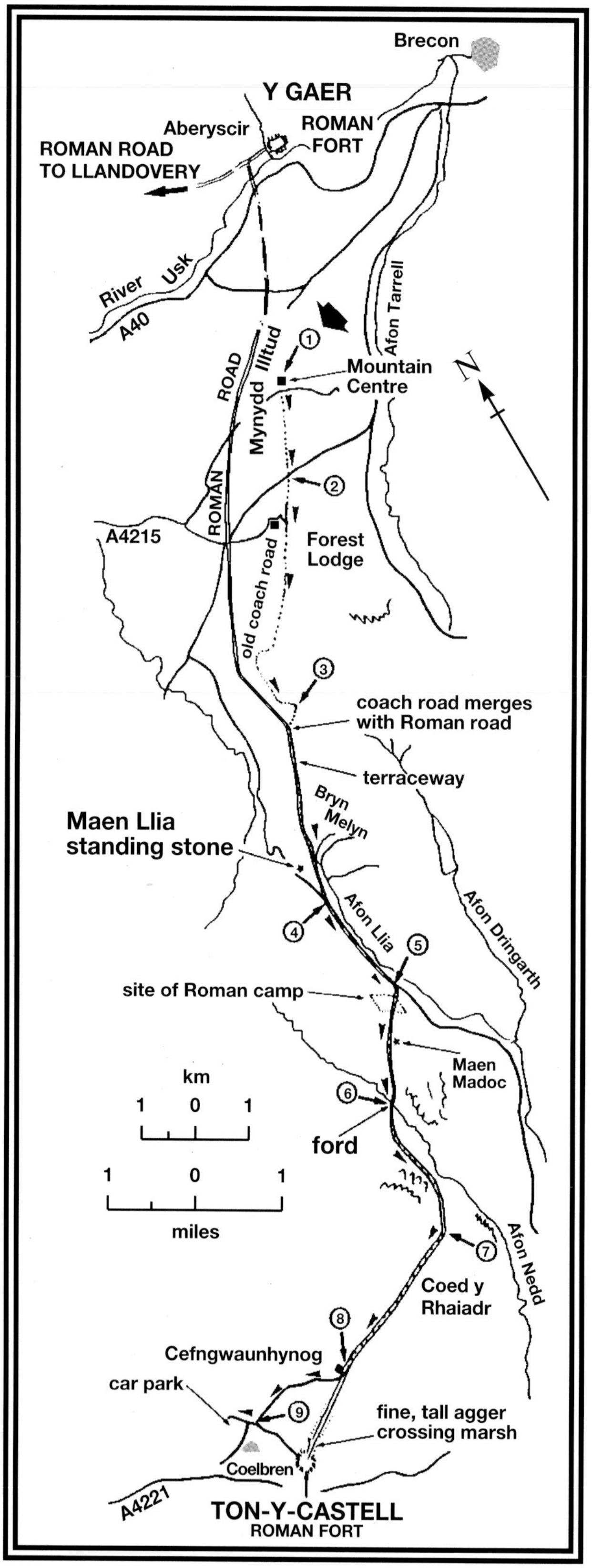

Brecon
Y GAER
ROMAN FORT
Aberyscir
ROMAN ROAD TO LLANDOVERY
River Usk
A40
ROMAN ROAD
Mynydd Illtud
Afon Tarrell
Mountain Centre
N
A4215
Forest Lodge
old coach road
coach road merges with Roman road
terraceway
Bryn Melyn
Maen Llia standing stone
Afon Llia
Afon Dringarth
site of Roman camp
Maen Madoc
km
1 0 1
1 0 1
miles
ford
Afon Nedd
Coed y Rhaiadr
Cefngwaunhynog
car park
fine, tall agger crossing marsh
Coelbren
A4221
TON-Y-CASTELL
ROMAN FORT

it climbs over Bryn Melyn as a terraceway. Keep on along the road, which becomes a hollow way, down towards the Afon Llia.

4. Bear left on to the lane along the valley bottom with the stream on your left.

5. Go over the cattle grid and turn right through the gate on to a track up through the plantation. Go through the site of a Roman marching camp and down into the valley.

6. Ford the Afon Nedd close to the site of the Roman ford. Take care as this can be deep. Continue up the hillside.

7. On the hilltop the Roman road changes alignment. Continue along the Roman road alongside the Coed y Rhaiadr plantation. Continue straight through the gate on to the metalled lane, which now follows the Roman line.

8. Keep to the lane which leaves the Roman road and go through the farmyard. Continue on to the T-junction.

9. Turn left to reach the fort site or right to the car park at Henrhyd Falls.

Below: *Descending to the Roman ford over the Afon Nedd.*

Inset: *On the top, heading for Ton-y-castell, the agger is visible.*

THE DEAN ROAD

The Roman road from Ariconium to Lydney

This Roman road is famous for the heavy stone paving and upright kerbstones that have been exposed in the Forest of Dean, and it has become known as the Dean Road. It is rather narrow for a Roman road, the paving being only about eight feet wide, though the actual distance between the pronounced side-banks is considerably greater than this. The age of the side-banks is not known, and they are probably more recent than the road itself. The narrowness of the paved surface has led some people to query the Dean Road's Roman origin. However, the balance of evidence suggests that this is a Roman road.

The Dean Road left the now-vanished Roman town of Ariconium to head along a ridge of relatively high land to Mitcheldean, now followed by the B4224. It runs along Green Bottom to Littledean, continuing along Sutton Bottom to Upper Soudley, where this short walk begins.

The road fords the stream and continues through the forest to Blackpool Bridge, lying just to the west of the forest ride. At Blackpool Bridge the main Roman road fords the stream. Blocks of stone which paved the ford are still visible. Interestingly, there was a loop road here which crossed by bridge — did packhorse traffic need to keep dryshod? — and a double line of kerbstones can be seen leaving the main road at an angle to head for the site of the Roman bridge. The walk ends near Blackpool Bridge, but the Dean Road runs on through Cockshoot Wood to Oldcroft and Allaston, making straight for Lydney and the Coast Road.

The Roman iron-mining industry of the Forest of Dean was centred on the small Roman town of Ariconium, and the sites of many bloomeries are known. It is now apparent that much of the iron ore was transported not by road but by ship — up and down the Severn Estuary and along the coast. Thus the Dean Road was not a long-distance route, nor was it a military road, but it served a local purpose, probably to transport iron ore from the place of production to the quay for shipment by barge.

There was a truly civilised strip of land which ran along the Severn Estuary and reached the height of its elegance in the late fourth century. It can be seen most highly developed in the temple complex at Lydney, which consists of a temple to an otherwise unknown god, Nodens (who seems to have been associated with hunting and healing, and possibly with the sea), a sanctuary and a large guest house. It seems incredible that the site was not built until after AD 364, a time of insecurity in Roman Britain as the barbarians invaded ever more frequently, and a time by which Christianity was growing in stature.

OS maps:
1:50,000 Landranger sheet
162

1:25,000 Outdoor Leisure sheet
14 [Wye Valley & Forest of Dean]

Distance: 1¾ miles

Pubs/hostelries:
On the walk: Soudley
Nearby: Parkend

Roman engineering works:
paved Roman road
Roman road loop at Blackpool Bridge
paved ford at Blackpool Bridge

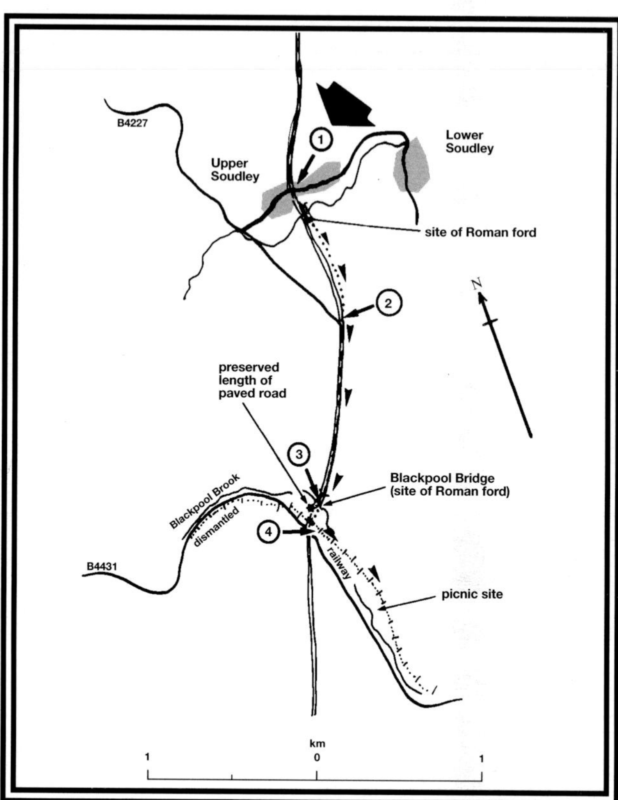

30. A WALK BETWEEN UPPER SOUDLEY AND BLACKPOOL BRIDGE

This easy, sylvan walk in the popular Forest of Dean follows the Roman road from Ariconium to Lydney and includes one of the few examples of a paved Roman road in Britain.

Instructions

1. Start at Upper Soudley and cross the stream heading south. Go along the forest ride.

2. Continue on to the lane straight ahead, along the Roman line.

3. Carry on to Blackpool Bridge and the preserved length of Roman road, visible on the right just before the disused railway bridge.

4. Turn left along the line of the dismantled railway through the forest to the picnic site and car park.

Below: *Bridge over the stream at site of Roman ford.*

THE ROMAN ROAD FROM TILLINGTON TO ABERGAVENNY

This road ran from Welsh Watling Street near Tillington in a south-westerly direction through the Roman town of Magnis, modern Kenchester, to the Roman fort of Gobannium at Abergavenny. It was an important route, for at Kenchester it crossed the major road from Stretton Grandison to Brecon and at Abergavenny it joined with the important Caerleon-Llanfair Clydogau road.

This was an early military road, possibly dating from the governorship of Ostorius Scapula, and formed part of the system of roads by which the difficult country of South Wales and the Marches was broken into conveniently sized blocks, well supplied with forts. It continued in importance since it was included in the Antonine Itinerary.

This road leaves Welsh Watling Street about a mile north-east of Tillington and runs straight to Kenchester, marked today by a minor road. Kenchester is the site of Magnis, a Roman town that covered some 22 acres. It now lies sleeping under the fields, nothing visible on the surface and most of its stonework stolen long, long ago. Its ghost survives in the hexagonal-shaped outline of the town walls, followed by modern field boundaries.

From Magnis the road turns southwards to cross the River Wye at Huff Pool, where the original alignment is resumed, followed by hedgerows and a straight, narrow lane known locally as Stone Street, close to the village of Madley, where the walk starts. The Roman road then curls its way over wooded Brampton Hill in a couple of open zig-zags, today followed by a track. It zig-zags again to climb the next ridge at Kerry's Gate. From here a great vista opens westwards into Wales, the unmistakable purple-blue profiles of Skirrid Fawr and the Sugar Loaf standing as beacons above the road's destination at Abergavenny.

The Roman road descended into Golden Valley and crossed the River Dore before turning south-eastwards through Abbey Dore, where the walk ends. The road continues to Ewyas Harold and Pontrilas. In Golden Valley the Roman line runs through the fields, roughly parallel with the dismantled railway, but beyond Pontrilas its course to Abergavenny is not known. It is assumed to have turned south-westwards again and run either along the line of the modern A465 or possibly as a ridgeway route along the crest of Campston Hill and the southern slopes of Skirrid Fawr.

Since the close of Roman times this old road has slumbered gently, ceasing to be the main through route once the Wye crossing at Huff Pool had become derelict. It has watched the comings and goings of other overlords: in the Middle Ages came the great expansion of the monastic

OS maps:
1:50,000 Landranger sheet
149 or 161

1:25,000 Pathfinder sheets
1040 [Hereford (south) & area]
1039 [Golden Valley]

Distance: 6½ miles

Pubs/hostelries:
On the walk: Madley
Abbey Dore

Roman engineering works:
agger visible in places
open zig-zags over the hills

Below: *The Tillington-Abergavenny Roman road as a little lane near the start of the walk.*

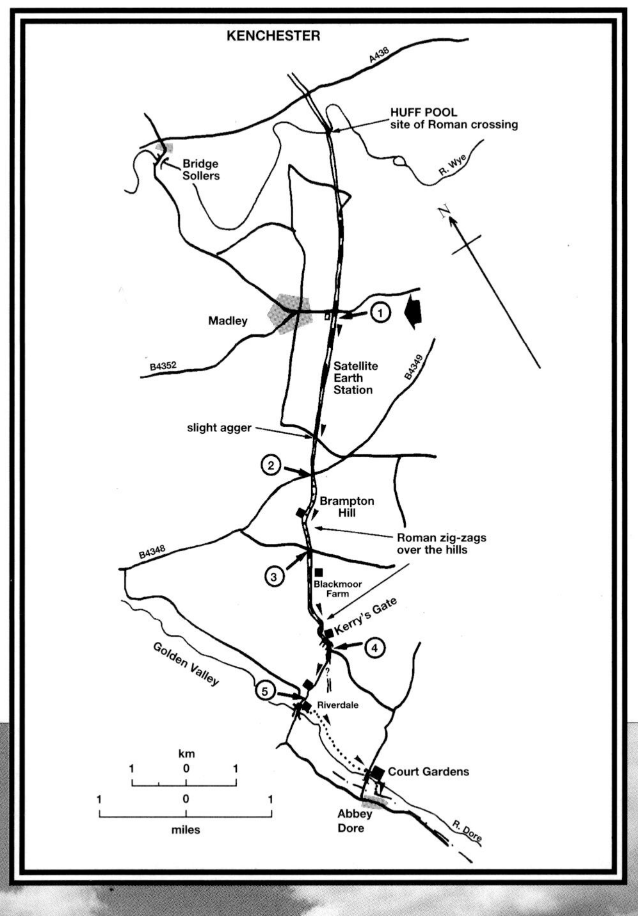

houses, and in 1147 the Cistercian Abbey Dore was founded in Golden Valley. This grew to be the most extensive monastic estate in the Welsh Marches, and the size of the surviving buildings, chiefly the church, hint eloquently of its former splendour. Wool gave the abbey its wealth and by the late 13th century Abbey Dore fleece was famed far and wide, fetching the highest price of all English wool. Large tracts of woodland were cleared for cultivation, though not to everyone's satisfaction; Gerald of Wales complained that the monks were 'changing an oak wood into a wheat field ...'.

Now the monastic splendour has gone, but the beauty remains and, when seen in evening sunlight with the spire of Peterchurch rising from the meadows, the valley seems truly named.

31. A WALK FROM MADLEY TO ABBEY DORE

The walk along this Roman road, now only a small lane, climbs over two ridges of hills before descending into beautiful Golden Valley.

Instructions

1. Start at the pub on the crossroads to the east of Madley [SO425384]. Head south-west along the Roman road. Pass the satellite station and continue over the crossroads at Brampton. Continue along the lane opposite, which becomes rather sunken but is on the line of the Roman road.

2. Cross the B4348 and continue up Brampton Hill. Go through the gate by the ruined farmhouse and down the track.

3. Bear slightly to the left to go straight across the minor road into the lane. Pass Blackmoor Farm and carry on along the lane to Kerry's Gate. Here the Roman road veered to the right to descend into the Golden Valley, but its exact course is not yet known.

4. Leave the line of the Roman road and follow the modern lane round to the left. Turn right down the lane into the Golden Valley.

5. Turn left at Riverdale to follow the footpath alongside the River Dore to Court Gardens. Cross the minor road, turn left and then right back on to the footpath. Follow the path round to the right and turn left along the river. Cross the river and take the footpath to Abbey Dore.

— VII —

NORTH WALES AND CHESTER

'Helen bethought her to make high-roads from one castle to another throughout the island of Britain. And the roads were made ... and the men of the island of Britain would not have made these great roads for any save for her ....'

The Mabinogion
(translated by Lady Charlotte Guest)

The Romans in North Wales and Chester

The Roman army reached North Wales in AD 48-49 when Ostorius Scapula, moving in from Wroxeter and Chester, harried the Decangli of present-day Clwyd. He forced them back, but soon had to fight a major battle against the Ordovices, the largest and most powerful tribe of the region, whose base was in the mountain fastness of Snowdonia.

Caratacus, fugitive son of the great king Cunobelinus, had first reappeared as a leader of the Silures in South Wales. After their defeat at the hands of Scapula, Caratacus had, with ease it seems, moved into the lands of the Ordovices, where he became commander of the united opposition to the Romans. A major battle was fought in AD 49, probably on the banks of the River Severn. The actual site is unknown, though several have been suggest-

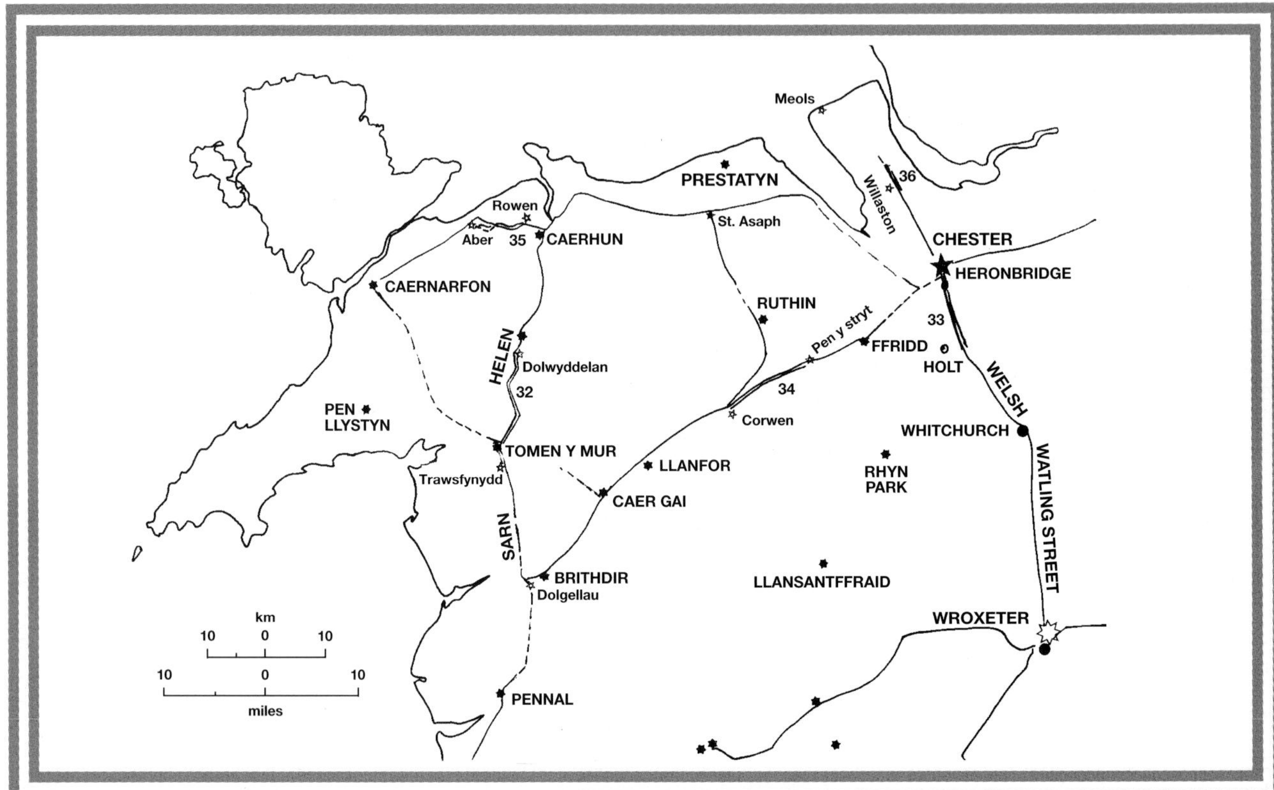

Below: *The mountain fastness of North West Wales — stronghold of the Ordovices and difficult for the Romans to police. Here mist descends into the valley near Capel Curig.* **Right:** *Walls of Roman Chester.* **Top:** *Diarama of Chester fort. Chester Museum.* **Above:** *Model of Chester amphitheatre. Chester Museum.*

ed. The Romans were victorious. Caratacus fled for refuge to Queen Cartimandua of the large pro-Roman tribe, the Brigantes, which now formed a client kingdom in Northern England. Cartimandua, however, loyal to her agreement with Rome, handed him over to his enemies without more ado. He was taken to Rome and displayed with other captives at a great triumphal procession. The emperor Claudius, impressed by his bearing, granted him and his family free pardon. In so doing Claudius was acutely aware that he was living up to the high calling that the poet Virgil had expounded to the Romans 'to show mercy to the defeated'.

Following the capture of Caratacus, political turmoil in Rome meant that there was little Roman military activity in North Wales, though it remained unsubdued, until the arrival in Britain of Suetonius Paulinus in AD 58. In the interim, Claudius had been succeeded by his stepson, Nero, who initially considered abandoning Britain. Suetonius had considerable experience in mountain warfare and had excelled himself in campaigns in the Atlas Mountains of North Africa. He was anxious to prove his merits in Britain and fought through the difficult terrain of North Wales, so that by AD 60 he was set to storm Anglesey. This was the final stronghold of the Ordovices and a place of refuge for the Druids. Tacitus sets the scene:

'The enemy lined the shore in a dense armed mass. Among them were black-robed women with dishevelled hair like Furies, brandishing torches. Close by stood Druids, raising their hands to heaven and screaming dreadful curses.

This weird spectacle awed the Roman soldiers .... But then they urged each other (and were urged by the general) not to fear a horde of fanatical women. Onward pressed their standards and they bore down their opponents, enveloping them in the flames of their own torches ....'

Although victory was assured, and the Romans were busy destroying the Druid's sacred groves, Suetonius Paulinus had to turn away with his troops and hurry back down Watling Street to quell the Boudiccan revolt.

It was not until AD 78 that the Roman army returned to North Wales and Julius Agricola finally brought the Ordovices under Roman rule. Like South Wales, this broken, mountainous region was thereafter controlled by forts and fortlets strung together by a network of roads.

The legionary fortress at Chester was the hub of this system, responsible for keeping North Wales in order. It is possible that a Roman military installation was set up at Chester as early as AD 60, but if so it has left no trace. In AD 74-5 Julius Frontinus set up the new legionary base there on the sandstone cliff above the River Dee, superbly sited for defensive purposes. It had good communications via the river as well as providing a perfect centre for roads into Wales, the Midlands and the North. The fortress was completed in AD 79 and garrisoned at first by the II Adiutrix Legion, who had been moved from Wroxeter to build it. In AD 87, the Emperor Domitian recalled the II Adiutrix from Britain to reinforce the Danube frontier and the XX Legion, Valeria Victrix, was withdrawn from Scotland to replace it. This legion remained at Chester till the end of the Roman occupation, finally leaving in about AD 380. Under Trajan (AD 98-117), the fortress was rebuilt in stone and is larger than those at Caerleon (*Isca*) and York (*Eboracum*).

The Roman fort is buried under the medieval and modern city of Chester, but the outline of its walls and buildings is known. Many a Chester basement contains Roman remains — part of a hypocaust, an altar, a fragment of a tombstone. It is thought that the famous black and white raised arcades — the 'Rows' — were built as they are because of the large amount of Roman rubble lying about. The medieval city walls are built of Roman stones, while the grid-iron street pattern reflects the layout of Roman roads within the fort. The Roman legionary hospital stood where the great cathedral now stands. Outside the south-east corner of the fort was the huge Roman amphitheatre, which could seat 7,000 and is the largest known in Britain. Only half of it can be seen — the rest lies under a convent — but it is one of the most interesting and remarkable of Chester's Roman relics.

North Wales remained even more military in nature than South Wales. Indeed, towns and villas are unknown in the region, which was mined extensively for metals — lead, copper and silver — and for stone, both limestone and red sandstone. There were also other industrial pursuits, the largest of which was the tile factory at Holt on the River Dee, south of Chester.

Roman Roads in North Wales and Chester

The road system in North Wales is not as well known as that in South Wales, nor in all likelihood was it ever so complete a network. There is no central route centre comparable to Brecon, since Chester, the important radial centre, lies on the east of the region. From it ran roads to Wroxeter (Welsh Watling Street), Dolgellau, Caernarfon and the Wirral peninsula. The main road to Carlisle and the northern frontier also originated at Chester. It ran eastwards towards Manchester before turning its face to the north.

As in South Wales, the roads pass through difficult terrain as well engineered terraceways, and the network is based on two roads which run southwards down either side of the Cambrian Mountains. In the east runs Welsh

Watling Street, from Chester to Wroxeter, and in the west Sarn Helen climbs over the mountains from Caerhun in the Conwy valley via the lonely outpost fort of Tomen-y-mur near Trawsfynydd and so through Dolgellau to Pennal.

Two cross-country routes head west from Chester connecting Welsh Watling Street with Sarn Helen. The north coast road to Caernarfon runs through St Asaph and Caerhun, where it crosses Sarn Helen, and continues over the northern part of the Snowdonian mountains before keeping along the coast to *Segontium*, an important Roman fort. The Dolgellau road runs south-west from Chester through Ffridd, the Roman fort at Caer Gai at the head of Bala Lake, and over the mountains to Dolgellau, where it joins Sarn Helen.

A third cross-country route lies further south and runs over the Long Mountain from Wroxeter through Forden Gaer to Newtown and Caersws.

Two other roads deserve mention. One runs south-east from Caernarfon through Tomen-y-mur and over the desolate Arenig Mountains to Caer Gai at the head of Bala Lake. The other is the recently discovered road from St Asaph which runs south down the Vale of Clwyd to the Chester-Dolgellau road north of Corwen.

The Roman roads of North Wales are particularly splendid. They are all commanding, clear-sighted routes, very Roman in attitude as they stride along ridgetops and terrace steep hillsides.

SARN HELEN

The Roman road from Caerhun to Pennal

Sarn Helen is the Romans' great route through western Wales, running south from Caerhun through Pennal and on to Carmarthen. The name needs some explanation. The first half is easy as *Sarn* is Welsh for causeway, but *Helen* is a little more difficult to understand. There is a long-standing tradition, found in the Welsh epic the *Mabinogion* and in the writings of Geoffrey of Monmouth, which connects the road with Helen, wife of the Roman Emperor Magnus Maximus. This is a good story, and although we now know that the road was built long before his time, it is certain that Maximus did march through Wales in AD 388, gathering an army to assail Rome in his bid for the imperial throne. Whether he was married to a lady called Helen, daughter of a Welsh chieftain, is not known. There is, though, a more prosaic explanation. It is arguable that *Helen* is not a personal name at all, but a corruption of *Lleng*, Welsh for legion, making Sarn Helen neither more nor less than *Sarn-y-Lleng*, the 'legion's causeway'.

The road follows a magnificent, lonely and exposed route. It branches from the north coast road near Ty'n-y-groes on the western bank of the River Conwy and runs south past the fort at Caerhun (*Canovium*). The course is lost in the low-lying meadows between *Canovium* and Dolgarrog, but from Dolgarrog to Trefriw the present road probably marks its course. Here, Sarn Helen divides and two different routes carry the road south-westwards to Dolwyddelan, one a valleyside terraceway through Bettws-y-Coed and the other climbing directly over the mountains.

At Dolwyddelan, where this walk starts, the two roads unite to pass along the west side of the deep defile of Cwm Penamnen, zig-zagging up at the head of the cwm on to the naked moorland. Here the road has been destroyed by quarries, but can be traced again descending to the crossing of the Afon Gamallt and continuing to Bont-Newydd. Beyond Bont-Newydd the road passes through Forestry Commission land but reappears splendidly to pass the isolated fort of Tomen-y-mur, where the route from Caernarfon to Caer Gai crossed it, heading across the wild Arenigs. Sarn Helen descends towards Trawsfynydd, where the walk ends. It then runs along the hillside through Plas Capten to join the lane at Pen-y-stryt, whence it passes along the western side of Craig Penshilen and through Bwlch-y-Ffordd ('pass of the road') to drop down towards Dolgellau and its junction with the road to Chester. It runs along the foot of Cefn y Clawydd, and descends to the Llefenni valley, crosses the Afon Dulas

Below: *Model of a British war chariot found at Llyn Cerrig Bach, Anglesey: British chariots did not have knives attached their axles. National Museum of Wales.*

and continues through Pennal into South Wales.

This road was probably built during or soon after Agricola's successful Welsh campaign in the late summer of AD 78, though there is the possibility that it was used during Frontinus' campaigns in AD 74-75.

Although Sarn Helen was a military road, the region through which it runs was also industrial. The Roman kilns on Sarn Helen south of Trawsfynydd at Pen-y-stryt were attached to a factory known to have been working between AD 80 and AD 150. It produced domestic pottery and roof and floor tiles. Farther south there were important copper mines.

Tomen-y-mur is perhaps the loneliest of all Roman forts in Britain and was garrisoned not by legionaries but by auxiliary troops. It stands in splendid isolation above the Vale of Trawsfynydd on marshy moorland surrounded by a ring of high mountains. Built initially by Agricola in late AD 78 on a 4-acre site, the walls were rebuilt in stone during the reign of Hadrian, probably about AD 110. The fort was evacuated as early as AD 140. Today the Hadrianic stone walls have vanished — their stone has contributed to the field walls that cross and recross the Roman earthworks — and the rather marshy site is dominated by a Norman motte, built within the fort.

Tomen-y-mur is the only auxiliary fort in Britain to have its own amphitheatre, though that seems too grand a word to describe the small, reedy hollow beside the lane where the troops of this lonely outpost were entertained. Its size, only about 25 yards across, makes it no more than a cockpit. The amphitheatre was probably also used for military training. The parade ground attached to the fort is still visible as an artificially levelled square to the south-east. A series of practice camps, built at Dolddinas on the moorland nearby, is evidence that the troops were kept busy.

Top: *Above Bont Newydd: the Roman road ascends through the forest passing a lonely farmstead.* **Above:** *Pottery vessels from Holt. Pottery such as this would have been in use at Tomen y mur. The white vessel is an example of the 'best' ware. Museum of Chester.* **Right:** *Looking back to Manod Mawr as Sarn Helen approaches Tomen y Mur.*

The civil settlement attached to the fort lay to its south-east along the line of Sarn Helen as it descends to the Nant Tyddyn-yr-yn. The Roman road bridged this stream, and part of the northern abutment is visible as an eight-foot-high earthen embankment. This would have supported a wooden bridge. The abutment on the opposite bank has been eroded by the stream.

Up here the wind blows and the surrounding mountains hide their tops in cloud. There is a sensation of loneliness and a bloody past and at the old fort, where sheep are the present garrison, the works of man are writ large in one of Nature's desolate spots.

32 A WALK FROM DOLWYDDELAN TO TRAWSFYNYDD

This wild mountain and moorland walk provides incredible views along the best-preserved stretch of Sarn Helen.

OS maps:
1:50,000 Landranger sheets
115 & 124

1:25,000 Outdoor Leisure sheets:
16 [Snowdonia: Conwy Valley area]
18 [Snowdonia: Harlech & Bala area]

Distance: 12½ miles

Equipment:
walking boots
warm waterproof clothing
compass
OS maps

Pubs/hostelries:
On the walk: Dolwyddelan
Trawsfynydd
Nearby: Ffestiniog

Roman engineering works:
agger visible in places
terraced stream crossing with abutment
terraceways

Other antiquities
Tomen-y-mur Roman fort

Instructions

1. Start at Dolwyddelan church [SH736524] and head south over the Afon Lledr, the railway and the Afon Maesgwm. Follow the forest road round to the left into the deep Cwm Penamnen. Continue past Gwyndy-newydd to Ty'n-y-cwm.

2. Turn left just beyond Ty'n-y-cwm and cross the Afon Maesgwm again. Follow the waymarked Sarn Helen as it climbs through Forestry Commission land up the steep head of the cwm as a Roman terraceway. Emerge out of the forest on to the bare moorland.

3. Cross the stile. Turn right along the forest boundary fence. Cross another stile and go uphill, still keeping the forest on your right.

4. When you arrive at the next cross-fence do not go over the stile but turn left along the fence, keeping it to your right for over half a mile to reach a mine road.

5. Turn left (east) along the mine road and continue along it as it bears under the shoulder of Manod Mawr.

6. Turn right about three-quarters of a mile farther on, just before a deep disused working. Follow the grassy track, which is not very clear, up the hillside, passing a small

shallow lake. Continue and bear left beside a stream to a ruined building and turn right to reach a fence with a stile.

7. Climb over the stile and turn left. Follow the track downhill to a gate and stile on the edge of the forest. Climb over the stile and turn left to follow the edge of the forest. Continue past the rocky crags to a stile over the fence at the point where Sarn Helen emerges from the forest.

8. Turn right and head south along Sarn Helen, a flat, green track. Cross two streams and keep going through a little cutting and past a small lake. Follow the Roman road as it descends steeply to the Afon Gamallt, easing its fall by small zig-zags.

9. Cross the wooden bridge over the stream and continue along the track for about 200 yards.

10. Leave the main track and turn right up the hill along Sarn Helen, which becomes very clear again, with the Iron Age hillfort Bryn y Castell on your left. When you reach a junction of tracks turn right and keep to the track downhill. Leave the Roman road at the gas sub-station and follow the track to the B4391.

11. Turn left along the B-road and then right over the stile on to Sarn Helen — here very clear — and follow it downhill. It is a right of way but you may have to climb some fences which obstruct it. Cross the field on the same alignment and arrive at a lane. Turn left along the lane into Bont-Newydd and reach the A470.

12. Turn left along the A470, crossing over the Afon Cynfal. Turn right along the minor road and keep left back to the A470. You have to leave Sarn Helen here for just over a mile. Turn right along the main road for 500 yards.

13. Turn left along the forest track, following this through the trees and bearing round to the right where another track carries straight on. Emerge from the forest and continue along the lane. Sarn Helen comes in from the left. Keep going to the point where the lane turns abruptly to the right. Ahead of you is Tomen-y-mur, the isolated Roman fort, with its tiny amphitheatre beside the road just before the cattle grid.

14. Turn left past the amphitheatre and go through the gate, heading south with a wall and the fort on your right. On the left is the raised bank of the parade ground. Continue through another gate and go downhill past the

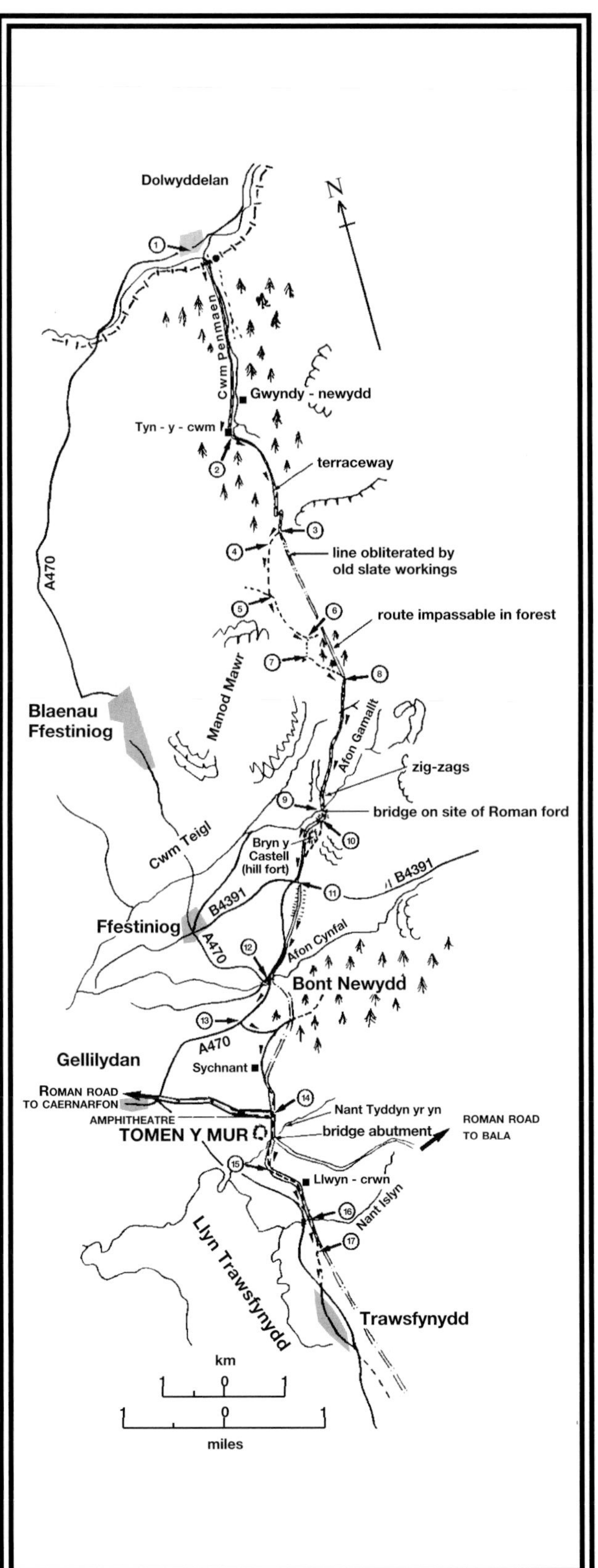

overgrown remains of the bathhouse to Nant Tyddyn-yr-yn and the remains of the bridge abutment [SH707386]. Cross the stream and climb up the far side, bearing to the right past a tumbledown barn. Cross the field to a gate in the stone wall.

15. Turn left into a green lane. Follow it past a barn and over a stream, bearing to the right where other tracks cross near Llwyn-crwn. Keep on over the railway towards the A470.

16. Just before you reach the main road turn left through a gate into a walled lane. Follow the lane downhill and over the Nant Islyn, continuing uphill on the other side. Keep straight ahead where the lane turns left under the railway. Keep beside the wall through a gate and over a stile.

17. Leave Sarn Helen and bear right. Cross over the Nant-y-Cefn and continue past a stone barn and over a stile, keeping on through gates to the A470. Cross the main road and follow the lane into Trawsfynydd.

WELSH WATLING STREET

The Roman road from Chester to Wroxeter

Welsh Watling Street runs down the eastern side of Wales linking the legionary fortresses at Chester and Caerleon through the important town of Wroxeter (*Viroconium*). It was a cornerstone of policing the region under Frontinus and Agricola and continued to be a very important road, included in the Antonine Itinerary. The northern stretch from Chester to Wroxeter is explored in this chapter, while the southern stretch is covered in Chapter 6.

The road runs south-east from Chester, where both walks begin, past Heronbridge, an important industrial centre during the 2nd century. Its site on the River Dee made it a good choice for a riverside receiving station for goods from the legionary factory further upstream at Holt. The Holt site was originally set up to supply building materials to the new stone fortress at Chester and produced, among other things, bricks, roofing tiles, water pipes, hypocaust pillars and pottery such as jugs, dishes and cups. These were shipped by sailing barge downriver to Heronbridge to be carried to Chester by cart along Welsh Watling Street. At Heronbridge workshops, houses and other stone buildings have been excavated as well as the dock at which the goods came ashore.

Little more remains to tell of the Roman activity here. Indeed, the defensive earthwork on the site today was constructed after the Romans had left Britain. It has been linked with a battle fought in the seventh century between the Britons and King Aethelfrith of Northumbria. Possibly the site holds a British war cemetery, as 20 mutilated skeletons were discovered during the course of excavation.

The Roman road fords the River Dee and changes to a more southerly alignment at Aldford church on its hill. It continues as a green lane through Churton, where Walk 33b ends, to Malpas and Whitchurch Heath. At Whitchurch a branch road runs in a south-easterly direction to link up with famous Watling Street, but the main Welsh Watling Street turns south over Prees Heath to Wroxeter.

Both these walks are pleasant rambles and both include the site of Heronbridge, where the River Dee makes for a peaceful scene, past activity and slaughter forgotten. Bulrushes line the river and yellow water lilies float like island-stars. Willows overhang the dark waters and now and then a boat passes, its oars flashing silver light. The Heronbridge site is hummocky and under long grass with here and there a thistle stirred by the wind as if mocking the desolation of the place.

33a. A CIRCULAR WALK NEAR CHESTER

This walk follows the main Roman road into Wales, from the legionary base at Chester to Eccleston and back along the banks of the Dee passing, at Heronbridge, the site of a Roman riverside quay and settlement and post-Roman earthworks.

33b. A WALK FROM CHESTER TO CHURTON

This walk follows the main Roman road into Wales from the legionary base at Chester via Eccleston and Aldford to Churton and includes a stroll alongside the River Dee and down an enchanting green lane on the Roman line.

Instructions

1. Both walks start in Bridge Street, Chester, and head south through the medieval Bridge Gate to cross the River Dee. The present Dee Bridge is more or less on the site of the Roman one. Once across the River Dee follow the road round to the right.

2. Bear left into Eaton Road, which continues the line of the Roman road. The road which bears to the right here is the start of the Roman road from Chester to Dolgellau.

3. Pass Heronbridge, now marked by the pink house on your left. The Heronbridge site can be reached through a kissing-gate on the left. Continue over the Chester bypass (A55) to Eccleston.

4. At Eccleston turn left and then bear right. At the gate to the Duke of Westminster's Eaton Estate the Roman

road carries straight on through the park. There is no public right of way.

5. Turn left (west), leaving Watling Street, and go down the road to the River Dee at the site of the old ferry.

Walk 33a

6. Turn left at the old landing and follow the riverside path back to Chester via Heronbridge.

Walk 33b

6. Turn right at the old landing and follow the riverside footpath past the Eaton Stud. Bear right along the path through the woods away from the river and across the neck of the big meander known as Crook of Dee. On regaining the river continue along the riverside footpath.

7. Turn left to cross the Dee over the blue and white painted Iron Bridge (inscribed 'William Shuttle, Junior Founder, 1824'). The Roman road probably forded the river here.

Right: *Wroxeter, destination of this northern half of the road, is dominated by the 'Old Work' a stretch of the ruined wall of the basilica.*

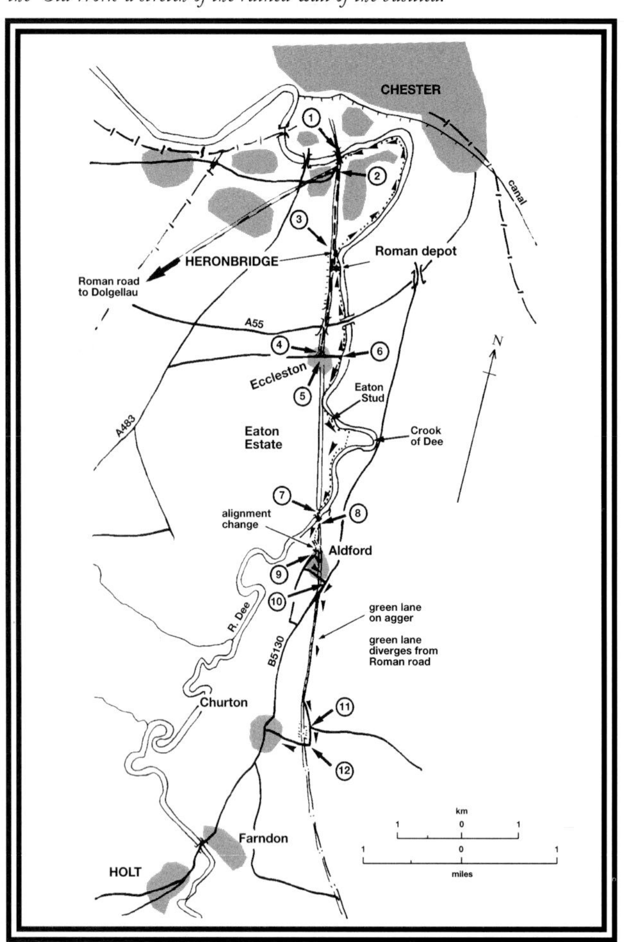

OS maps:
1:50,000 Landranger sheet 117

1:25,000 Pathfinder sheets
774 [Chester (east)]
790 [Farndon, Holt, Tattenhall]

Distance:
Walk 33a — 6 miles
Walk 33b — 6½ miles

Pubs/hostelries:
On the walk: Chester, Eccleston, Aldford, Churton

Roman engineering works:
agger visible in places
terraceway

Other antiquities:
site of legionary depot and settlement at Heronbridge

Above: *Bridge over the river Dee at the site of a Roman ford.*

8. Continue along the drive for about 150 yards with the Roman road as a hollow way on your right. Turn right through the kissing-gate and strike off to the left up the field (the footpath is only faintly visible) to the Norman motte near the church. The Roman road is very obvious here.

9. Go through the white gate to the right of Aldford Church and turn left into Church Lane. Turn right opposite the church gate and go down Middle Lane past the post office/stores. Turn left along Rushmere Lane, crossing the line of the Roman road.

10. Turn right along the B5013 and then bear left into Lower Lane. Continue when this becomes a green lane which diverges from the Roman line.

11. Continue into the lane which comes in sharply from the left.

12. Turn right with the lane. Head uphill into Churton.

THE ROMAN ROAD FROM CHESTER TO DOLGELLAU

The Chester-Dolgellau road was probably built under Julius Frontinus during his North Wales campaign of AD 74-75 and it parallels the more important coast road. The age of the Roman forts along it confirm it as part of the military network laid down during the pacification of the region. Caer Gai, the Roman fort situated at the south-west end of Bala Lake, was occupied between AD 78, when it was built, and AD 125, when it was abandoned. The road is not included in the Antonine Itinerary.

The road branches from Welsh Watling Street just south of the River Dee at Chester. Its course is not known for certain till it reaches Ffridd, whence it is followed by lanes and a stretch of main road (A5104) through Bwlchgwyn and Pen-y-stryt, where this ride begins.

From here it follows a magnificent course along a ridge of high land between the Morwynion valley and the Vale of Clwyd. This old highway is in use today as a very quiet, almost forgotten, lane. But it is superbly engineered to take advantage of the ridge, running almost entirely along the crest as a series of short, straight alignments — the usual method for a Roman road in broken country.

The wide verges bordered in part by hedges hint at side-ditches buried beneath, and an *agger* is visible in places, though in others the road has become a sunken lane. On reaching the Dee valley near Corwen, where the ride ends, the Roman road coincides with the main road and then runs on a conspicuous *agger* across the parkland of Rug to Druid, where its line is taken up first by the A494 and then by a terraced lane from Glan yr afon to Bethel.

It is used again by the main road through Bala and along

Bala Lake and then it crosses the fields to the fort at Caer Gai. Beyond Caer Gai, although the modern and Roman roads run in the same direction, they rarely coincide. The road joins Sarn Helen at Coed, 1½ miles east of Dolgellau.

This is an easy road with wide views to the Welsh mountains. Harebells, gorse and grasses line the verges, hogweed towers nobly, and yarrow, a herb sacred in antiquity, grows in profusion. The Druids used the stems of yarrow to divine the weather in the coming season, and the herb was also known as 'woundwort' and the 'soldier's herb' because of its value on the battlefield to staunch wounds. It is fitting indeed that it should grow along a Roman road! In the upland stretch bracken borders the road, and the sharp wind blows the distant barking of dogs while near at hand sheep bleat and buzzards mew overhead.

The whole sense of this road is very Roman — open and dominant. From it you look north down the fertile Vale of Clwyd a great patchwork of lush green and ripening gold; southwards the purple-crowned Berwyns loom like gigantic molehills and to the west lie the peaks and precipices of Snowdonia, the Arenigs and the Rhinogs.

OS maps:
1:50,000 Landranger sheets
116 & 125

1:25,000 Pathfinder sheets
788 [Ruthin]
805 [Corwen]

Distance: 11 miles

Pubs/hostelries:
On the drive: Corwen
Nearby: Gwyddelwern

Roman engineering works:
agger visible in places
luxuriant verges denote buried ditches in places
alignment along the ridge between the Morwynion and Clwyd valleys

Other antiquities:
Iron Age fort at Caer Drewyn, Corwen

34 A CYCLE RIDE/DRIVE FROM PEN-Y-STRYT TO CORWEN

This important road languishes as a half-forgotten, unfrequented lane which commands stunning views across North Wales into Snowdonia.

Instructions

1. Start at Pen-y-stryt [SJ198518]. Head south-west along the A5104 to the roundabout at SJ188510. Take the second exit, continuing on the A5104 (signposted Corwen, Bala).

2. Almost immediately turn right on to the Roman road. Carry on at the crossroads and pass the entrance to Rhoslydan.

3. Bear right, briefly leaving the alignment of the Roman road, which continues across the little col and up the field opposite.

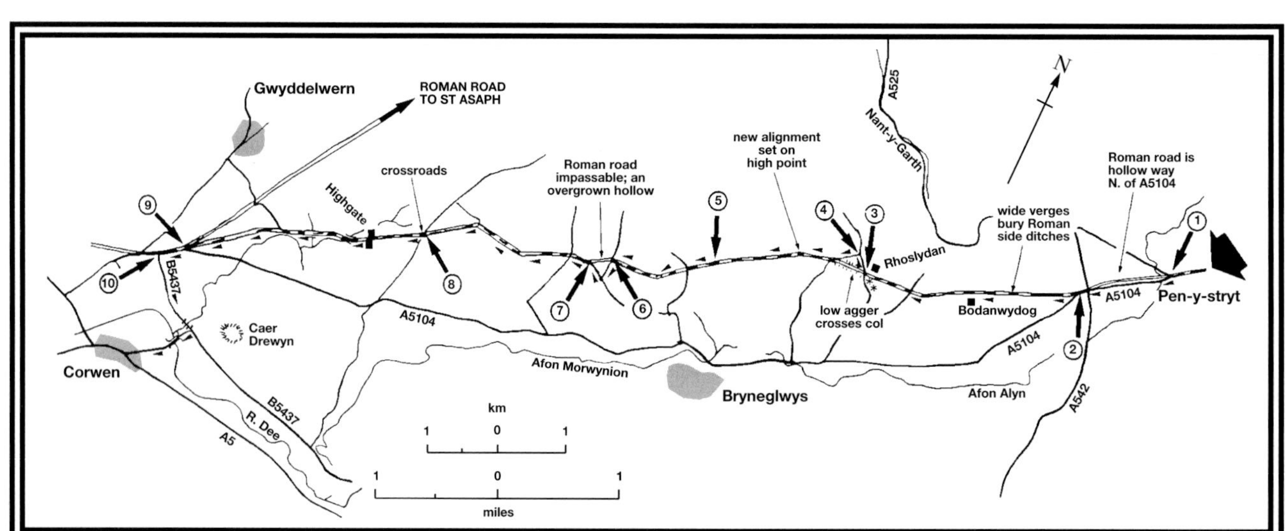

Above: *The little lane on the Roman line, with its wide verges.*

4. Turn left on to the lane to rejoin the Roman road. Continue, climbing to a high point where a new alignment was set. Carry on to the next high point, which commands superb views.

5. Continue over another high point, and downhill to the T-junction. The Roman road goes straight across but its course is now impassable, though it is marked as a track even on up-to-date maps.

6. Turn left away from the now-obstructed Roman road, and when you reach the next T-junction turn right.

7. After 200 yards the modern road turns to the left and continues on the line of the Roman road. Continue, ignoring roads coming in from the right and left.

8. At the staggered crossroads turn left and then right to get back on to the Roman line, which now becomes rather windy and continues past Highgate to the main A5104.

9. Bear right along the A5104 for 300 yards.

10. Turn left leaving the Roman road and go along the B5437 and then right to cross the River Dee into Corwen.

THE ROMAN ROAD FROM CHESTER TO CAERNARFON

This road from Chester to Caernarfon was probably used by the Romans from the time of their earliest forays into North Wales. It was the road whereby Suetonius Paulinus successfully invaded Anglesey in AD 60, before having to withdraw with speed on account of the Boudiccan rebellion. Certainly Julius Frontinus and Julius Agricola travelled upon it as they successfully snapped the last cord of Ordovician resistance. The emperors Hadrian and Septimus Severus both came this way and it is included in the Antonine Itinerary. It is no mere trackway over the hills.

The Roman road probably left Chester along the same route as the road to Dolgellau and branched from it once past the head of the Dee estuary, which in those days stretched farther inland. Here it swings north-westwards to Holywell, and then turns west across the northern part of the Clwydian Range, its line followed by the A55. It descends into the Vale of Clwyd at Rhuallt, and then its course lies across fields south of St Asaph ([?] *Varae*).

Beyond the River Elwy its line is taken up by the switchback road (B5381) through Glascoed and Betws-yn-Rhos, and thence it runs through broken, hilly country to Tal-y-Cafn, where it crosses the River Conwy.

The present road from the river is on the line of the Roman road through Ty'n-y-groes and as far as Roewen, where the walk begins. It climbs steeply out of Roewen up the slopes of Tal y fan to Rhiw at a gradient of 1 in 3 before bearing south-west to join a Bronze Age track, which was modernised by the Romans through the Bwlch y Ddeufaen (the 'Pass of Stones'). This area had long been densely populated, and on either side of the road are standing stones and stone circles that were old when the Romans came and have given the pass its name. Once through the pass, the Bronze Age track, now the more clearly marked of the two roads, continues through Bont Newydd to Aber, where the walk ends, passing the British fort of Maes y gaer.

The Roman road branches off north-west through Rhiwiau and zig-zags down to Gorddiniog, south of Llanfairfechan. Two Roman milestones found at Rhiwiau show that this Roman road was repaired on at least two occasions. The earlier milestone, of the time of Hadrian, records the eighth mile from Caerhun and must have originally stood in the Bwlch y Ddeufaen. It relates to the Emperor's visit to Britain in AD 121. The other milestone dates from the reign of Septimus Severus who, in AD 280, was in North Wales on a similar visit to reaffirm Rome's possession of the region.

Once on the coastal strip opposite Anglesey the Roman

road turns south-west. It is paralleled by the A55 but runs along the hills higher up the slope than the modern road. It crosses the Afon Ogwen and continues along the ridge between the rivers Cadnant and Seiont through Waen Wen and straight for Caernarfon.

The stretch of this route beyond Roewen is an amazing road with some astounding views over the Menai Straits to Anglesey, the windswept island where Suetonius Paulinus fought and won his great battle over the Ordovices in AD

OS maps:
1:50,000 Landranger sheet 115

1:25,000 Pathfinder sheets
753 [Conwy and Colwyn Bay]
752 [Llanfairfechan]

Distance: 6 miles

Equipment:
walking boots
waterproof clothing
compass
OS maps

Pubs/hostelries:
On the walk: Roewen
Aber

Roman engineering works:
terracing
zig-zag to Gorddiniog

Other antiquities:
standing stones
stone circle
cromlech
burial mounds
Maes y gaer

60. His soldiers were hacking down the sacred groves of the fearsome Druids when the news came that southern England was aflame with rebellion. This road was their direct route back to the south. Laboriously the soldiers tramped back from Anglesey to the River Dee, from the Dee down Welsh Watling Street to Wroxeter and so on to Watling Street through the Midlands to London.

Today the road is peaceful, save for the occasional scream of a jet overhead, and larks sing, winging upward high about the hills and the sea while the scent of gorse blossom hangs heavy and sheep bleat. The walking is fairly easy, with the exception of the steep ascent behind Roewen — after all, this was a major Roman road.

35. A WALK FROM ROEWEN TO ABER

A magnificent walk over the mountains on the edge of Snowdonia with wide views over Anglesey.

Instructions

1. Start at Roewen. Follow the 'Youth Hostel' sign, turning right up the hill. Go straight over at the T-junction and follow the Roman road very steeply uphill to the Youth Hostel at Rhiw.

2. Continue through the gate and along the Roman road.

3. Carry on to where the metalled road comes in from the

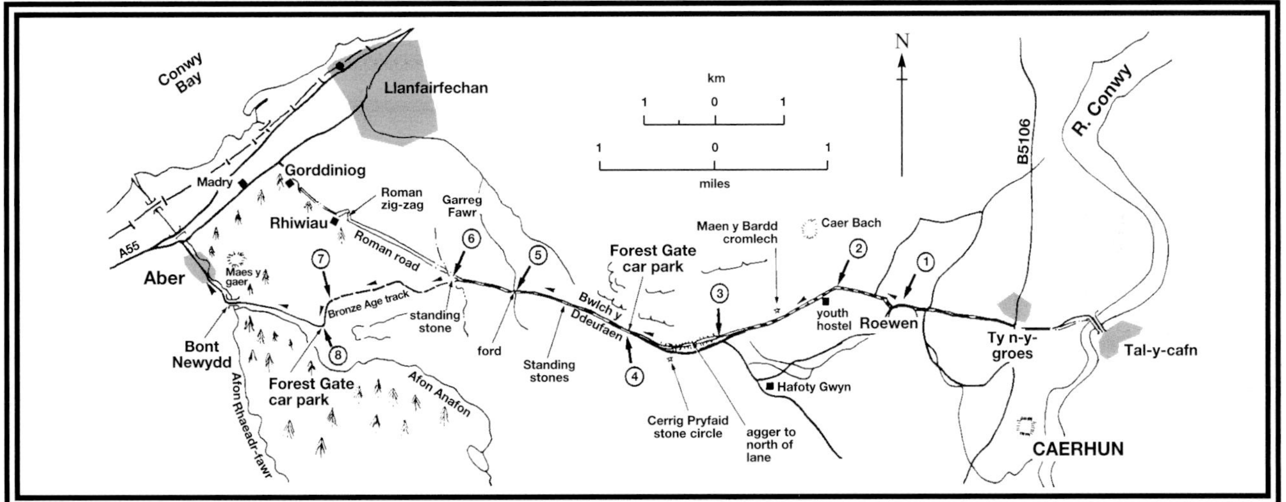

Top left: *The broad beautiful Vale of Clwyd: a recently discovered Roman road passed down the vale from St Asaph to join the Chester–Dolgellau road at Corwen.* **Bottom left:** *The Chester–Caernarfon Roman road at the Bwlch-y-Ddeufaen.* **Above: left:** *A standing stone. The Roman road leaves the Bronze Age Trackway just beyond this ancient marker.* **Above right:** *A lane runs on the Chester–Meols Roman road near Street Hey.*

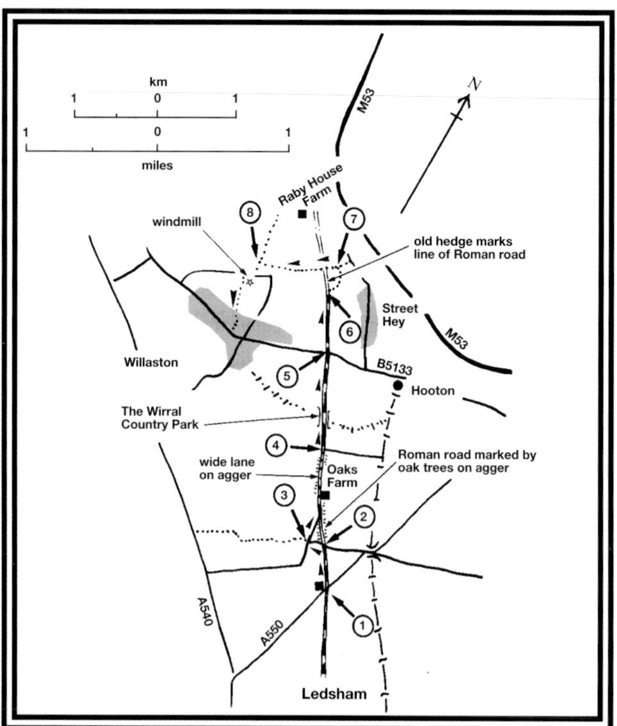

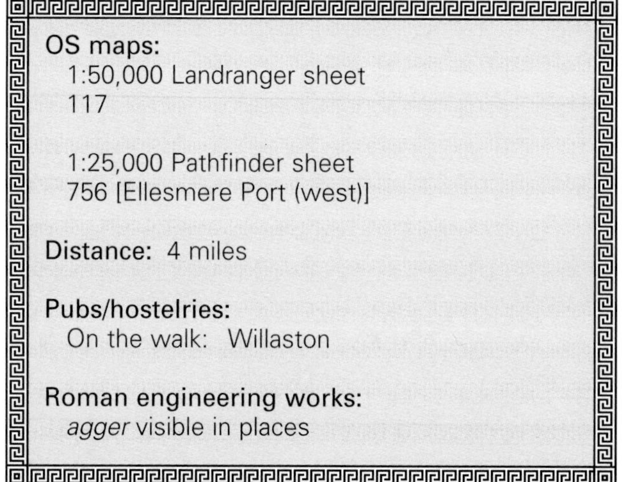

OS maps:
1:50,000 Landranger sheet 117

1:25,000 Pathfinder sheet 756 [Ellesmere Port (west)]

Distance: 4 miles

Pubs/hostelries:
On the walk: Willaston

Roman engineering works:
agger visible in places

left along the line of the Bronze Age trackway. The Roman road carries straight on, taking up the Bronze Age route.

4. Pass the small car park at the Forest Gate [SH721715] and continue along the Roman road into Bwlch y Ddeufaen, passing close to the two standing stones that give it its name. Go through the gate.

5. Ford the stream and continue, crossing another, smaller, stream and going uphill to where a standing stone marks the route.

Above: *Oak trees guard the agger of the Roman road near Oaks Farm.*

6. The stone marks an important road junction in pre-Roman times. Shortly beyond the stone the Roman road turned off to the right, but its diversion from the Romanised Bronze Age track is hard to recognise today. Continue along the well marked Bronze Age trackway, following it downhill.

7. Bear left to the small car park at the Forest Gate [SH676716].

8. Turn right and follow the lane downhill to Bont Newydd across the Afon Rhaidr-fawr and on to Aber.

THE ROMAN ROAD FROM CHESTER TO MEOLS

The Wirral peninsula, the tongue of land between the Dee and the Mersey, has seen its fair share of coastal change since Roman times. Its blunt head is a profile shortened and straightened by coastal erosion, while the saltings of the River Dee have expanded since Roman days. Marshland has been drained, reclaimed and enclosed and the treacherous tidal waters of the Dee estuary reduced in size. Where now sheep graze and marsh birds feed, Roman ships eased their way towards numerous little harbours and Romano-British fishermen plied their trade.

A Roman road ran from Chester on a single alignment for at least 10 miles up the centre of the Wirral peninsula.

It was designed to serve the many small ports and harbours on the shores of the Wirral, both those on the Dee Estuary and those on the Mersey, by acting as a link-road from which lanes could run down to the quays. It was heading for a more important port at the top of the Wirral peninsula. This final destination may never be known for certain, because of the coastal change. None the less, the alignment of the road suggests a final destination that now lies out to sea somewhere between Hoylake and New Brighton. Meols has frequently been suggested as the probable site because Roman material has been found offshore here, including brooches, agricultural implements, fish hooks, net sinkers, pins, beads and sections of wall. We can suggest that Meols — or rather, a site near it — was the Roman port to which this road was making its way and that the inhabitants were involved in coastal trade and in fishing, but this is not known.

The road was probably built in the AD 70-80s as a supply route for the developing settlement and fortress at Chester. Certainly the road seems to have been built with commercial thoughts uppermost, but we do not know what goods were carried along it. Probably a whole variety of merchandise passed this way — from pottery to foodstuffs, from specialised imports to local wares — but it is likely that heavier goods, such as building stone, were shipped around the coast and up the rivers.

The road left the Roman fort of *Deva*, its course represented today by the A540. On the far side of the Shropshire Union Canal it now runs across fields to Mollington, beyond which it is followed by a line of footpaths and lanes to Ledsham, where the walk begins. From Ledsham the road is raised on an *agger* as Ledsham Hall Lane. At Oaks Farm it can be seen crossing a field and from there it is followed by lanes to north of Street Hey, where it is marked by a line of hedgerows as far as Radley Hall Farm before the line is lost.

36 A WALK FROM LEDSHAM TO WILLASTON

This is an easy-going walk on the Wirral peninsula through gentle scenery along a little-known Roman road.

Instructions

1. Start where the Roman road crosses the A550 [SJ354756]. Head north-west along the Roman road.

2. Turn left along Badgers Rake Road, briefly leaving the Roman road, which goes straight ahead where oak trees and the remains of an *agger* mark its course.

3. Turn right along the private drive to Oaks Farm, which is followed by a footpath although it is unsignposted. The driveway bears right to rejoin the line of the Roman road, which it then follows.

4. At the end of the lane Heath Road comes in sharply from the right and turns north along the line of the Roman road. Carry on along it and over the dismantled railway, now in the Wirral Country Park. Continue to the crossroads.

5. Go straight over into Street Hey Lane, which is on a noticeable *agger*. The lane bends slightly and becomes an unsurfaced track on the edge of a small wood.

6. The walkable stretch of the Roman road ends where the woodland track turns abruptly to the right. The line of the Roman road marches straight on across the field as an old hedge.

7. Turn right along the woodland path, leaving the Roman road. Bear left with the path. Where the path divides turn left over the stile. Follow the footpath, recrossing the line of the Roman road at the field boundary. Continue along the footpath.

8. Turn left when you reach the bridleway and emerge on the road. Turn right to the windmill and left down the footpath to Willaston.

— VIII —
NORTHERN ENGLAND

'Lo! what high mounds immense divide the moor,
stretched from the southern to the northern shore!
These are but relicks of the Roman way,
Where the firm legions marched in dread array ...'

FRANCIS FAWKES
Branham Park (1745)

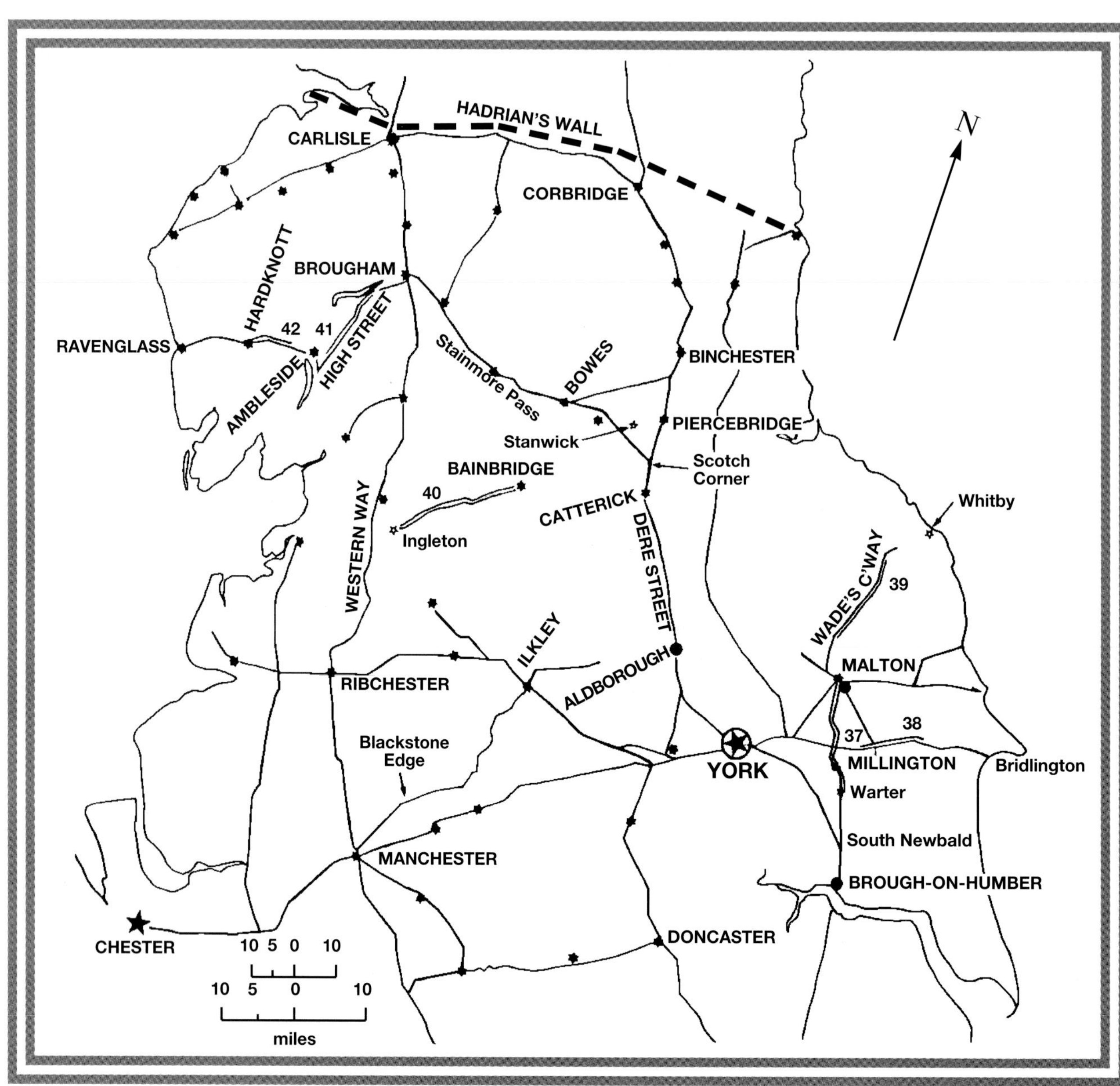

Above: *The northern tribes were cattle breeders.*

The Romans in Northern England

At the time of the Roman conquest most of Northern England was in the hands of the Brigantes, though the Parisi, related to the Gauls of the Champagne region, held lands on the east coast. These northern tribes were cattle breeders, less civilised than the Britons further south, though the Parisi soon developed some communications with the Romans and traded in luxury items like bronze brooches.

Cartimandua, Queen of the Brigantes, was friendly towards Rome. She accepted client kingdom status in AD 43 and the vast Brigantian territory, with its grazing herds and roaming cowboys, became a 'buffer zone' between the new Roman province and the tribes of Caledonia. Cartimandua's husband, Venutius, led the Brigantian anti-Roman faction and civil war broke out on several occasions, notably after Cartimandua had handed the fugitive Caratacus over to Rome, when Roman intervention was necessary to restore her to her throne.

In AD 69 Venutius succeeded in dethroning the queen, who had divorced him for his armour bearer, Vellocatus. On this occasion Cartimandua had to be rescued by Roman cavalry, a scene surely more fitting to a Western than to ancient history! Northern England was now a serious threat and prepared to rise in revolt under Venutius, who set about reinforcing the huge British fort at Stanwick. Indeed, as Tacitus remarks:

Above: *The remains of the bridge at Piercebridge, where Dere Street crossed the River Tees — the sockets for the iron rivets that held the wooden superstructure of the bridge can still be seen.*

'The throne was left to Venutius, the war to us ...'

The former legate of the II Augusta Legion, Vespasian, became Emperor that same year and sent his son-in-law, the daredevil Petillius Cerialis, to Britain as the new governor. Cerialis had been commander of the IX Hispana Legion during the Boudiccan rebellion, so was no stranger to British warfare. He made all haste to annex the Brigantian territory, advancing from Lincoln with the IX Legion and crossing the Humber into the friendly lands of the Parisi. He passed swiftly to Malton and from thence to York, where in AD 71 he founded a new legionary fortress.

From York, Cerialis swung north-west to storm and capture the vast Brigantian stronghold at Stanwick. The Brigantian resistance collapsed and Venutius probably went into hiding, vanishing for ever from the pages of history. Cerialis continued across the Stainmore Pass to join up with other Roman troops that had moved up the western side of the Pennines. Northern England was incorporated into the Roman Empire.

York (*Eboracum*) became the military capital of Roman Britain, and the settlement that developed beside the legionary fortress grew and prospered to such an extent that in the 3rd century it became a *colonia*. In AD 213 Britain was divided into two provinces and York became capital of the northern one, *Britannia Inferior*. The north was to remain a garrisoned zone, and few other towns were founded, the chief ones being Brough-on-Humber (*Petuaria*), Aldborough (*Isurium*) and Malton (*Derventio*). Eastern Yorkshire was the most civilised, with many villas. Lead was mined, jet was collected on the beaches of the north-east, and there were several centres of pottery manufacture.

The Roman Roads in Northern England

The Roman roads of Northern England are based on two principal routes, one on either side of the Pennines. Both run northwards to Hadrian's Wall. The Western Way passes from Manchester, through Ribchester to Carlisle. The eastern route is a continuation of Ermine Street that crossed the Humber by ferry and continued to York. An alternative road avoiding the ferry strikes north-west from Lincoln through Doncaster to York. From York Dere Street is the main highway and forges northwards through Piercebridge, where it bridged the River Tees, and on to Corbridge, shadowed by another northern road which runs through Thirsk and Thornton-le-Street.

Cross-country roads over the Pennines link the two north-south highways. Pre-eminent, then as now, was the road over the Stainmore Pass which leaves Dere Street at Scotch Corner and runs to Brougham near Penrith, where it meets the Western Way coming up from Manchester. This road lies almost entirely beneath the A66.

Other roads across the Pennines run from Ingleton to Brough-by-Bainbridge; from Ribchester via Ilkley to Tadcaster; from Manchester to Ilkley, a road made famous by the extraordinary paved incline on Blackstone Edge; and from Manchester to York, this road continuing eastwards from Stamford Bridge towards Bridlington.

Cerialis' campaign route of AD 71 heads north from the Humber through Millington to Malton, a Roman route centre. From here Wade's Causeway strikes off northwards towards Whitby, its sandstone slab foundations visible as it snakes over Wheeldale Moor.

In the west, the Roman roads of the Lake District follow incredible routes. High Street climbs across 2,000-foot-high mountains, superbly aligned to give the easiest possible gradient, while the road from Ambleside to Ravenglass crosses dangerous Hardknott Pass and gives unparalleled views.

The Roman roads of northern England offer truly superb walking, and there are times when the walker is conscious of the ghostly tramp of marching feet and the creak of cumbersome Roman carts. Certainly something of the spirit of the Roman eagles hangs around these roads, weaving around them a sense of indomitable purpose.

THE ROMAN ROAD FROM SOUTH NEWBALD TO MALTON

Cerialis' road to the north

This road branches from the Brough-on-Humber to York road near South Newbald and heads straight on over the Wolds. It predates the supposed continuation of Ermine Street from Brough to York, and follows the route taken by Petillius Cerialis in AD 71, when he passed through Parisian territory before assaulting the great Brigantian stronghold at Stanwick. It continued to be an important road and is followed by the Antonine Itinerary, passing *Delgovicia*, thought now to be Millington.

East Yorkshire saw considerable prosperity under Roman rule, in marked contrast to most of northern Britain. Despite the dominating presence of the great legionary fortress of the IX Legion at York, the region was generally peaceable and some towns developed. Villas and other civilian buildings have been found along the walk in the Millington valley and at Langton. Langton villa was the centre of an important estate and a range of corn-processing equipment has been found there, ranging from a threshing floor to a corn-drying oven, storage barns and millstones.

From South Newbald to Market Weighton the Roman road lies under the A1034. Then it continues straight along the hillside east of the town as a track still known as Humber Street. However, from this point to Warter, where the walk begins, there is little of the Roman road to be seen. There was a change of alignment to the north-west at Warter, which may some day yield Roman remains since Roman ornaments and coins have been found here.

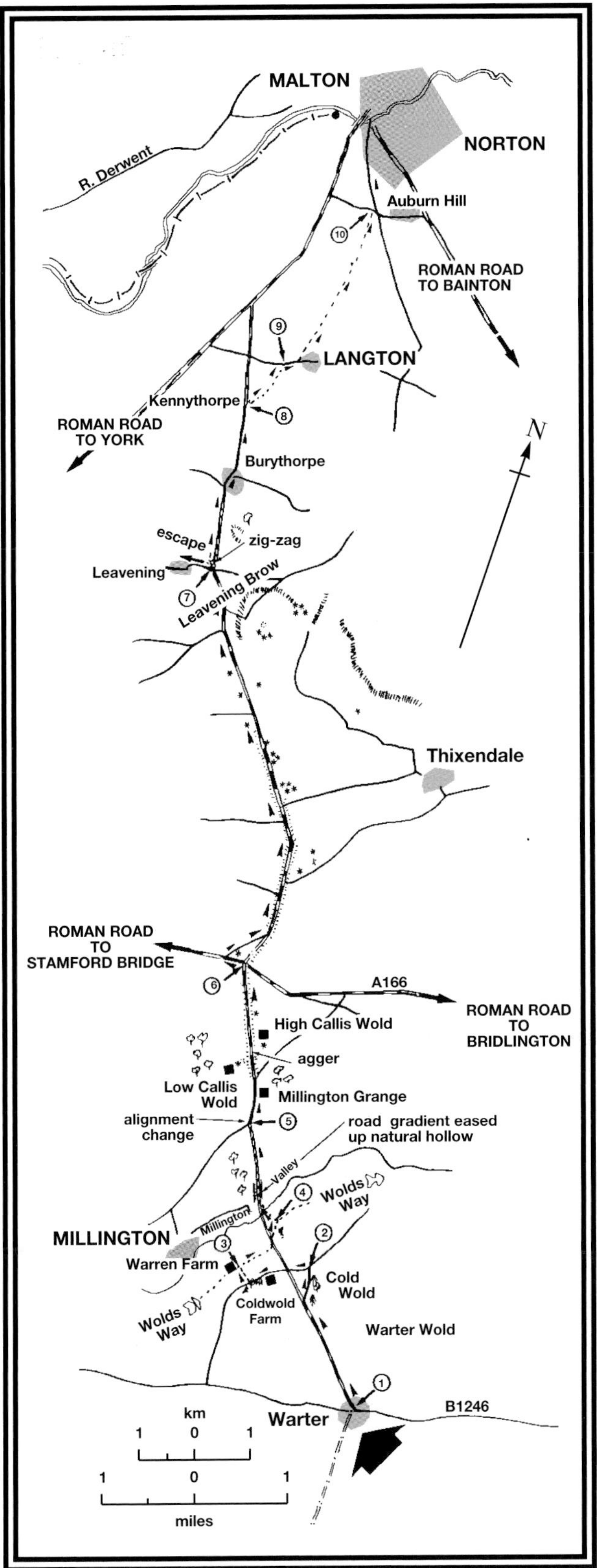

The road heads straight up on to Cold Wold, still in use as a lane, and descends into the Millington valley, the steep gradient eased by a terraceway which has fallen out of use. It crosses the stream, where traces of road metalling have been found, and then climbs out of the valley, making use of a natural hollow.

On the top the alignment changed and the Roman road, raised on an *agger*, runs in short, straight lengths to cross the Stamford Bridge-Bridlington Roman road. It follows the western edge of the Wolds as a little lane with superb views over the vale till it reaches Leavening Brow, which it descends by a typical zig-zag. From the bottom of the hill it runs through Burythorpe and Kennythorpe, where the walk leaves the road, and joins the road from York into Malton.

Cerialis developed Malton as his base in AD 71-72, and Julius Agricola built a fort here in AD 79 which was rebuilt in stone during the reign of Trajan (AD 98-117). It was a focus of routes and a civil settlement grew up between the fort and the River Derwent which developed into a sizeable town. It spread south of the river into the Norton area, where an extensive pottery industry developed. This 'Norton Ware' is distinctive — hard grey to blue-grey pottery of good quality including flagons, dishes, bowls, face-vases, mortaria and unusual beakers with an appliqué design.

37 A CYCLE RIDE/WALK FROM WARTER TO MALTON

This pastoral walk/cycle ride over the Wolds takes the route used by the Governor of Britain, Petillius Cerialis and the IX Hispana Legion in AD 71 on their way to subdue Brigantia.

Instructions

1. Start at Warter. Head uphill north-west along the lane to Cold Wold.

2. The Roman road went straight down into the valley where there is now no right of way. Instead, turn left past Coldwold Farm. Turn right by the covered tank down a wide, pebbly farm track. This is a public footpath so cyclists must dismount.

3. Turn right at Warren Farm on to the footpath. Follow the path along the top of a post-Roman embankment on the edge of the steep Millington valley. After nearly half a mile the footpath bears to the left and down into the valley.

4. Bear left, leaving the Wolds Way, to cross the stream at approximately the Roman crossing point. Go uphill along

the line of the Roman road and cross the modern road. Cyclists remount. The Roman road makes use of a small natural hollow to help ease the gradient, and the *agger* is faintly visible.

5. Turn right at the road past Millington Grange, Low Callis Wold and High Callis Wold to the A166.

6. The A166 lies on the Roman road from Stamford Bridge to Bridlington and the Roman road from Millington crossed straight over here. The route has been ploughed out and there is no right of way, so a brief detour is necessary. Turn left along the A166 for about a quarter of a mile and then turn right along a minor road. In about half a mile rejoin the Roman road, which continues northwards as a lane to the T-junction on Leavening Brow. To

take the 'escape route' turn left at this junction along the modern road into Leavening and end the walk there.

7. Go through the gate immediately opposite and follow the grassy Roman zig-zag downhill and through the next gate. Carry on along the hollow way which follows the Roman road over the stream to Burythorpe. Follow the lane to Kennythorpe.

Top left: *Roman gemstone. National Museum of Wales.* **Left:** *The stream crossing in the Millington valley — the site of a Roman ford.* **Above:** *Roman zig-zag at the top of Leavening Brow. Malton lies ahead.*

8. Leave the Roman road here and turn right opposite High Farm to follow the edge of the field and then the track to Langton, site of the Roman villa.

9. Turn right on to the road into Langton and then first left through the gate on to the bridleway. This is a minor Roman road from Langton into Malton. Follow the bridleway for about 2 miles to the stables.

OS maps:
1:50,000 Landranger sheets
106 & 100

1:25,000 Pathfinder sheets
666 [Kirby Underdale and Garton-on-the-Wolds]
656 [Sledmere]
655 [Burton-le-Willows]
643 [Malton and Gilling East]

Distance:
full walk/ride to Malton —17½ miles
to Leavening only — 11 miles

Pubs/hostelries:
On the walk: Malton
Nearby: Thixendale
Leavening

Roman engineering works:
agger visible in places
terraceways
cutting
zig-zag

Other antiquities:
tumuli
Roman sites in Millington valley
Roman Derventio (Malton)

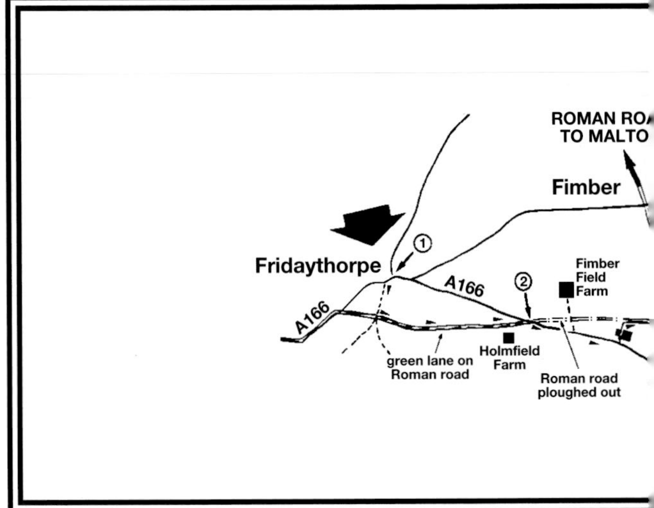

Top: *Tall beech trees guard alongside the Roman highway as it crosses the wolds.*

Above: *'Wold Gate', the straight Roman road beyond Kilham.*

10. Turn right and then left on to Langton Road and the final mile to the River Derwent and Malton.

THE ROMAN ROAD FROM STAMFORD BRIDGE TO BRIDLINGTON

This Roman road headed east from Stamford Bridge through Fridaythorpe and across the Wolds to a lost harbour near Bridlington. The exact destination is unknown as it has been destroyed by coastal erosion. The road was probably built in about AD 80 under Julius Agricola when he was consolidating Roman control over this part of the province before his push for the far north. Clearly the road was an important link between the coast and the legionary fortress at York.

There were rich farmlands on the Yorkshire Wolds in Roman times. Wheat was the main crop, and no doubt some of it went to supply the garrison at York, since all landowners had to provide wheat to feed the army. Oats, barley and fodder crops were also grown and herds of cattle and flocks of sheep grazed the uplands. Native farms continued to exist throughout Roman times, but in general this farming economy was based on large estates — villas — and the labour was provided by slaves, probably native Britons either captured in the wars or born into the bondsman class. There is a concentration of villa sites in eastern Yorkshire: at least 15 are known, and those at Rudston and Kilham are near to this Bridlington road.

The villas rose to their grandest during the fourth century, when many were given mosaic pavements. The Rudston villa is known for its 'Venus mosaic', in which the goddess, rather oddly shaped it must be admitted, is portrayed looking into her mirror.

The Roman road lies under the A166 from Stamford Bridge till about half a mile from Fridaythorpe, where the walk begins, passing along a green lane with traces of an *agger*. Further green lanes carry the road onwards along the high ground of the Wolds, where during the Dark Ages it was fortified as a defensive earthwork still visible today. A straight lane with wide verges takes up the line to Kilham, site of a Roman villa, where the walk ends.

Beyond Kilham the Roman road is still a wide, straight lane known as Wold Gate which comes to an abrupt end on the outskirts of Bridlington.

This road possesses a magnificent sensation of being on top of the world, in communion with a greatness untouched by mortality. This is a characteristic of the best

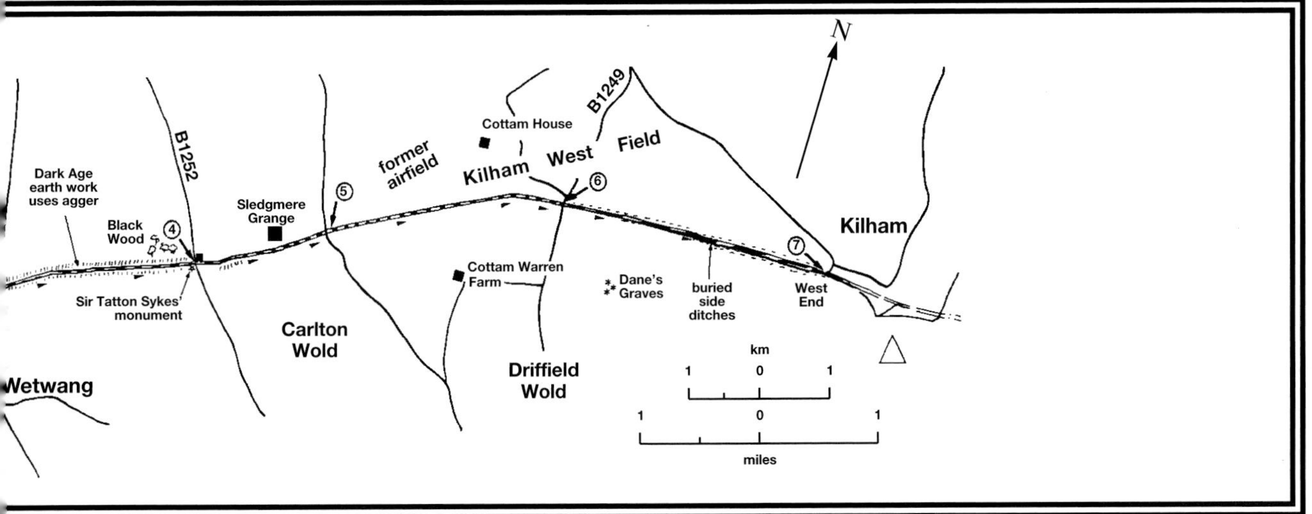

Roman roads, a feeling of vast size which communicates the determination of Rome to dominate the whole world. This road still strides ahead over the soft Wolds landscape of folded hills, its wide verges growing luxuriant over infilled ditches abundant with flowers.

OS maps:
1:50,000 Landranger sheets
106 & 101

1:25,000 Pathfinder sheets
666 [Kirby Underdale & Garton-on-the-Wolds]
656 [Sledmere]
657 [Bridlington]

Distance: 13 miles

Pubs/hostelries:
On the walk: Fridaythorpe
Kilham
Nearby: Wetwang
Langtoft

Roman engineering works:
traces of *agger* in places
buried side-ditches show up as wide, luxuriant verges

Other antiquities:
site of Romano-British cemetery
Dark Age earthwork parallel to the Roman road
site of villa at Kilham

38 A WALK FROM FRIDAYTHORPE TO KILHAM

This walk follows an east-west Roman road, now dwindled to a line of green lanes and a minor road, and gives wide views across the Yorkshire Wolds.

Instructions

1. Start at Fridaythorpe. Head south down the little lane opposite the school signposted 'Wolds Way'. Turn left where the little lane meets a green lane. Continue to the A166.

2. Turn right along the A-road and turn up the second track on your left, passing the farm. Turn abruptly to the right with the track. This brings you back on to the Roman road. Continue to the B-road, where the Malton-Bainton Roman road crossed.

3. Cross the B-road and carry on along the green lane opposite, passing the site of a Roman cemetery. Continue along the green lane straight ahead. Cross over the lane and carry on with the partially levelled remains of an earthwork running alongside to Sir Tatton Sykes' Monument.

4. Cross the B1252 and continue along the Roman road past Sledmere Grange and down into the valley. Cross the lane in the valley bottom.

5. Climb up the bank, go through the gate and climb out of the valley along the bridleway to Kilham West Field.

6. Cross the B1249 and carry on along the Roman road, now a straight lane with wide verges. Keep on straight over

the high ground to West End, Kilham, where another lane comes in from the left.

7. Carry on into Kilham.

hold the sandstone slabs in place. The road was cambered and surface water was carried beneath it in culverts overlain by large cover stones. Sadly many of these were broken by tanks during the war, though some still remain

WADE'S CAUSEWAY

The Roman road from Malton to Whitby

Wade's Causeway must be the most famous Roman road in Britain; certainly the stretch on the top of Wheeldale Moor is the best preserved. This remarkable slab surface stretches away giving a weird sense of timelessness, as if the Romans were here for only a few years back rather than over fifteen centuries.

Legend holds that this road is named after a giant, Wade, who built the causeway for his wife, Bel, so she could pasture her cattle on the moors. Archaeology holds, no less romantically, that Wade's Causeway was built during the Agricolan advance northwards in AD 79.

Much is made of this small stretch of preserved road, which has survived the depredations of time largely through its remoteness from human habitation, since elsewhere the road has long ago been robbed of its stones. In the great period of drystone wall building of the 17th and 18th centuries this stretch of road was so remote that its stones just weren't worth the trouble in time and effort to cart them away.

The present appearance of the road is misleading for, unlike the Dean Road and the road on Blackstone Edge, Wade's Causeway was not a paved road. The layer of sandstone slabs, which form the present surface, are part of the foundations and were covered by a 'metalling' of sand and gravel. Kerbstones were set along the sides of the road to

— looking as if they were constructed far more recently than the 1st century AD!

The stretch of road on Wheeldale Moor is part of the through-route from Malton to Whitby, which crosses the Vale of Pickering to Wrelton, where the walk begins, and then climbs to the Roman camps at Cawthorne. From here it descends the steep slope to the north and continues through Cropton Forest, rising on to the famous stretch on Wheeldale Moor. Here, though the construction of the road is excellent, it does not keep to a single straight alignment, but was constructed as a series of short, straight lengths which introduce an element of winding. It descends into the Wheeldale Beck valley and crosses Wheeldale Gill, rising out again as a modern farm track to pass Hazel Head and Hollin House Farm to Julian Park. Here it turns north towards the site of a Roman camp at Low Burrows and veers north-eastwards along the Lease Rigg ridge before dropping to Grosmont, where the walk ends. Beyond Grosmont Wade's Causeway is not easy to follow. First it crossed the River Esk and then turned to a more easterly course via Aislaby to Whitby.

The question of why the road winds about on Wheeldale Moor is a vexed one. Why is it not straight? The winding is clearly intentional. Perhaps it was built by contingents of Roman soldiers being taught the art of road construction, especially how to change alignment. In this context it has been suggested that this was a purely military route which never took on a commercial role and was disused within 40 years.

Top left: *Wade's Causeway at Rutmoor Beck: the sandstone slab surface snakes across the moor.* **Left:** *A culvert with its large cover-stone intact.* **Below:** *Goathland.*

None the less, it is probable that so well constructed a route would have continued in use. It was a direct link between the north-east coast and the fort and thriving town at Malton. Moreover, the shiny black stone, jet, was an important product of the north-east coast during Roman times. Most of it was collected from the beach shingle in the Whitby region and there is good reason to suppose that it found its way along Wade's Causeway to Malton and thence to York to be worked into jewellery, particularly rings, medallions and beads.

39 A WALK FROM WRELTON TO GROSMONT

This exciting walk includes the best preserved length of Roman road in Britain.

Instructions

1. Start at Wrelton. Head north towards Cawthorne along the lane. At the T-junction turn right.

2. Turn left down the road to Keldy.

3. Turn right at the bottom of the hill, and follow the bridleway across the Sutherland Beck into the plantation. Continue along the bridleway, which emerges from the trees and bears to the right after about half a mile. The right of way diverges from the Roman road.

4. Turn left and continue along the bridleway, joining a track to a T-junction just north of Stape.

5. Turn left and follow the road northwards. Carry straight

on along the forest track just west of the Roman road. Cross Rutmoor Beck.

6. Turn right on to the famous stretch of Wade's Causeway along the hillside and then downhill to cross Wheeldale Gill.

7. Turn left to follow the terraced lane past Hazel Head and Hollin House Farm to Julian Park.

8. Turn left and head north along the lane, which merges with the Roman road past Strunty Carr.

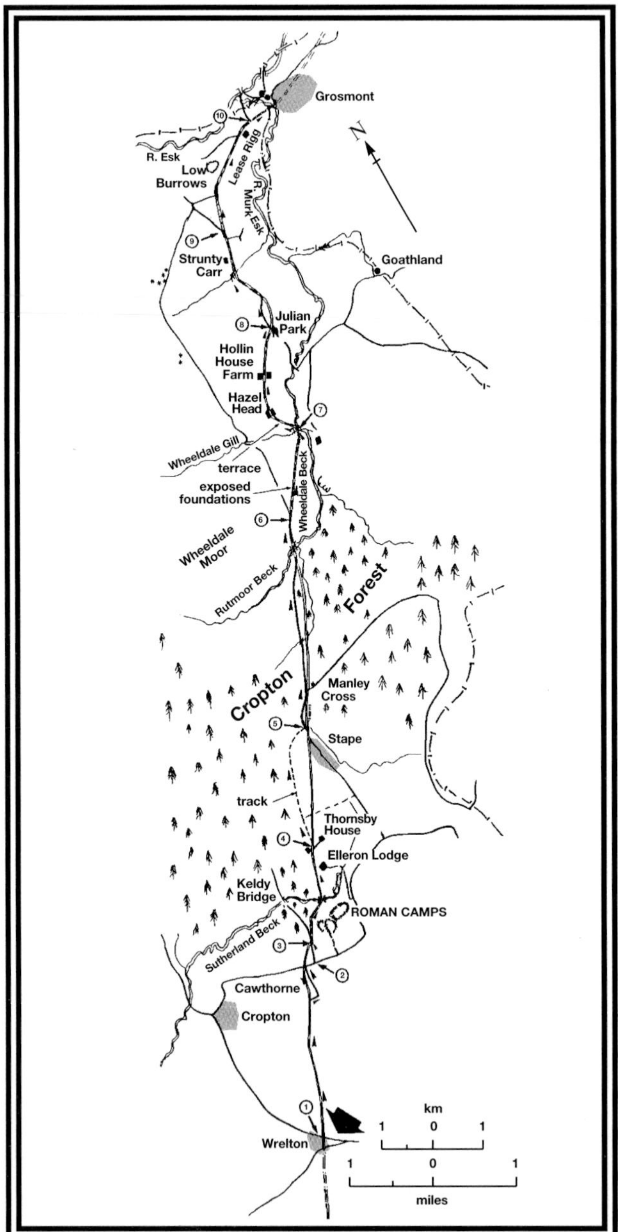

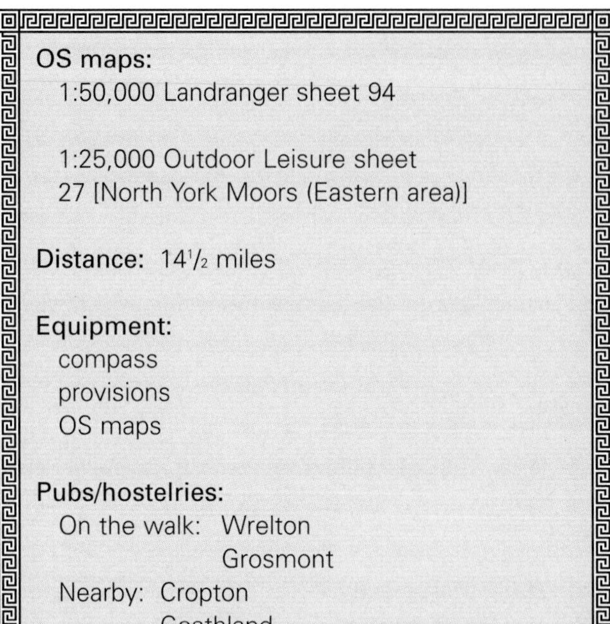

OS maps:
1:50,000 Landranger sheet 94

1:25,000 Outdoor Leisure sheet 27 [North York Moors (Eastern area)]

Distance: 14½ miles

Equipment:
compass
provisions
OS maps

Pubs/hostelries:
On the walk: Wrelton
Grosmont
Nearby: Cropton
Goathland

Roman engineering works:
agger visible in places
terracing
sandstone block foundations
culverts with stone covers

Other antiquities:
Cawthorne Roman practice camps
Low Burrows Roman fort site

Below: *The ancient Manley Cross in Cropton Forest, just off the road.*

9. Turn right on to the bridleway, rejoining the lane after about half a mile, past the site of a Roman camp at Low Burrows and continue to Lease Rigg.

10. Turn to the right between the buildings leaving the Roman road briefly. Turn left to rejoin the alignment of Wade's Causeway, now a track, and follow it steeply downhill. When you reach Grosmont turn left through the kissing-gate signposted 'Railway Trail' and follow the footpath past the school and over the river to the village.

THE ROMAN ROAD FROM INGLETON TO BROUGH-BY-BAINBRIDGE

The Roman road from Ingleton to the fort at Brough-by-Bainbridge (*Virosidum*) crosses the magnificent landscape of the Yorkshire Dales. It passes beneath the frowning crags and scars of Ingleborough and Whernside, giving splendid views to both these mountains. At length the road drops into fruitful Wensleydale.

The walk follows the entire road, which today seems to begin and end in splendid isolation. During Roman times it was part of the road network and probably continued south-west of Ingleton to join the Western Way, perhaps near Lower Bentham, and eastwards from Brough probably along Wensleydale, heading for the legionary fortress at York.

The Ingleton road keeps to a north-easterly alignment despite the steep slopes and awkward valleys that had to be

Right: *The Roman road running along the valleyside north-east of Ingleton.*

Below: *Looking to Bainbridge along the final straight alignment.*

negotiated in crossing the fells. This demonstrates the superb skill of the Romans in choosing the route, for deviations from the straight are remarkably few. The surveying and engineering of the route could not be bettered. First it follows the valley of the Doe from Ingleton to Chapel-le-Dale along a much more level course than the B6255, which runs along the opposite side of the valley.

The modern road joins the Roman road to climb over Ribble Head, but shortly beyond this they part company and the Roman road crosses the Gayle Beck. It is terraced up the steep slopes of Cam Fell, which keeps the gradient remarkably smooth. From Oughtershaw Side to the final alignment at Wether Fell the road runs in a series of straight lengths on a remarkably even gradient and then descends smoothly to Brough along a spur of the fell.

The road was built as part of the process of pacifying Brigantian territory and was probably laid out under Petillius Cerialis. The great Agricola completed the pacification of the region and built a string of forts, including Brough, which is perched on a little hill above the confluence of the River Bain and the River Ure as it swirls along the bottom of Wensleydale. The Agricolan fort was replaced by a later stone fort and *Virosidum* remained garrisoned right to the end of the fourth century. The Roman name for this fort, *Virosidum*, means 'high seat' and is an apt description! The fort has undergone extensive excavation since the 1950s, but was mentioned as long ago as 1586 by the indefatigable William Camden.

The road is generally about 15 feet wide and raised on a

OS maps:
1:50,000 Landranger sheet
98

1:25,000 Outdoor Leisure sheets
2 [Yorkshire Dales (Western Area)]
30 [Yorkshire Dales (Northern and Central Areas)]

Distance: 19½ miles

Pubs/hostelries:
On the walk: Ingleton
Chapel-le-Dale
Bainbridge
Nearby: Hawes

Roman engineering works:
terracing
terraced descent to river crossing
zig-zag
paving
culvert covers

Other antiquities:
Roman fort at Brough-by-Bainbridge

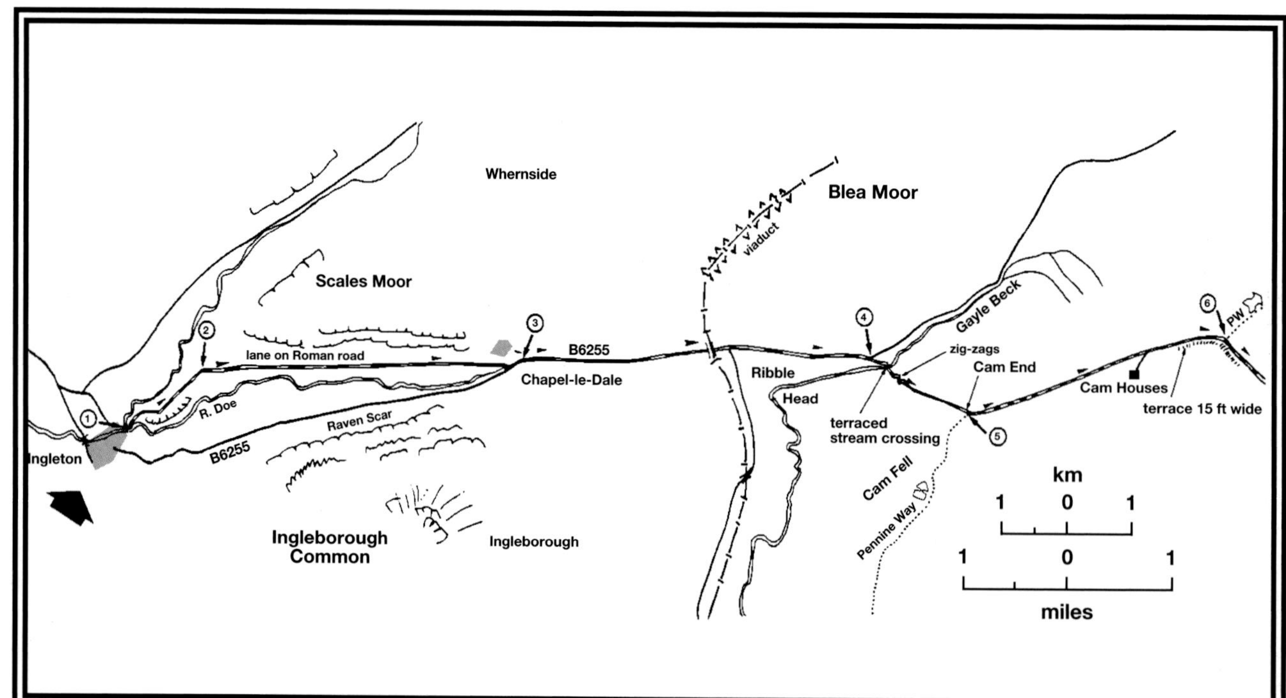

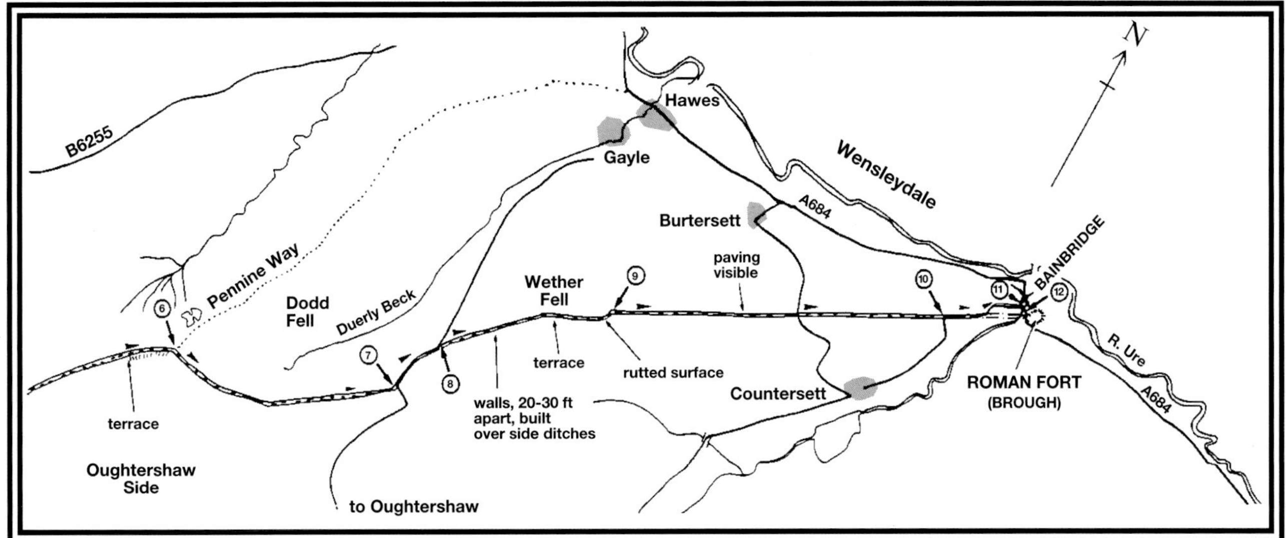

slight *agger*, and in places the wide, lush verges hint at buried side-ditches while one of the most exciting features of this road are the cart ruts cut into the limestone rock. Were they worn by the passage of Roman waggons or are they of more recent origin?

40 A WALK FROM INGLETON TO BROUGH-BY-BAINBRIDGE

This long and interesting walk travels through spectacular countryside along one of the most exciting Roman roads in Britain.

Instructions

1. Start at Ingleton and head north along Mill Lane, which climbs steeply in short, straight lengths.

2. Bear right with the road, which turns north-east to Chapel-le-Dale as a straight valley-side road. Turn right along the modern lane to the B6255.

3. Turn left along the B-road. In about a quarter of a mile, just before the inn, the Roman road comes in from the left and the B6255 bends to the right to take up the alignment, which it follows for the next 3½ miles. Go under the approach to Ribblehead viaduct.

4. Keep straight ahead where the B6255 turns left. Follow the track, which slants downhill as a Roman terrace. Cross Gayle Beck and follow the zig-zag uphill. Carry on to Cam End [SD802805].

5. Here the Roman road is joined by the Pennine Way and bears north-east, resuming its old alignment for the steady ascent to Cam Houses. Continue along the fine Roman terraceway, cut out of the rock, past the turn-off on the right for Cam Houses Farm, where the Pennine Way turns off to the left [SD829834].

6. Follow the Roman road as it bears more to the east to swing along Oughtershaw Side around the south of Dodd Fell keeping to a very level gradient at about 1,900 feet.

7. Go through the gate where the road from Oughtershaw (signposted Kettlewell 14½) comes in from the right [SD861846] and continue straight along this modern road.

8. Continue straight on where the road turns left, following the Roman line. Follow the track, which bears slightly to the right and then to the left to pass as a terraceway around Wether Fell.

9. The final alignment for Bainbridge was set out on the eastern edge of Wether Fell. The Roman surveyors ingeniously avoided crossing a small but deep valley by turning a sharp angle [at SD882871] from which the final alignment was set out along a spur of the fell. Continue along this impressive walled lane. Cross over the Burtersett-Countersett road and carry on along the Roman road.

10. Continue where the Countersett-Bainbridge road comes in from the right and turns on to the Roman road. Bear left with the modern road away from the Roman road and go steeply downhill into the village.

11. Turn right along the A684 for about 50 yards, crossing the River Bain.

12. Turn left on to the footpath to the fort.

HIGH STREET

The Roman road from Brougham to Windermere

The Roman road called High Street has given its name to a 2,600ft-high Lake District mountain across whose summit it strides with the assurance and determination so characteristic of the Romans. In the 15 miles of its course between Winder Hall Farm near Pooley Bridge and Troutbeck Park, it passes no human habitation at all and crosses some of England's wildest, most inhospitable landscape. It is arguably the most amazing course followed by a Roman road in Britain, and undoubtedly the most daunting.

High Street was a military road. It heads south from the fort at Brougham, near modern Penrith, towards Windermere, although where it was actually going we do not know. Even so, the course chosen is extraordinary, and can only be explained as a conscious attempt to dominate the land around and break up the landscape into patrollable blocks. It was constructed during the early years of Agricola's governorship as part of his campaign for the pacification of the north-west. Perhaps it was built as it was in an attempt to speed up the campaign so that he could embark for Ireland, a project which Tacitus tells us was close to Agricola's heart.

OS maps:
1:50,000 Landranger sheet
90

1:25,000 Outdoor Leisure sheets
5 [English Lakes (North East)]
7 [English Lakes (South East)]

Distance: 15½ miles

Equipment:
waterproof clothing
compass
OS maps

Pubs/hostelries:
On the walk: Troutbeck

Roman engineering works:
grassy *agger*
terraced stream crossing
spectacular terraced descent to Troutbeck

Other antiquities:
stone circle

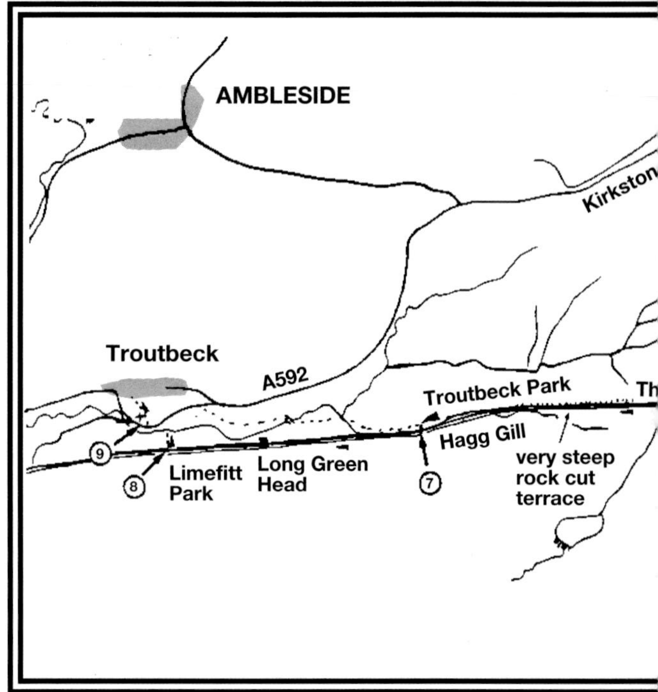

High Street can be traced south-west from Brougham through Eamont Bridge and Yanwath, beyond which the B5320 follows it as far as Tirril. It continues along the same alignment over the fields to Celleron, where the walk begins, and passes Winder Hall Farm, in use as the farm track. It runs along the side of Heughscar Hill at the head of Ullswater. After crossing the Elder Beck by a typical terraced Roman crossing it climbs, now visible as a grassy *agger*, up on to Loadpot Hill, crossing the 2,000ft contour.

On gaining the ridge it turns southwards and crosses near the summits of Wether Hill, Red Crag, Raven Howe, High Raise and High Street itself, all of them well over 2,000 feet high and offering a magnificent panorama of the land below. It descends to Trout Beck by a steep, terraced route at a remarkable gradient of 1 in 5, parallel to and east of the Kirkstone Pass. At Troutbeck Park it crosses the Hagg Gill and keeps along the east side of the Trout Beck valley as a terrace past Long Green Head and Limefitt, where the walk turns from it to Troutbeck. It probably continued its straight alignment into the vicinity of Windermere.

In later years the route was used by pack-horse traffic — no waggon would dare try ascend it — and by the 13th century it had become known as Brettestrete, the road of the Britons. The flat summit of High Street itself became the location of an annual shepherds' meet and fair day, the last of which took place in 1835. The people of the valley farms climbed to the mountain top and horse races were held on the fine natural course.

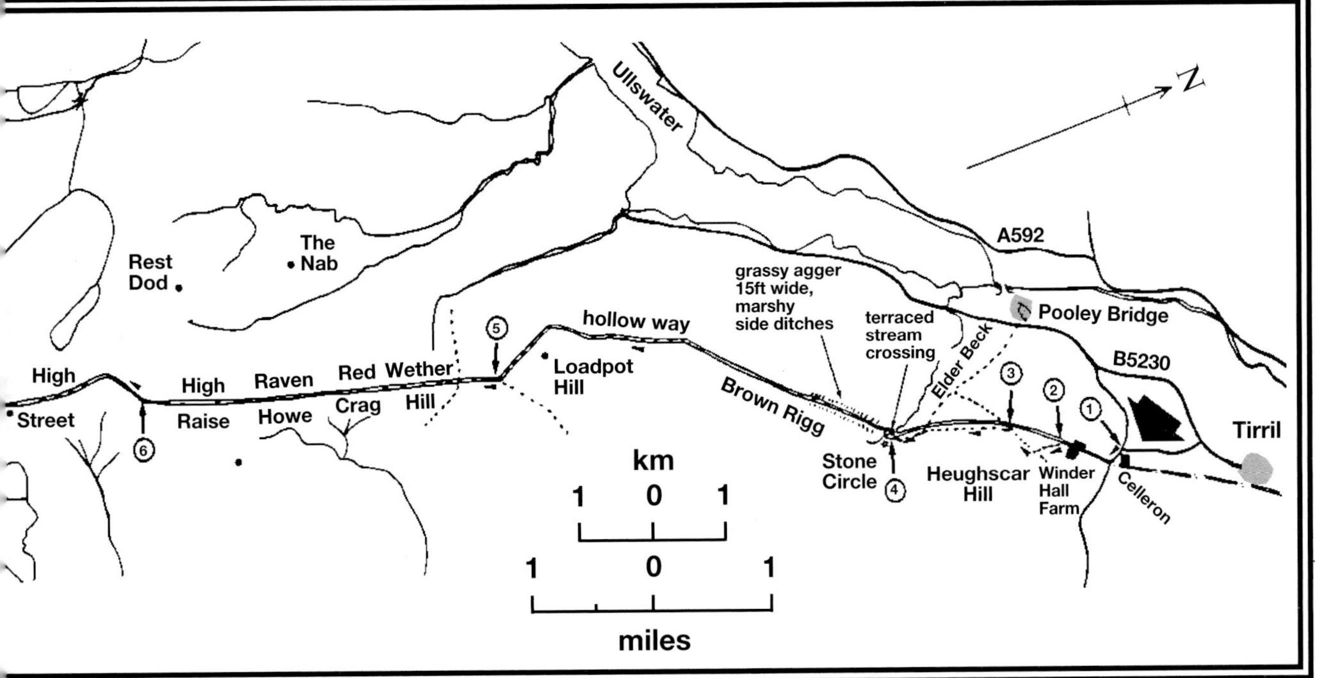

41 A WALK FROM CELLERON TO TROUTBECK

This testing and exciting walk follows the crest of some Lake District mountains with superb views.

Instructions

1. Start at the entrance to Celleron Farm [NY495253]. Head south-east along the lane. In about a quarter of a mile turn right up the farm road to Winder Hall Farm (signposted 'public bridleway to High Street'). Go past Winder Hall Farm and through the gate.

2. Once through the gate strike uphill to the left, to the corner of the wall behind Winder Hall Farm. Turn right on to the worn path.

3. Bear left to follow a clear trackway under Heugh Scar. The Roman road is the faint terrace on the right.

4. Carry on over the crossroad of tracks to the stone circle at the headwaters of Elder Beck [NY483223]. Bear to the right past the stone circle and cross Elder Beck. This is not the Roman crossing point, which is just a few yards downstream. Bear round to the left on to High Street itself, which becomes increasing clear, showing up as a bright green strip. Continue along the Roman road up the slopes of Brown Rigg and on to the lower slopes of Loadpot Hill, where the road has become a hollow way. The ascent is remarkably smooth and gradual, so that the 2,000-feet contour is passed with little difficulty. The Roman road bears left for the final, considerably steeper, ascent of Loadpot Hill and then descends slightly to a junction of bridleways.

5. Turn right and follow the Roman road along the ridge over the series of summits, all over 2,300 feet high.

6. Bear round to the right with the Roman road on to the mountain called High Street. Keep going along the ridge till you reach Thornthwaite Crag, where the steep descent begins. Go downhill along the rock-cut terraces at the uniform gradient of 1 in 5.

Below: *Winder Hall Farm, looking back along the Roman road.*

Above: *Blea Water with the 2,600 ft high mountain, High Street, behind it. The Roman road runs along the snow covered crest from right to left.*

7. Cross the Hagg Gill at the first footbridge, so as to keep to the bridleway rather than take the footpath, which continues straight ahead. Once over the stream turn right and continue past Long Green Head.

8. At Limefitt Park camping site turn right and follow the road through the campsite and over Trout Beck. Turn left along the A592.

9. Turn right along the bridleway past the church into Troutbeck.

THE ROMAN ROAD FROM AMBLESIDE TO RAVENGLASS

This Roman road was far more important than may at first appear. It connected the broken country of the lakes, a potential festering ground for resistance to Rome and a place of refuge for bandits, with a major harbour and coastal fort at Ravenglass (*Glannaventa*). This meant that troops could be deployed speedily to any trouble-spots and that supplies could be brought in to maintain them. Moreover, regular policing of the area, by patrols from the three forts along its 20-mile course, would help to keep the

Pax Romana, and travellers could be escorted across the dangerous Hardknott and Wrynose passes through which the road runs. That it was an official route which continued in use throughout Roman times is demonstrated by its inclusion in the Antonine Itinerary.

This road was originally thought to have been constructed in about AD 80 under the famous governor, Julius Agricola, as part of his plan to subdue Ireland. He was thought to have planned to embark from Ravenglass, but it is now considered more likely that the road was built later in the first century.

It is a masterpiece and runs from Ambleside (*Galava*), at the head of Windermere, along the valley of the River Brathay to Little Langdale, where this walk starts, and where the road is now a walled green lane. Beyond Little Langdale it keeps to the south side of the dale to Fell Foot and the ascent to the Wrynose Pass. It crosses Wrynose and Hardknott passes, where the modern road shadows it, and continues to the south of the Roman fort at Hardknott (*Mediobogdum*), where the walk finishes. Beyond this the road drops down into Eskdale and carries on to the coast at Ravenglass.

The Roman fort at Hardknott is undoubtedly one of the most astounding sites of Roman Britain. Overlooked from the north by Scafell and from the east by Hard Knott, the site is very open, perched 800 feet up on a spur of land that seems to hang above the fertile plains of Eskdale, a lonely eyrie where the Roman eagles could sit and and brood, keeping watch over their dominions. Today sheep graze within the broken walls, but there is still much to see. The fort walls stand to a height of some eight feet — partially rebuilt — and within are the remains of various buildings. The bath house lies just outside the south gate. The parade ground, 200 yards from the east gate, is an artificially levelled area, the best example in Britain of a Roman military parade ground. Somehow it has been squeezed into this confined site between the fort and the mountain.

There are conflicting views as to the age of the fort and its probable purpose. A fragmentary inscription found in 1964 suggests that Hardknott was built (or rebuilt?) in the reign of Hadrian (AD 117-138), and names the builders as the fourth cohort of Dalmatians from the Balkan Adriatic coast. After the end of the 2nd century Hardknott appears to have been partly evacuated, leaving only a small caretaker force, or even becoming an inn or wayside rest house. This suggests a brief occupation of only some 50 years, a short life indeed when compared to other Roman forts in northern Britain such as Brough-by-Bainbridge, Ambleside and Ravenglass, which were garrisoned into the fourth century.

Below: *The stone granaries at Hardknott Fort.*

The fort was soon forgotten, its lonely, broken walls left to decay. Indeed, it was not until 1694 that its Roman origin was recognised. An antiquary from Leeds, Ralph Thoresby, rode over Hardknott Pass on 17 September of that year and was astonished by the view that met his eyes. Since Thoresby's time many others have stood at the top of Hardknott Pass and looked down with surprise at the fort below, its plan standing out clearly, with the individual buildings within the walls and outside them the parade ground, the bath house and the faint lines of the approach roads, and have felt their imagination stir and time edge backwards to those few years when the fort bristled with life.

42 A WALK FROM LITTLE LANGDALE TO HARDKNOTT

This spectacular walk through Wrynose and Hardknott passes finishes at the extraordinary Roman fort at Hardknott.

Instructions

1. Start at Little Langdale [NY316034]. Head south down the road and cross the River Brathay. Turn right along the green lane to Low Hall Garth. Follow the green lane along the Roman road to Fell Foot.

2. Turn left along the modern road, shadowed by the Roman road. Climb steeply uphill along the modern road, which gradually closes with the Roman road (by now a fine causeway) and crosses it not far from the Three Shire Stone on Wrynose summit. Go through the Wrynose Pass.

3. Turn right to cross the River Duddon and turn left along the footpath. The Roman road soon joins it along a wide causeway.

4. Cross Mosedale Beck and go straight up the lane signposted to the Youth Hostel at Black Hall. This is the Roman road.

OS maps:
1:50,000 Landranger sheet 90

1:25,000 Outdoor Leisure sheet 6 [English Lakes (South West)]

Distance: 7 miles

Equipment:
walking boots
compass
OS maps

Pubs/hostelries:
On the walk: Little Langdale

Roman engineering works:
cutting
terracing
causeway
short stretch of conspicuous agger
zig-zags

Other antiquities:
Roman fort at Hardknott

5. Keep left along the footpath where the lane turns to Black Hall. Follow the footpath on the Roman road, which in places is still 20 feet wide, as it zig-zags up the mountainside to Hardknott Pass.

6. Turn left along the modern road. The Roman road shadows the modern road here, first to the north and then to the south of it, and then to the north again as it makes for the fort at Hardknott. There are spectacular views from here over the Irish Sea to the Isle of Man.

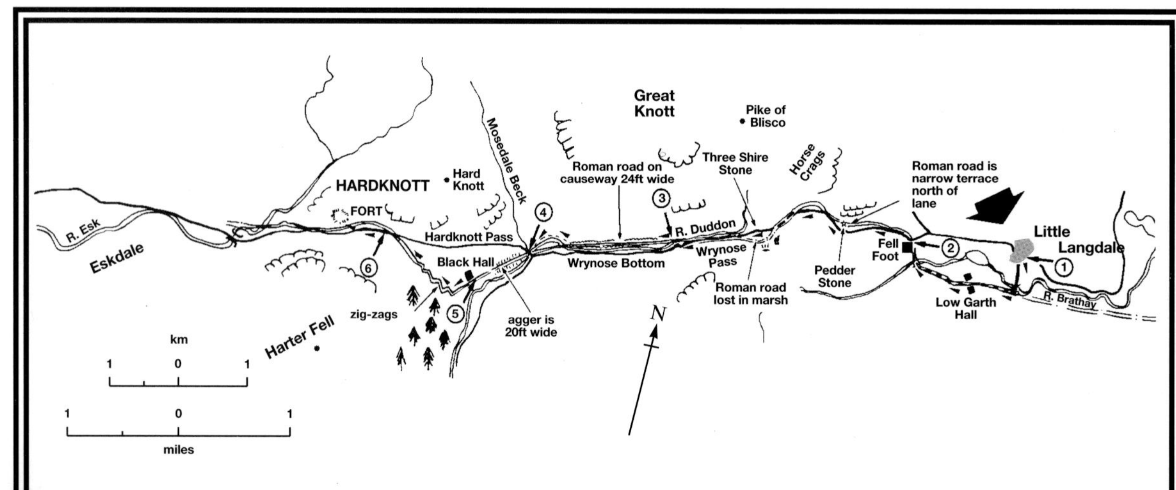

— IX —
HADRIAN'S WALL

'And so, having reformed the army in the manner of a king, Hadrian set out for Britain. There he corrected many faults and was the first to build a wall, 80 miles long, to separate the Romans from the barbarians.'

Scriptores Historiæ Augustæ
4th Century AD

Above: *The temple of Mithras on the Wall, flooded in early 1994. The Mithratic cult was very popular in the Roman army prior to the arrival of Christianity.*

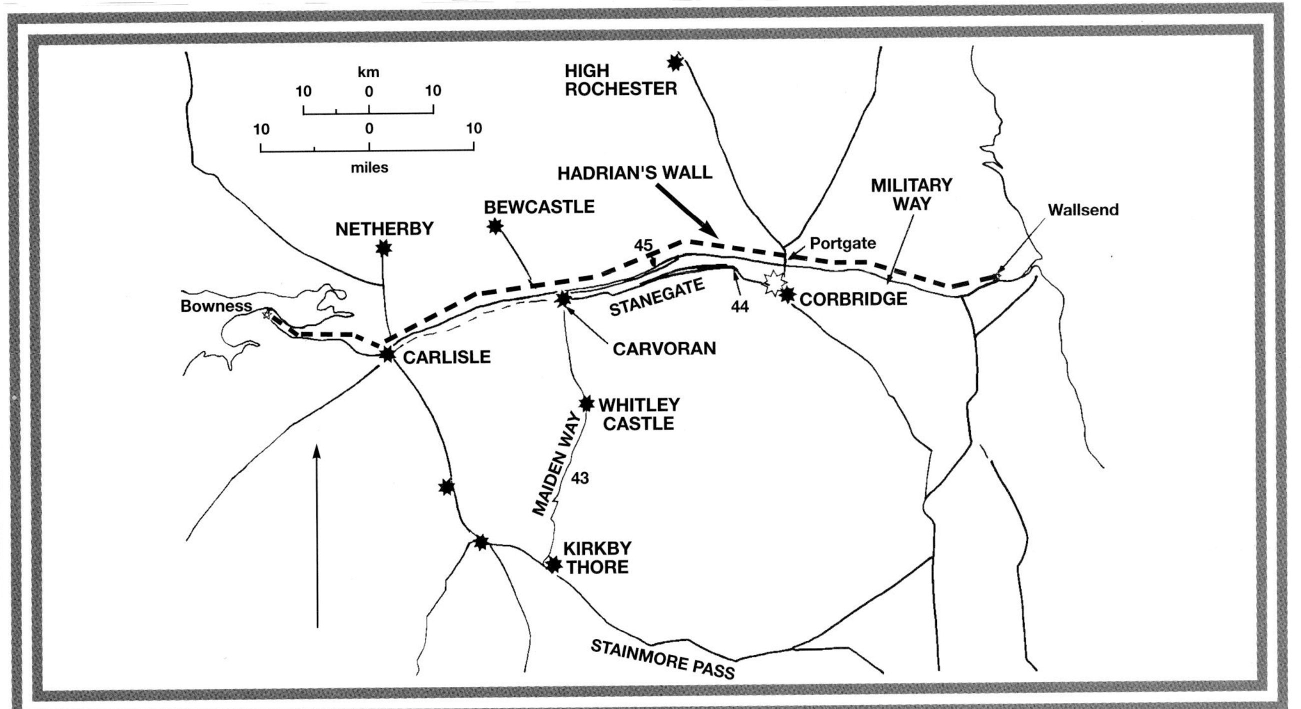

The Romans in the Hadrian's Wall Area

Julius Agricola was the first Roman to lead his troops into the area between the Solway and the Tyne, later to be made famous by the great wall of Hadrian, the most important Roman structure in Britain. The IX Legion arrived from York along Dere Street and founded a fort at Corbridge (Corstopitum), while the XX Legion marched up the Western Way from Chester and built their fort at Carlisle (Luguvalium). From these two new forts Agricola launched his famous two-pronged attack on Caledonia in AD 80-81.

At the same time, probably in AD 80, the army built a road between Corbridge and Carlisle. This was later known as the Stanegate and was initially no more than a cross-country road guarded by a line of forts.

Rome seems not to have had the available resources to conquer and hold Caledonia, and its grip upon this distant land was only tenuous. By the reign of the Emperor Trajan (AD 98-117) the army had drawn back to the Stanegate. The probable reason for halting here was that the isthmus marked the northern boundary of Brigantian territory, and the Brigantes had been incorporated into the Roman

sea to sea, forming a barrier across which any movement could be strictly controlled. It may not be fanciful to see the Wall as the emperor's response to the loss of the IX Legion.

The great Wall took some six years to build, the work being started in AD 122 when Aulus Platorius Nepos, a close friend of Hadrian, was governor of Britain. The Wall was built by all three legions in Britain at the time, with the legionaries working in gangs allotted to specific tasks. Once the Wall was built it was garrisoned not by the legions but by auxiliary units of both cavalry and infantry.

The course of the Wall was chosen with an eye to magnificence. From Newcastle

Left: *The Corbridge Lion; a funeral object. The Romans used symbolism of the lion devouring its prey to depict the final triumph of death over life. It was a favourite device for ornate tombs.* **Below:** *Looking east from Steel Rigg along the fearsome cliffs of the Whin Sill with the Wall snaking along the top.* **Below right:** *Burnstones; the start of Walk 43.*

Empire for some time, first as a client kingdom in AD 43 and more recently as a part of the province.

So the Stanegate became a frontier. The forts along it were modified, new forts were built, watch towers were added and the road was continued east of Corbridge and west of Carlisle. Trajan's aim was to police the frontier and control movement into and out of the province. We have no evidence to show how well this policy worked; probably it was not entirely successful. Indeed, it may be that it holds the key to one of the enduring mysteries of Roman Britain — the disappearance of the IX Legion, Hispana. Inscriptions show that the legion was at York in AD 107-8, but after this there is no record of it anywhere in the Roman Empire. Was this simply because the IX Hispana was moved from Britain to work on the continent and was later annihilated, possibly in the fierce struggle in Judea in AD 132-135, or is there a more sinister explanation, namely that it suffered a crushing defeat on Britain's northern frontier?

In any event, the northern frontier was causing considerable trouble when Hadrian, Trajan's great nephew and his successor, arrived in Britain in AD 122. Under Hadrian the VI Victrix Legion arrived at York to take the place of the IX — perhaps this in itself is significant. Hadrian was a great builder, responsible for walls and frontiers in Germany and North Africa as well as here, so it is not surprising that his answer to the problem was that most inspiring and solid of all Roman remains in Britain, his great wall. It stretched 73 miles (80 Roman miles) from

westwards it keeps to the high ground on the northern edge of Tynedale before passing on to the great crags of the Whin Sill, which turn their rugged cliffs to the north. It continues along the Whin Sill to the River Irthing and then, still keeping to high ground, carries on along the north of the river to the Solway Estuary.

As originally conceived, Hadrian's Wall was envisaged as an adjunct to, rather than a replacement of, the line of forts along the Stanegate. It was to consist of a wall of stone or turf pierced by fortified gateways to allow the passage of both civilian and military traffic. These gateways, spaced about a mile apart, were to be guarded by fortlets or milecastles. Between these, watch towers, or turrets, spaced about a third of a mile apart, allowed a close watch to be kept on the frontier. The main garrison was still to be stationed at the Stanegate forts. North of the Wall, save where the Whin Sill crags made it unnecessary as a deterrent, a V-shaped ditch was dug, some nine feet deep and 27 feet wide.

For some reason this planned set-up was not completed, and at some time after the Wall had been started, probably in AD 124, a new plan was drawn up and employed. The Stanegate was abandoned as a frontier and forts for the main garrison were built on the Wall itself. Initially there were 12 forts on the Wall, but this number later rose to 16. Perhaps at the same time the decision was taken to reduce the width of the Wall from 10 feet to eight feet. These changes have resulted in the Wall being a complex structure. In addition, the building materials varied. West of the River Irthing the Wall was originally constructed of turf — a traditional building material for the Roman army — and later rebuilt in stone, while to the east of that river the Wall was built in stone from the beginning.

The new plan for the Wall, in which the Stanegate ceased to function as a frontier and became once again merely a cross-country road, had as its very essence the creation of a military 'zone' which everyone except the Roman army and authorised people were prohibited from entering. The southern boundary of the zone was demarcated by the vast and impressive linear earthwork called the Vallum. This is a deep, flat-bottomed ditch with two flanking mounds. Causeways cross it to the gateways of each fort, and it was probably built after the forts had been constructed.

Above: *Paving stone shows along the Maiden Way in starting the descend to the Glendue Burn. Is this Roman or later handiwork?*

The Wall suffered a chequered history. In AD 142, when southern Scotland was once again part of the Roman province and the Antonine Wall was built further north, the garrison on Hadrian's Wall was severely depleted and the Wall evacuated. It was recommissioned in about AD 158, but once again, with the revived fortunes of the Antonine frontier, the Hadrianic barrier was later evacuated. In AD 163, with the final abandonment of the Antonine Wall, Hadrian's Wall was once again recommissioned. From that date until the final withdrawal of Roman troops from Britain, Hadrian's Wall was the northernmost frontier of the Roman Empire. On several occasions it was stormed and had to be rebuilt. Particularly damaging was the destruction of about AD 203, after which wholesale rebuilding was necessary.

The area around Hadrian's Wall was always military in nature, the civilian settlements being no more than adjuncts to the forts. This was especially so in the fourth century AD when the organisation of the army was more relaxed and soldiers were allowed to marry. There were several outpost forts to the north of the Wall Zone which were kept garrisoned and sent back news of the movements of the northern tribes. Just south of the Wall Zone proper, in the dangerous and lonely northern Pennines, were important lead mines guarded by the vast Roman fort at Whitley Castle.

The Wall effectively divided the Brigantes of northern England from the Votadini and Selgovae of south-eastern Northumberland and southern Scotland, and doubtless this was one of its aims. Its formidable southern aspect, notably the Vallum, was obviously designed to prevent movement northwards as verily as the northern ramparts were designed to stop the aggressive northern tribes penetrating south.

Roman Roads in the Hadrian's Wall Area

Dere Street and the Western Way pass across Hadrian's Wall near Corbridge and Carlisle to head north. Approximately half-way between them another road, the Maiden Way, arrives at the Wall from the south. This road, which branches from the Stainmore pass at Kirkby Thore, crosses the wild heights of the Alston Block via the fort at Whitley Castle. At Carvoran the Maiden Way joins the Stanegate, the major cross-country road and one-time frontier that was used for the transport of goods as well as deployment of troops.

The late second-century Military Way shadows Hadrian's Wall from end to end. It starts at Wallsend and runs through Carvoran and Carlisle to the western limit of the Wall on the Solway Firth at Bowness.

These frontier roads all possess a sense of adventure. They are exhilarating roads, built on the edge of the Roman world under huge, hurrying skies.

THE MAIDEN WAY

The Roman road from Kirkby Thore to Carvoran

This lonely road treads over the spacious northern fells in a silence disturbed only by the jarring calls of grouse and the endless crying of the wind. It branches north from the important road over the Stainmore Pass at Kirkby Thore to cross the northern Pennines west of Alston and reach the Stanegate at Carvoran. It is possible that Agricola's men were the builders of the Maiden Way, but it seems more likely that it is a later first or early-second-century road built to help consolidate pacified land. In the early 17th century Reginald Bainbrigg, headmaster of Appleby Grammar School, wrote of 'a street called the Mayden Way, which is paved with stones throughout the moors ...' It was described in detail in 1845 and, because it crosses such an isolated area, much of it has survived in something like the same state.

From Kirkby Thore little of the Maiden Way remains visible until, beyond the isolated hamlet of Kirkland, it climbs up over Melmerby Fell joined by a track. It then descends obliquely downhill into the valley of the Rowgill Burn, where a bridge probably carried it across the stream and one of the earthen ramps is still to be seen. Beyond Rowgill Burn it climbs on to Gilderdale Forest heading for the large Roman fort at Whitley Castle, one of the highest Roman forts in Britain. This was built in the second century AD to guard important lead mines, the lead being transported under military protection along the Maiden Way.

Beyond Whitley Castle the modern A689 runs on top of the Roman road along the South Tyne valley through Slaggyford to Knarsdale, where the walk begins. Here the modern and Roman roads part company, with the modern road keeping nearer to the river and the Roman road, now some 12 feet wide and used by the Pennine Way, heading along the hillside. Both roads have to cross the deep valley of the Glendue Burn, and the modern road has to turn a sharp bend to do so, crossing at virtually the same point as the Roman road. The Roman road slants down to the crossing as a well engineered terrace and a footbridge carries the walker across at approximately the site of the Roman ford.

Beyond the Glendue Burn the Maiden Way, raised on an 18-foot-wide grassy *agger* some two feet high, climbs up on to Hartleyburn Common continuing straight ahead at Lambley under a lane, raised on an *agger* and with wide, grassy verges growing over the infilled side-ditches.

At the crossing of the Glencune Burn, on the southern edge of Featherstone Common, the Maiden Way, visible as a grassy *agger*, continues ahead over fields to the west of Waterloo and heads up to the Roman fort at Carvoran. However, this section has fallen out of use and the walk finishes at the Glencune Burn.

43. A WALK FROM BURNSTONES TO FEATHERSTONE COMMON

This walk over the hills follows one of the most isolated of all British Roman roads. Initially a quiet stretch of the Pennine Way, this length of the Maiden Way is then marked by a line of little lanes.

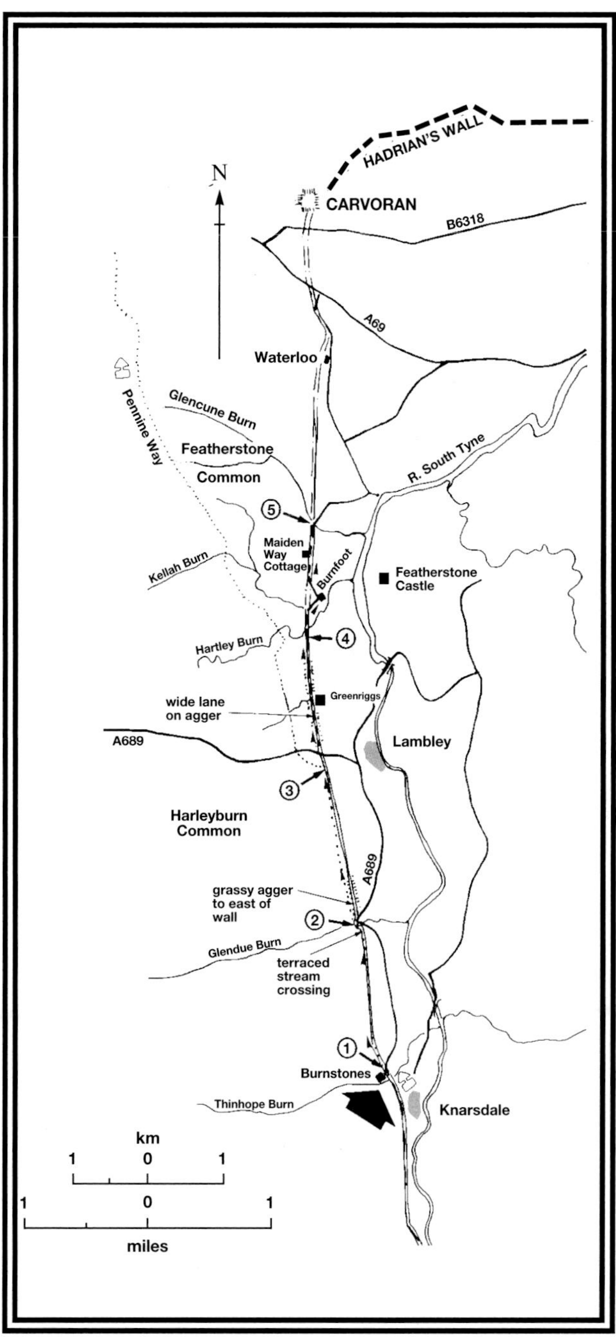

OS maps:
1:50,000 Landranger sheet
86

1:25,000 Pathfinder sheets
559 [Slaggyford]
546 [Haltwhistle and Gilsland]

Distance: 5 miles

Equipment:
waterproof clothing
compass
OS maps

Pubs/hostelries:
Nearby: Knarsdale

Roman engineering works:
stream crossing
conspicuous grassy agger
terraceways

Instructions

1. Start at Burnstones [NY75545] under the disused railway viaduct near Knarsdale. Go up the drive signposted to Burnstones and the Pennine Way. Turn right along the Pennine Way up the hill, joining with the Roman road which comes in from the right. Continue over two small streams and descend to the crossing of the Glendue Burn.

2. Cross the Glendue Burn by the wooden footbridge and turn right up the hill, waymarked Pennine Way. The right of way is to the left of the stone wall, while the *agger* of the Maiden Way is to the right of it. The going here is fairly rough, over peat bog and heather. Continue along the Pennine Way, which runs along the Maiden Way over Lambley Common.

3. Do not turn left along the Pennine Way, but carry straight on to the A689 near Lambley. Cross the main road and go down the minor road opposite signposted to Featherstone and Haltwhistle. Cross the Black Burn and pass Greenriggs.

4. Cross Hartley Burn and Kellah Burn, where the Maiden Way continues straight ahead and the modern lane negotiates a double bend up the hill to rejoin it. Continue past Maidenway Cottage and the shrine-like war memorial.

5. Descend into Glen Cune [NY 665615] on the edge of Featherstone Common, beyond which the Maiden Way is now lost.

Left: *Newbrough. On the Stanegate.* **Below:** *Looking north from Stanegate across Grindon Lough to Hadrian's Wall.*

THE STANEGATE

The Roman road from Corbridge to Carlisle

The Stanegate was built by Agricola in AD 80 as a cross-country road to link Dere Street and the Western Way, the two great routes along which his army penetrated into Caledonia. It was important in the late first century AD before becoming the northern frontier of the Roman province in the years prior to the construction of Hadrian's Wall. It was to continue as a major road for non-military traffic, such as corn waggons bringing supplies to the troops, traders and civilians.

The Stanegate left Corbridge (*Corstopitum*) as a continuation of the main east-west road within the fort. It crossed the Cor Burn on well engineered terraceways and continued westwards. The course is uncertain from here to beyond the River North Tyne, where it has been traced heading towards Fourstones, 16½ feet wide and set on a foundation of sandstone blocks.

Beyond Fourstones it turns west and the modern road runs on it for the next few miles through Newbrough, where the cycle ride starts, and past Settlingstones, with wide views northwards to Hadrian's Wall, about a mile

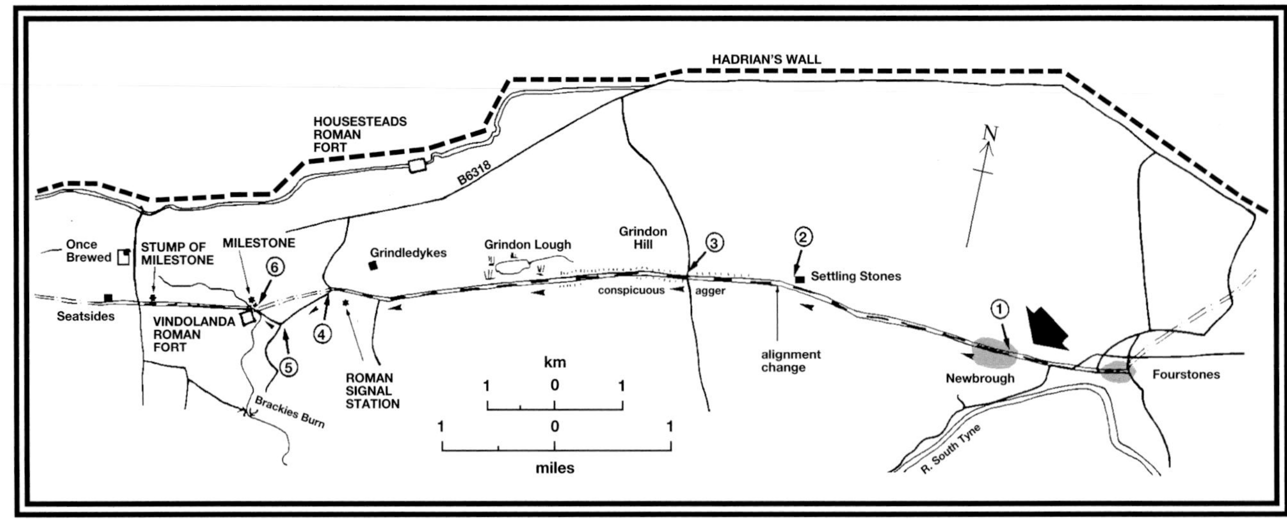

OS maps:
1:50,000 Landranger sheet 87

1:25,000 Pathfinder sheets
547 [Hexham and Haydon Bridge]
546 [Haltwhistle and Gilsland]

1:25,000 Map of Hadrian's Wall.

Distance: 6½ miles

Pubs/hostelries:
On the drive/ride: Newbrough
Nearby: Once Brewed

Roman engineering works:
agger
terraceway at stream crossing

Other antiquities
Roman milestone in original position
Roman fort, Vindolanda.

away. Along this stretch it is raised on a fine *agger*, some 27 feet wide. The modern road bears off just before the fort at *Vindolanda* and the Stanegate descends across fields to the Brackies Burn, where a Roman milestone stands in its original position in a grove of trees beside it. There is no lettering visible, but the stone, a cylindrical column some 6 feet high, is an eloquent reminder of those who have travelled the Stanegate before us.

A trackway joins the Stanegate at the stream and continues past *Vindolanda*, where the cycle ride ends. The Stanegate continues on to Seatside, but beyond the farm it exists only as traces of *agger* across the rough ground. The B6318 crosses it near the Mare and Foal standing stones and the two roads then run approximately parallel over Haltwhistle Common and on to Carvoran. From here to its destination at Carlisle the only visible remains of the Roman road are at stream crossings, where deep cuttings and embankments helped ease the gradient of the road.

44. A CYCLE RIDE/DRIVE FROM NEWBROUGH TO VINDOLANDA

This cycle ride/drive along the Stanegate affords views towards Hadrian's Wall across the wild Northumberland landscape and finishes at the Roman fort at Vindolanda, where a Roman milestone stands in its original position beside the road.

Instructions

1. Start at Newbrough, where the Stanegate is used by a minor road. Carry on to Settlingstones.

2. Here the Stanegate reaches high ground (615ft). Shortly beyond is a slight change of alignment and the road runs on a conspicuous *agger*. There are glorious views.

3. Go straight over the crossroads on Grindon Hill and continue past Grindon Lough.

4. Bear left when another road comes in on the right to head downhill into the deep valley of the Brackies Burn, leaving the Stanegate, which heads straight downhill across the fields to the right.

Above: *Great Chesters. Altar and grass-grown stones.*

5. Turn right towards the car park for the Roman fort. Continue by foot towards the Roman fort.

6. Bear left with the road and rejoin the Stanegate. The famous Roman milestone stands in the trees on the right, just before the Stanegate crosses the Brackies Burn. Continue to the fort.

HADRIAN'S WALL MILITARY WAY

The Roman road from Wallsend to Carlisle

Hadrian's Wall Military Way runs the entire length of the Wall from Wallsend in the east to Bowness on the Solway Firth, a distance of 73 miles. It was built in the late second century, designed as a service road for the Wall, and passes through the main forts, though not through the milecastles and turrets.

The Military Way is a superbly graded road, though today it is grass-grown all along most of its length; and yet after the building of General Wade's Military Road (the present B6318) in the 1740s carters for long preferred to use this old Military Way as it had a more even gradient. In the pursuit of this good grading the road does not slavishly follow the course of the Wall, for where the latter crosses broken terrain, as at Housesteads, the Military Way keeps well to the south on more level ground, with spur roads running up to the turrets and milecastles on the Wall.

Today, Hadrian's Wall is among Britain's tourist honeypots, and every inch of it is well walked. It is unlikely that you will tread the Wall alone; even in blinding sleet and a bitterly cold wind I met some visitors intent on 'doing' Walltown Crags. The Military Way which shadows the Wall so faithfully is not tramped with quite the same zeal. Indeed, few people give it a thought as they are overawed by the majesty of the Wall, and are no doubt unaware of the road's existence, imagining, perhaps, that the Wall itself served as a road. I doubt my acquaintances noticed the Military Way at Walltown Crags, where the walk begins, though it is a conspicuous grassy terrace thereabouts, some 18 feet wide, on the south side of the Wall. Probably more people notice the superbly neat zig-zag with which it climbs the rocky cliff beneath Steel Rigg, if only because the public footpath runs along it and there is no alternative way up.

The Military Way is a good road: great piled clouds pass overhead in stately procession, driven by the keen wind, birds sing and today all seems prosperity and peace. It is the Wall rather than the road that provides outstanding views, so that you look out for miles across the northern limit of the Roman world. Instead, on the Military Way, you are in that world, walking through the forts not past them, and treading in the footsteps of those who guarded it, of those who traded with them, and all the time the sinuous Wall sweeps along the crag-top beside you.

There can be no greater contrast than that between the two forts visited; Great Chesters (*Aesica*) and Housesteads (*Vercovicium*). Housesteads, where the walk ends, is one of the most frequented sites of antiquity in Britain — visited daily by many hundreds of people. It may be busier today than it was during Roman times, when it was surrounded by a bustling civil settlement in which the people who followed the army lived and worked and played. Where the crowds throng today from car park and visitor information centre to museum and labelled ruins, there were houses, shops, taverns, workshops and so on, which stretched down from the fort walls towards the present B-road and on either side of the fort. By contrast, Great Chesters is sleeping under the turf. It has been excavated and the famous *Aesica* brooch was found here, but today it is an extension of the nearby farmyard and the farm cat hunts beside the broken altar, black cattle graze among the fallen stones and crows caw noisily overhead. Time rests at Great Chesters even when an Air Force jet screams its way above the Wall, sending one's mind tumbling down the centuries to wonder what the Romans would have made of that.

Wall and milecastle at Cawfields.

45. A WALK FROM WALLTOWN TO HOUSESTEADS
(or finishing at Cawfields or Steel Rigg)

This breathtaking 8½-mile walk follows the Roman Military Way beneath Hadrian's Wall from Walltown Crags via Great Chesters to the famous Roman fort at Housesteads.

OS maps:
1:50,000 Landranger sheet 86

1:25,000 Pathfinder sheet 546 [Haltwhistle and Gilsland]

1:25,000 Map of Hadrian's Wall.

Distance:
Walltown to Housesteads — 8½ miles
Walltown to Cawfields — 2¾ miles
Walltown to Steel Rigg — 5½ miles

Pubs/hostelries:
Nearby: Milecastle Inn
Once Brewed

Roman engineering works:
agger visible in places
terraceways

Other antiquities:
Hadrian's Wall
Roman forts — Carvoran, Great Chesters, Housesteads
milecastles and turrets

Instructions

1. Start at the car park at Walltown [NY676663]. Climb up the hill to turret 45A.

2. Turn right on to the Military Way, here used by the Pennine Way, past milecastle 45 and continue past turret 44B. Beyond this the Military Way is very clearly marked, lying to the south of the Wall and keeping an easy gradient, passing close to a Roman milestone in use as a gatepost.

3. Pass through the belt of woodland and continue along the Military Way to enter the Roman infantry fort at Great Chesters by the west gate.

4. Cross the fort and leave it via the steps over the walled-up eastern gate. Continue to the road at Hole Gap at Cawfields Quarry.

To 'escape' here, turn left to the car park at the quarry.

5. The Military Way runs to the south of the disused quarry lake and car park and makes use of the northern berm of the Vallum. Turn right down the road and then sharply left so that the car park and quarry lake are between you and Hadrian's Wall. Continue along the Military Way, which diverges from the Vallum, and pass some way to the south of milecastle 42. Cawfield Crags are now to your left beyond the Wall.

6. Cross the road at Caw Gap (there is no car park here so it is not a convenient place to break the walk) and continue along the Military Way opposite, taking care to avoid the marshy hollow at Bogle Hole. Pass to the south of milecastle 41 and follow the zig-zag in the Military Way which climbs up to the Wall at Winshields Crag.

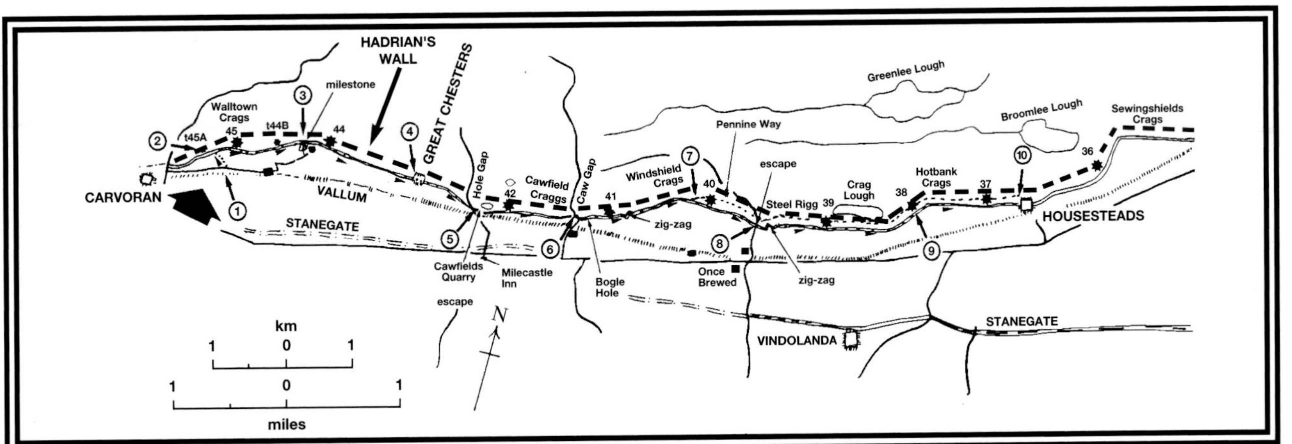

7. Just beyond the summit of Winshields Crag (1,120ft) the Pennine Way bears left with the Wall, but the Military Way bears right so that once again it lies to the south of the Wall. Follow the Military Way past milecastle 40 and down to the road at Steel Rigg.

To 'escape', turn left to the car park or right down the road to Once Brewed.

8. Keep straight on along the road, and then go over the stile (signposted the Roman Military Way). Carry on along this through the gate and negotiate the original Roman rock-cut zig-zag in the Military Way up the steep slope past milecastle 39. On the far side of the Wall the land falls away northwards down Whin Sill. Continue along the Military Way, which is very easy to follow, and which closes with the Wall, turning abruptly to the left to climb Hotbank Crags.

9. Pass milecastle 38, where in 1935 a Roman building inscription came to light denoting that the milecastle was built by the II Legion during the governorship of Aulus Platorius Nepos. Continue past milecastle 37.

10. Arrive at Housesteads.

Below: *Great Chesters. The arch to the strong room.*

— X —
NORTH OF HADRIAN'S WALL

'Britain was conquered and immediately abandoned.'

TACITUS
Histories

Below: *The coaching road on the Roman line approaching Ninemileburn.*

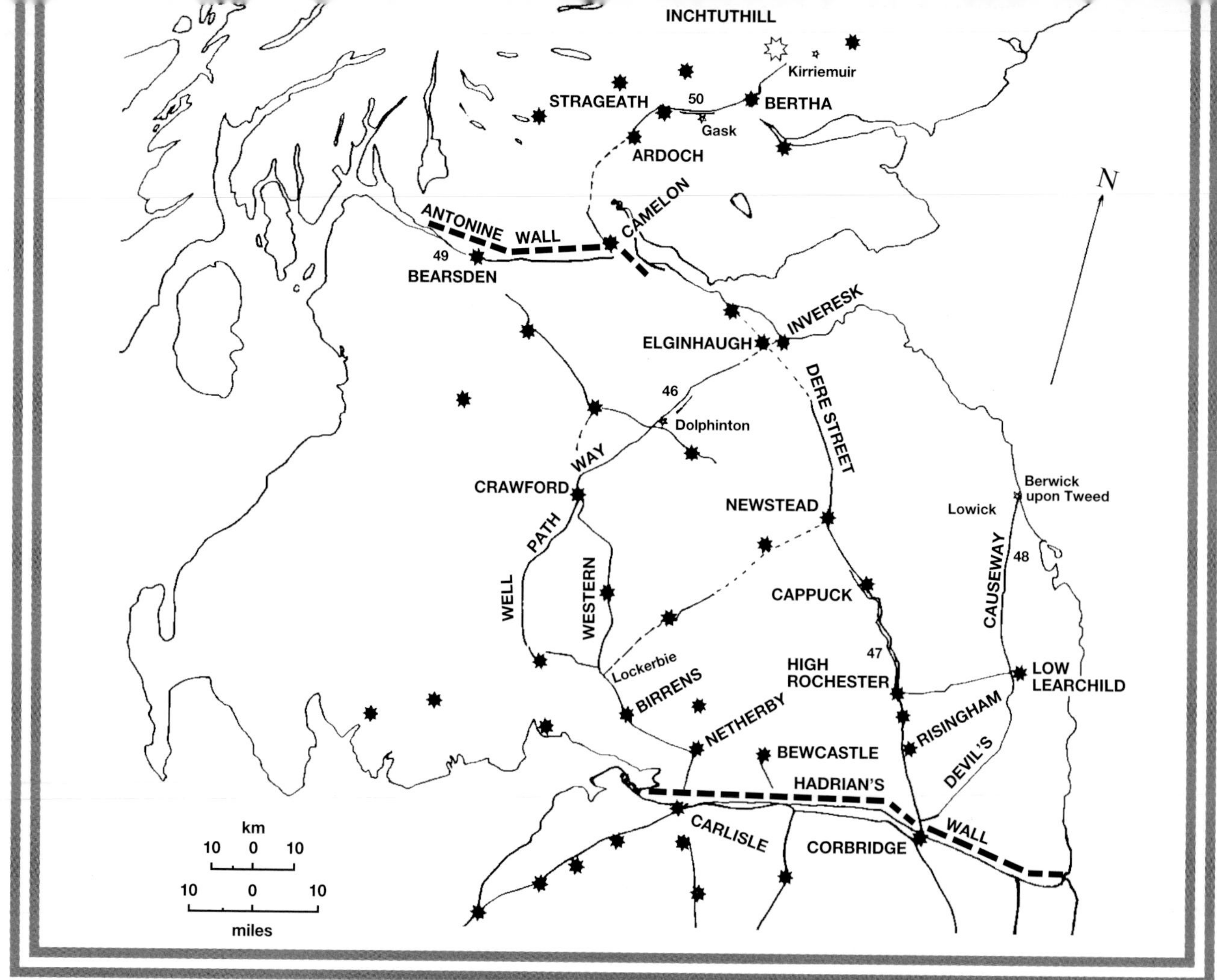

The Romans North of Hadrian's Wall

Roman involvement in the far north spans the years from Agricola's advance of the AD 80s to the end of the fourth century, when the outpost forts of Hadrian's Wall were finally abandoned. It is a story full of apparent contradictions, for here, in the northernmost outpost of empire, where the Roman way of life was roughened by rough landscape, rough weather and rough people, the political shenanigans in Rome itself were felt more keenly than elsewhere. Britain beyond the Hadrianic barrier was a good political football, kicked hither and thither in the play for power, so that it seems as if Rome was unable to make up its mind whether or not it wished to hold the region.

The initial plan was total conquest, and in AD 81 the governor Agricola advanced in a flanking movement to the Forth-Clyde isthmus. Supported by his fleet he pushed further north and, in AD 84, defeated the Caledonians in a pitched battle at Mons Graupius. The site of this decisive victory is lost, though many places have been suggested, ranging as far north as the Moray Firth. It unlikely that we shall ever know the exact location.

Agricola and the Romans thought that the whole of Britain had been subdued. A legionary fortress was started at Inchtuthill, near Perth, forts were built to guard the glens and the road network was begun. But policy changes were afoot in Rome and Agricola, who had already served the equivalent of two governorships, was recalled. The victory was never followed up, and instead there was a strategic withdrawal to a 'frontier' near Gask, south of the River Tay. In about AD 90 Inchtuthill was evacuated before it had even been completed, and by AD 122 the new Emperor, Hadrian, was in Britain to supervise the building of the wall for which he is famous. Rome had drawn back from total conquest. Not for long, however. In AD 139-142 Hadrian's successor, the emperor Antoninus Pius, sent Q. Lollius Urbicus to Britain to reconquer southern Scotland. Urbicus was North African by birth and, as he had been governor of Lower Germany before being moved to Britain, was a man of extensive experience in dealing with frontier politics. He began by rebuilding the fort at Corbridge, which he then used as a base, driving the northern British tribes back to the Forth-Clyde isthmus and building the Antonine Wall, more or less along a line of forts set out by Agricola 60 years earlier. It was completed within a year. Some 12 years later the wall was temporarily evacuated following a rebellion. It was rebuilt but, ever an uneasy frontier, was soon abandoned again, a victim of Roman politics and the need for troops on the Danube and Rhine frontiers. This second abandonment is now thought to have happened in AD 163. The Romans made only one further foray into the north, under the emperor Severus in AD 209-10, reaching at least as far as the Moray Firth. Severus' death at York in AD 211 resulted in the final withdrawal behind Hadrian's Wall, but even after this, four outpost forts were manned for another 150 years.

Roman Roads North of Hadrian's Wall

Hadrian's Wall is the great divide, for although the roads north of it were planned long before the Wall was even contemplated, its construction ensured that the northern network was never completed. Today we see only the beginnings of the grid that was to be laid down but which never materialised. None the less, exploring the roads in this area is a splendid experience. Rome's footfall trod but lightly here but the print was indelible and long lengths of the roads have hardly altered since the legions were recalled.

Dere Street and the Western Way continue north of Hadrian's Wall and converge south of Edinburgh. They shadow Agricola's two-pronged march into the north in AD 81. Dere Street was paralleled by another road nearer the coast, the Devil's Causeway, which branched from the main road north of Corbridge and ran at least as far as Berwick-upon-Tweed.

These highways were linked by cross-country roads. A major route ran from Newstead to Lockerbie via Craik Cross and Raeburnfoot over the inhospitable wilderness of Eskdalemuir. The other completed cross-country road ran from Newstead via Peebles to Carstairs, while yet another road linked Dere Street with the Devil's Causeway. A branch road from the Western Way led further west to the Roman sites in Nithsdale. This was the Well Path, which retains considerable traces of Roman work.

In the absence of a complete Roman network, prehistoric tracks were travelled extensively both by the native tribes and the Roman soldiers, but evidence for their use in Roman times is hard to come by. On the Cheviot Hills, for example, many ancient tracks exist, of which Chennell Street, to the east of Dere Street, is the best known. This was a route used by the Votadini, a roving tribe of British cowboys, typical of the northern Celts. Despite its name, Chennell Street was never Romanised.

Beyond the Antonine Wall there is just one road which ran north from Camelon, near Falkirk. How far this road ever stretched also remains unknown. Despite Mons Graupius the Caledonian spirit remained free. When it came to guerrilla warfare the dedicated Roman law-givers and road-builders were outclassed by the wild independence of the free-booting barbarians of the far north.

THE WESTERN WAY

The Roman road from Carlisle to Inveresk

This main route into Scotland formed the western prong of the Agricolan advance in AD 81. It is a military road and is lined with camps and forts, including those at Netherby, Birrens, Torwood and Crawford, and the Antonine Itinerary covers it as far as Birrens. It swept north from Carlisle (*Luguvalium*) for several miles before changing alignment to the north-west, a turn which enabled it to be engineered skilfully along a narrow ridge of dry land over the extensive coastal marshes of the Solway Moss and the difficult Esk valley. It continued along the same alignment to and beyond the important fort at Birrens (*Blatobulgium*).

It drove northwards up Annandale to Moffat and then climbed up over the wild moorland of Beattock Summit, eased by small cuttings, before curving as a terrace along the hillside to the head of the Clyde valley at Crawford. Beyond this the Roman engineers chose a hilly route rather than risk following the narrow defile of the Clyde. The road turned north-east and forged onward along the eastern flank of the Pentland Hills, where the walk is found, and on to Inveresk.

It is a well engineered road and demonstrates the Romans' supreme grasp of the region's geography and their skill at surmounting obstacles. Terraceways, cuttings and zig-zags were designed to ease gradients, while the approaches to river crossings are cleverly brought about.

The route varies in character considerably. Over the Solway Moss and in Annandale it hides from those who seek it, but across the Beattock Summit it proclaims itself heroically, shadowed by a derelict coaching road, the railway and the busy, motorway-like A74(T), which crowd together through the pass, arteries of communication squeezed through an historic gap.

The best walkable stretch of this road is along the eastern slopes of the bare Pentland Hills. Here the line of the Roman road was used by the builders of an early-17th-century coaching road. This fell out of use in 1830 when the present A702 was built, so that today a wide green lane follows the Roman line for 8 miles between Dolphinton and Ninemileburn.

Dolphinton once had the distinction of possessing two railway stations; now it is nowhere near a railway line. It gets its name from a local laird of the 12th century, Dolfin (or Dolphine), a kinsman of the 1st Earl of Dunbar, who

did indeed bear a dolphin on his coat of arms. From here to Carlops the walk follows the line of the old coaching road, with the Roman road running alongside, giving a wonderful opportunity to see fine Roman engineering features, including the terraced descent to West Water, where the Romans went straight across but the coaching road made a detour to its single-arched bridge, dated 1620, and the high embankment which spans a gully near Fairslacks.

At Carlops, which was founded as a weaving village in 1784, the road crosses the River North Esk and the modern, coaching and Roman roads coincide. The embankment of one of Agricola's marching camps has been found here, but there is nothing to be seen on the ground. The Allan Ramsay inn at Carlops is named after the poet who in 1725 published 'The Gentle Shepherd', a pastoral poem written in the old broad Scots dialect in which many local places are featured.

Between Carlops and Ninemileburn, the Habbie's How of Ramsay's ballad, the coaching road runs on top of the Roman road and, now a little lane, forges ahead as an open, urgent route heading busily for its destination watched over by smooth green and brown hills dappled in golden light as the wind sweeps great clouds across them.

46 A WALK FROM DOLPHINTON TO NINEMILEBURN

This pastoral walk follows the Western Way into Scotland along the foot of the Pentland Hills. Once used as a coaching road, the Roman road is now mostly a wide green lane.

Instructions

1. Start on the minor road north of Dolphinton [NT110479]. Walk north-east past Sandy Nick Cottage up the track to a disused sand pit. Bear left where the track forks and follow the old coaching road.

2. Pass Ingraston, beyond which the Roman road comes in on the right at NT124497.

3. Carry on along the lane past South Slipperfield Cottages and bear left downhill to the gate. Follow the coaching road to the bridge.

4. Cross the bridge and follow the coach road back on to the Roman alignment and past Mendickfoot. Turn right on to the road and continue past West Linton golf course.

5. Turn left at the T-junction and then right along the private road signposted 'public footpath to Carlops'. Go over the bridge. Continue past the entrance to Stonypath,

Left: *The modern road on the Roman line at Carlops.*

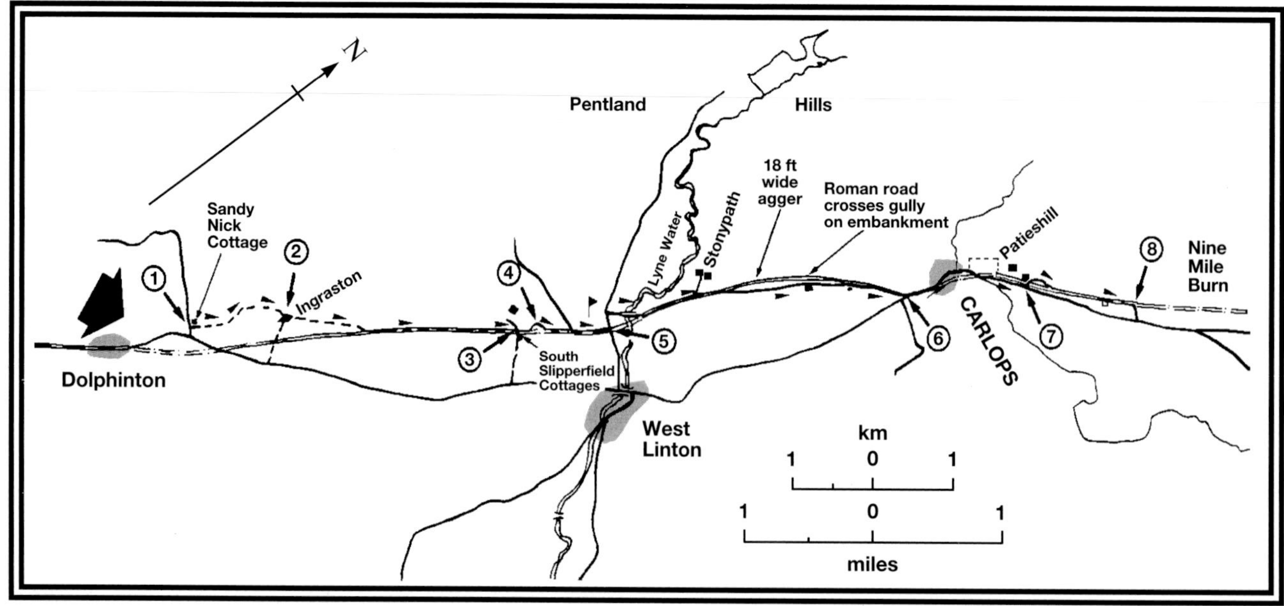

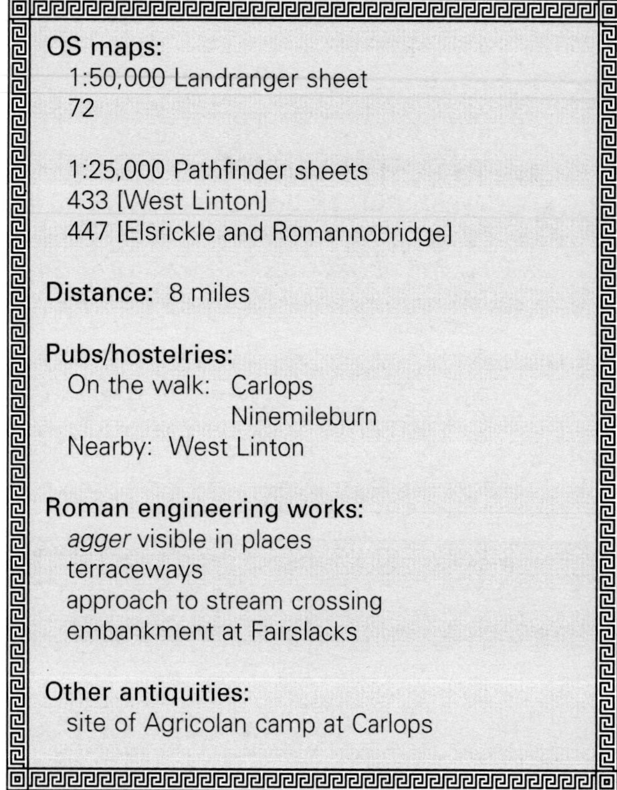
OS maps:
1:50,000 Landranger sheet
72

1:25,000 Pathfinder sheets
433 [West Linton]
447 [Elsrickle and Romannobridge]

Distance: 8 miles

Pubs/hostelries:
On the walk: Carlops
Ninemileburn
Nearby: West Linton

Roman engineering works:
agger visible in places
terraceways
approach to stream crossing
embankment at Fairslacks

Other antiquities:
site of Agricolan camp at Carlops

crossing the Roman road, which now continues on the left, and pass Fairslacks. Follow the lane to the right downhill towards the main A702(T) at Carlops.

6. Turn left along the pavement beside the A702(T) through Carlops and across the River North Esk.

7. Turn left towards Pateshill and right to rejoin the Roman road. Continue along the road under the lee of the Pentland Hills to Ninemileburn. The Western Way can be followed no further.

8. Leave the Roman road and turn right to the main A702(T).

DERE STREET

Agricola's road into Scotland

Dere Street is older than Hadrian's Wall, which it crosses north of Corbridge. From here it heads across the rugged and windswept lands of Northumberland, passing over the Cheviots and forging onward to Newstead (*Trimontium*), near Melrose. It was aiming for the fort at Elginhaugh, near Dalkeith on the Forth-Clyde isthmus. The Antonine Itinerary follows it from Corbridge to High Rochester (*Bremenium*).

'Monumental' is the word which springs to mind to describe this road. North of Hadrian's Wall the straight lengths of Dere Street leap to prominence and the abrupt changes of alignment seem more sharply focused than is the case further south. Between Corbridge and High Rochester the modern A68 runs on top of the worn *agger* for most of the way, and from Woodhouse to Blakehope the direct survey line crosses the grain of the country, involving the road in a series of sharp rises and precipitous falls. This is exciting, daredevil engineering, as impressive a stretch of Roman highway as exists anywhere, but motorists, beware! Despite the signs warning of blind summits, you can be taken by surprise on this switchback, for the road literally seems to fall away ahead as you top the crests.

Dere Street is a military road and was built through the territories of the Votadini and the Selgovae by Agricola's advancing army in AD 81, the eastern route of his famous two-pronged advance to the north. It continued in use throughout the Roman occupation, and camps and forts are scattered along it in profusion. The road is up to 50 feet wide including the side-ditches, and where the *agger* is visible it is about two to three feet high and metalled with local stone.

The finest walkable stretch of Dere Street begins at High Rochester, passing over desolate moors made more desolate by the presence of MOD firing ranges, which impart a feeling of restless unease to any who would dare loiter here. Not unfitting, this sense of disturbance, where the tarmac surface on top of the Roman military way is the most obvious mark of humanity to break the sweeping contours of the unkempt and naked moor.

Above: *The coaching road on the Roman line running beneath the Pentland Hills.*

Dere Street descends into Coquetdale by a terraceway now known by its medieval name, the Gamel's Path, and, unencumbered by modern metalling, arrives at Chew Green. This is a lonely spot, where the wind wanders among grassy embankments, all that remain of at least four Roman camps. Then Dere Street heads boldly into the Cheviot wilderness and crosses into Scotland. It follows a magnificent course, first climbing by a terraceway on to Brownhart Law, crowned by a Roman signal station, and then traversing, upon a fine grassy *agger*, a narrow ridge of land beneath Woden Law, site of an Iron Age fort. As the road bears north-west round the shoulder of this hill the view leaps out ahead, with misty blue mountains hanging on the horizon and Scotland spread out below. The Agricolan army were probably responsible for the destruction of the Iron Age fort, but later contingents of Roman soldiers, maybe stationed at nearby Pennymuir, used it for military exercises and built the spectacular practice siege-works just below the summit of the hill.

From Woden Law a line of paths and lanes runs along the Roman road to Whitton Edge and a final change of alignment, aiming for Newstead, under the shadow of the triple peaks of the Eildon Hills, 14 miles distant. This change of alignment turns Dere Street along a straight line of lanes and trackways to the River Teviot at Jedfoot, where this walk ends. Beyond the River Teviot, Dere Street continues across fields and open country to Newstead, beyond which point the course it took in its final push to Elginhaugh is disputed.

47. A WALK FROM HIGH ROCHESTER TO JEDFOOT

This magnificent and demanding walk traverses the wild and desolate Cheviot Hills along the main Roman military route into Scotland.

Instructions

1. Start at the entrance to the modern Redesdale Army Camp on the A68(T) north-west of Rochester. This first stretch of Dere Street heads through the artillery ranges, so do not proceed if the red flag or lights are showing. Follow the road northwards. Dere Street comes in from the right, and the modern road turns left on to it.

2. Bear right at Featherwood Farm to follow the modern track. Turn left at the junction of tracks and rejoin Dere Street.

3. Beyond Featherwood camps, turn right and descend to the River Coquet.

4. Cross the River Coquet to the Roman camps at Chew Green. The Pennine Way joins Dere Street from the left.

If you wish to avoid the part of Dere Street over the firing ranges, start here. You either have to drive westwards up the winding road through Upper Coquetdale to Makendon Farm [NT803093] and walk the last mile to join Dere Street, or follow the Pennine Way from the A68 at NT769025.

5. At Black Halls [NT789106] leave the Pennine Way and follow Dere Street to the left over the border to follow the ridge of high land to Woden Law.

6. Bear left into the col round Woden Law and head downhill.

7. Cross the Kale Water and follow the lane round to the right.

8. Go over the crossroads on to the track waymarked 'Dere Street'.

9. Turn left on to the road at Whitton Edge. Follow the road to the T-junction at Shotheids [NT715200].

10. Go straight across on to the path and continue to the lane near Cappuck.

11. Cross the lane to continue along Dere Street, now an overgrown terraceway down to Oxnam Water. Cross the Oxnam Water and continue uphill.

12. Cross the next lane and carry on along Dere Street.

13. Go over the crossroads and along the lane to Jedfoot.

Right: *Dere Street crossing the Cheviots.*

Inset: *Dere Street waymark.*

OS maps:
1:50,0000 Landranger sheets
74, 80

1:25,0000 Pathfinder sheets
510 [Otterburn]
498 [Catcleugh]
499 [Harbottle]
486 [Chesters and Hownam]
474 [Jedburgh]

Distance: 21 miles

Equipment:
waterproof clothing
maps
compass
food and drink — no shops within easy reach of the walk

Roman engineering works:
30ft-wide agger visible in places
terraceways

Other antiquities on route:
Iron Age fort, Woden Law
Roman forts — High Rochester (Bremenium), Cappuck
Roman camps — Silloans, Featherwood, Chew Green, Pennymuir
Roman signal station — Brownhart Law
Roman practice siege-works — Woden Law
Roman cemetery and remains of tombs 750yd south of High Rochester

DERE STREET

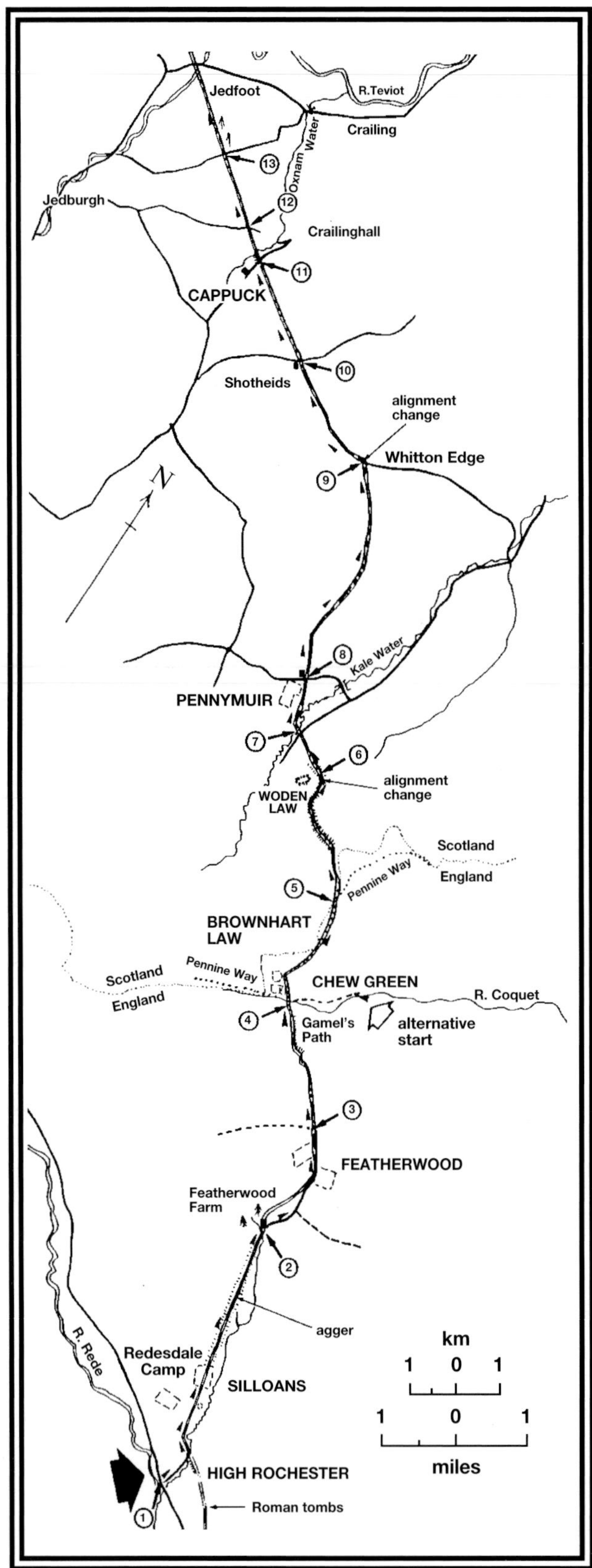

THE DEVIL'S CAUSEWAY

The Roman road from Corbridge to Berwick-upon-Tweed

The Devil's Causeway, a name by which this Roman road has been known since the Dark Ages, branches from Dere Street about 1½ miles north of Corbridge, and runs north-east to the River Coquet and then in a more or less northerly direction to Berwick-upon-Tweed.

This was a military road and, like the more important Dere Street, pre-dates Hadrian's Wall, having been built either during the Agricolan advance or soon afterwards. It was aiming for an as yet undiscovered fort and harbour on the North Sea coast near Berwick. Such a fort and harbour would reflect Agricola's strategy of using both fleet and army to subdue the northern tribes. It is probable that the road continued beyond Berwick to the Firth of Forth, but no traces of it have been found beyond the River Tweed.

The Devil's Causeway was planned to parallel Dere Street and partition the territory of the Votadini, the main Celtic tribe from Northumberland to the Forth. The Votadini were friendly towards Rome and may have enjoyed client kingdom status from the late first century onwards. Their old tribal centre, the hillfort Traprain Law, which dominates the coastal plain near Edinburgh, increased in prosperity during Roman times, suggesting some kind of 'special relationship'. This may go some way to explaining why only one major Roman fort is known along the length of the Devil's Causeway. This is at Low Learchild (*Alauna*) and it guarded an east-west road connecting the Devil's Causeway to Dere Street. There were two successive forts here and it is likely that the garrison was a cavalry regiment. It was probably not occupied after Hadrian's Wall was built. Nothing of the fort remains today.

The course of the Devil's Causeway is beautifully engineered, consisting of ten straight sections linked by nine changes of alignment, two of them at river crossings and the rest on high ground. The road was shown correctly on Warburton's 1716 map of Northumberland and was described in detail in 1864 before deep ploughing destroyed its surface in many places. In some respects it is a strange Roman road, for maps show it very clearly, striding across the countryside, followed in places by bridleways and lanes, but on the ground it is shy and retiring. West of Longhorsley the OS maps mark a line of bridleways running along the Roman road for two miles over high ground from Doe Hill to Todburn. Sadly, these bridleways are impassable: unmarked, wired off and ploughed out. None the less, at the point where they bisect the Longhorsley-Netherwitton road the Roman way can be seen to the north, crossing the meadows as a wide, green swathe towards Todburn Moor Farm.

OS maps:
1:50,000 Landranger sheet 75

1:25,000 Pathfinder sheet 464 [Lowick (Northumberland)]

Distance: 5½ miles

Pubs/hostelries:
On the walk: Lowick

Roman engineering works:
raised *agger*

Just to the west of Weldon Bridge a straight, narrow lane, gloriously raised on a high *agger*, follows the Devil's Causeway for a short stretch down to the River Coquet, but all traces of the Roman crossing have vanished. This is not really surprising considering the turbulent nature of this north country river, which destroyed the two predecessors of the 18th century Weldon Bridge in 1744 and 1752 respectively, and has presumably moved its channel considerably since Roman times.

Today the Devil's Causeway is a sequence of long, lost stretches, forgotten bridleways and lengths where the Roman road is still in use. The most notable stretch which can be followed lies north-east of the Cheviots and north of the River Till, where a modern lane runs upon the Roman road for 6 miles between East Horton and Lowick, a grey, windswept village which clusters at a modern crossroads and was once a centre for the lime trade, with large lime kilns located nearby. The road, which forges ahead straight as a ruled line, commands superb views to the Cheviots.

48 A CYCLE RIDE/DRIVE FROM EAST HORTON TO LOWICK

This is an exhilarating ride along an important Roman way now dwindled to a little lane swept by winds from the North Sea. The lane runs on a single, straight alignment surrounded by the wild Northumberland landscape and brooded over by the Cheviot Hills.

Instructions

1. Start at East Horton [NU028308]. Head north along the lane. The Devil's Causeway joins from the right. Continue northwards on the raised lane which runs on the Roman road. Cross over two crossroads.

2. Follow the lane over the Coal Burn and continue past Brownridge.

3. Arrive at Lowick. The Roman road carried straight on here along the same alignment, which points directly to Berwick castle.

ANTONINE WALL MILITARY WAY

The Roman road from Bridgeness to Old Kilpatrick

The Antonine Wall was built in AD 142-143 on the orders of the Emperor Antoninus Pius when the Romans reoccupied southern Scotland. The change of policy which took the frontier further north was probably related to politics in Rome and may even have been prompted by a desire for change for change's sake at the start of the reign of a new emperor.

The wall runs for 37 miles across the Forth-Clyde isthmus from Bridgeness to Old Kilpatrick. It was cleverly engineered, in a manner similar to Hadrian's Wall, to take advantage of the topography, so that there was a good field of view northwards aiming to check movement into and out of the province. Defence of the frontier was based on a line of forts built on the wall with associated fortlets and watch towers. The wall was not built entirely of stone, but

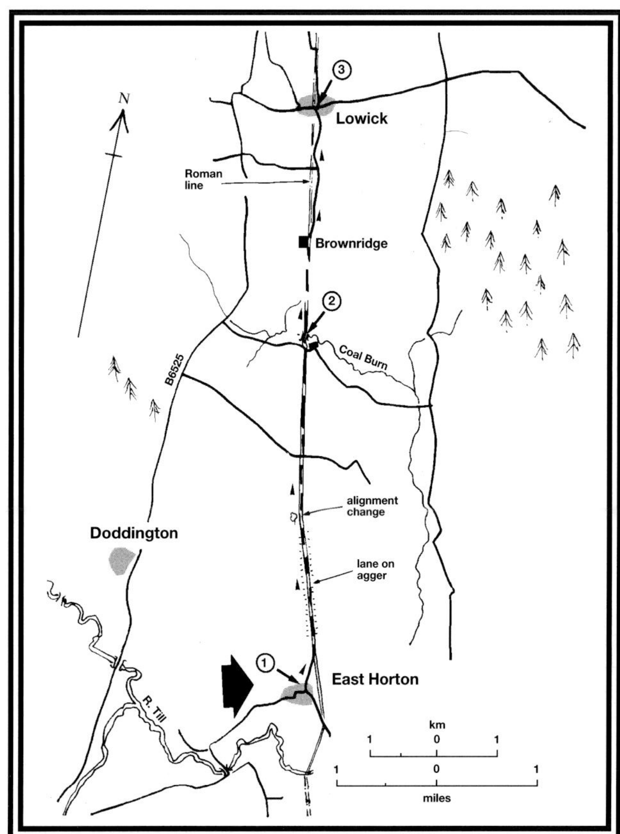

consisted of a stone base, pierced by culverts for good drainage, surmounted by a turf rampart, generally about 14 feet wide and perhaps 10 feet high. The Roman army was particularly handy at building with turves, and the use of this material rather than stone does not mean that the Antonine Wall was a second-rate structure in any way. Indeed, the stone distance slabs, which marked the limits of the work done by different gangs of legionaries, are extremely elaborate, much more so than those from Hadrian's Wall, their well executed artwork giving an impression of the wall's importance as the northernmost frontier of the Roman Empire. The rampart was topped by a timber patrol-walk. To the north of the rampart was an enormous ditch, at least 12 feet deep and some 20 to 40 feet wide, which in many places is the only part of the structure to have survived.

The Military Way runs behind the wall and more or less parallel to it, connecting all the forts, and where the wall crosses difficult ground the Military Way frequently chooses a less demanding course, with branch-roads leading to the forts. This provided bypasses for through-traffic. Along this road travelled all the goods needed by the Roman army, wine and oil from the Mediterranean, grain from arable lands further south; local products of milk, cheese and meat, fruit and vegetables; pottery vessels, metal work, and military supplies. Pottery found in Bearsden shows the extensive communications available with other parts of Britain and with Gaul: vessels have been unearthed here made in Dorset, the Colchester area, the Severn Valley, Yorkshire, Fent and France.

At the end of the 18th century the Military Way could be followed for most of its length. Today it has almost entirely vanished, ploughed out, destroyed or swallowed up in suburbia. The only walkable stretch of the road lies north of Glasgow, where it heads through the site of Bearsden fort and bypasses Castlehill fort on its rocky

Right: *The Devil's Causeway between East Horton and Lowick.*

Below: *In Lowick.*

knoll. The *agger* of the bypass loop is visible on the golf course, crossing the green as a gentle swelling, some 18 feet wide, beside stunted thorn trees, all that remains of a hedge.

Bearsden fort was formerly known as New Kilpatrick, but its Roman name is not known. It was first described in the early 18th century and was surveyed by General Roy in 1775, but by the end of the 19th century it had been swamped by Glasgow's spreading suburbs, buried beneath Victorian villas, and it has only been during redevelopment that the well preserved bath house has come to light. Roman baths were famous, not just as places for a soap and a scrub, but as leisurely, civilised complexes with hot, warm and cold chambers, similar to modern Turkish baths. The building inscription survives and shows that the fort was built by the XX Valeria Victrix from Chester. Nothing is known of the soldiers stationed at Bearsden, though they may have been cavalry troops, unusual on the Antonine Wall. Possible Bearsden was an outpost of Castlehill Fort where a mixed unit of cavalry and infantry was stationed.

Bearsden was occupied only once during the second century AD, for between 12 and 15 years. Every other fort so far investigated on the Antonine Wall was inhabited twice, before and after the disastrous uprising of AD 155. Bearsden, it seems, was not reoccupied, and traces of burnt debris were found where the garrison had fired their fort.

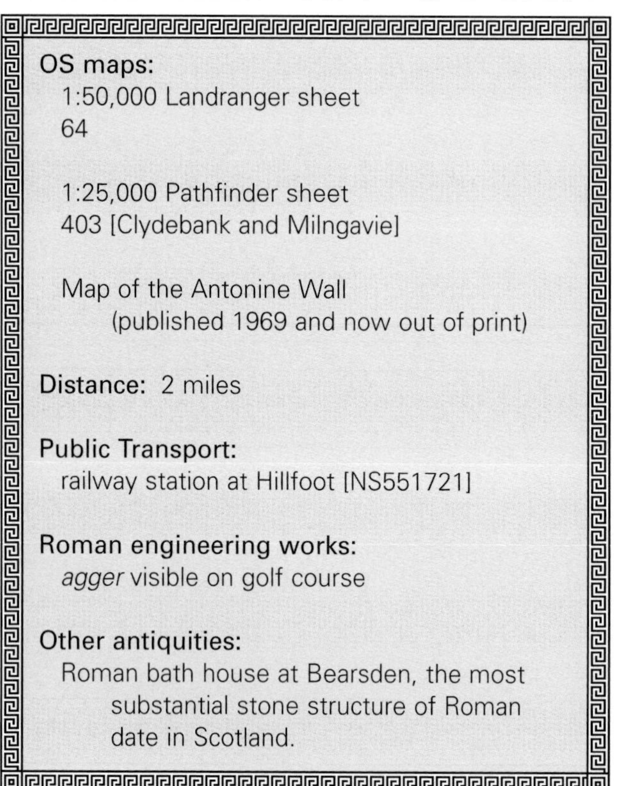

OS maps:
1:50,000 Landranger sheet
64

1:25,000 Pathfinder sheet
403 [Clydebank and Milngavie]

Map of the Antonine Wall
(published 1969 and now out of print)

Distance: 2 miles

Public Transport:
railway station at Hillfoot [NS551721]

Roman engineering works:
agger visible on golf course

Other antiquities:
Roman bath house at Bearsden, the most substantial stone structure of Roman date in Scotland.

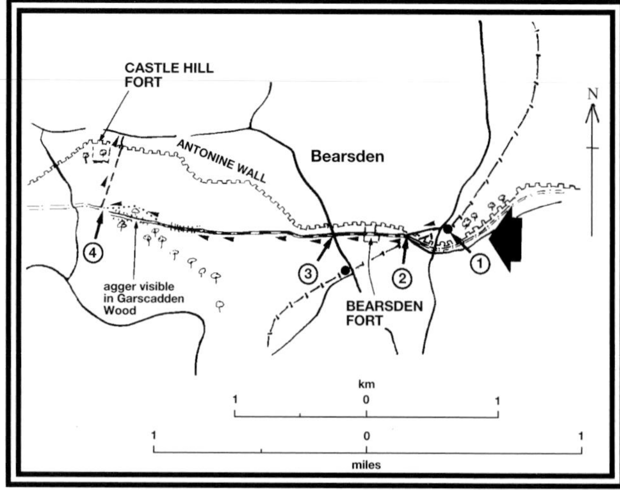

49 A WALK ALONG THE ANTONINE WALL MILITARY WAY AT BEARSDEN

This short walk follows the Military Way attached to the Antonine Wall, and runs along 'Roman Road' the most northerly use of the term as a road name in the lands once occupied by the Roman Empire.

Instructions

1. Start at Hillfoot station. Cross the road and walk up the hill opposite, across the line of the Antonine Wall.

2. Continue along Roman Road. This is on the line of the Antonine Wall Military Way and is the most northerly road in the Roman Empire to bear the name. Pass the Roman bathhouse on your right.

3. Go straight over at the crossroads, and continue along Thorn Road, which is also on the Military Way. Follow Thorn Road round to the left (signposted to the tennis courts) and continue across the golf course, where the *agger* is visible. Pass Garscadden Wood on your left.

4. Either retrace your steps or turn right on to the track, leaving the Military Way, pass the fort at Castle Hill and cross the line of the Antonine Wall. Continue to the main road, where there are buses back to Hillhead station.

ROME'S FARTHEST NORTH

The Roman road from Camelon To Kirriemuir along the Gask Ridge

This is the most northerly road in the entire Roman Empire. It was the route followed during Agricola's campaign into the Highlands, which culminated in his decisive victory over the Caledonians at Mons Graupius in

Above: *The grassy agger of the Military Way crosses the golf course.*

AD 84. It continued to be the main military road to the far north, though the abandonment of plans to conquer the whole of Britain meant that it never ran to its planned, but now unknown, destination.

It was designed to be the trunk route and branches must have been planned though none, so far, have been found. The road was well engineered, taking advantage of the topography so as to be laid out in a minimum of alignments with good all-round visibility.

The Roman road starts at Camelon near Falkirk and heads north-west to Stirling, passing to the west of Stirling Castle. It must have crossed the Forth near here, probably at Kildean, an old-established crossing place, though the actual spot used is not known. Its course is obscure through Dunblane and Greenloaning, but is visible passing Ardoch fort (*Alauna*). It continues north-east past the Roman signal station at Kaims Castle before turning abruptly eastwards to the major fort at Strageath.

From here it runs roughly parallel with the edge of the Highlands along Strathearn, crossing the River Earn, probably at Innerpeffray to follow the Gask Ridge, commanding good views to both north and south. It heads northwards to cross the River Tay at Bertha, near Perth, and runs through Scone Park and on past Inchtuthill fort to just beyond Kirriemuir. It must have continued further than this, but definite traces of a road have not been found.

The road varied in width from about 18 feet on the terraceways to some 27 feet elsewhere and was set upon an *agger*. Its construction was solid and it was built to last. Opposite Kaims Castle and near Ardunie on the Gask Ridge its substantial foundations have been excavated.

The stretch along the Gask Ridge is doubly important, not only as the most northerly walkable Roman road in the former lands of the Roman Empire, but also as the line of the first Roman frontier in Britain, a 'frontier' which took shape as a concept when the Roman high command drew back from the plan of total conquest of this island. Till the Gask frontier was designed, the Romans did not know the meaning of the word. Their Empire was continuously expanding, so that halts along any 'line' were temporary affairs, left behind as soon as the army advanced further into enemy territory. The Gask frontier, and its near-contemporary frontier in Germany, represent a fundamental change in thinking. Maybe the Empire would not go on expanding for ever, perhaps a line could be drawn around it ....

This was in the late AD 80s, when the far northern and western forts at Inchtuthill and at the entrances to the glens had been abandoned. The Gask frontier was not an impenetrable barrier in the manner of later frontiers, but was based on pre-existing forts along the Roman road. The Romans strengthened this line of defences south of the Tay by building a line of watch towers, most of those identified being along the Gask Ridge. These were not 'signal stations', as is frequently claimed, for there are too many of them too closely spaced. Rather, they would have kept a look-out over a wide swathe of cleared land north and south of the road so as to monitor all movement into and out of the province. They were fortified wooden

Main Picture: *View north from Crossgates on the Roman road, the first frontier in Britain.*

Inset: *The Roman road on the Gask ridge, looking west.*

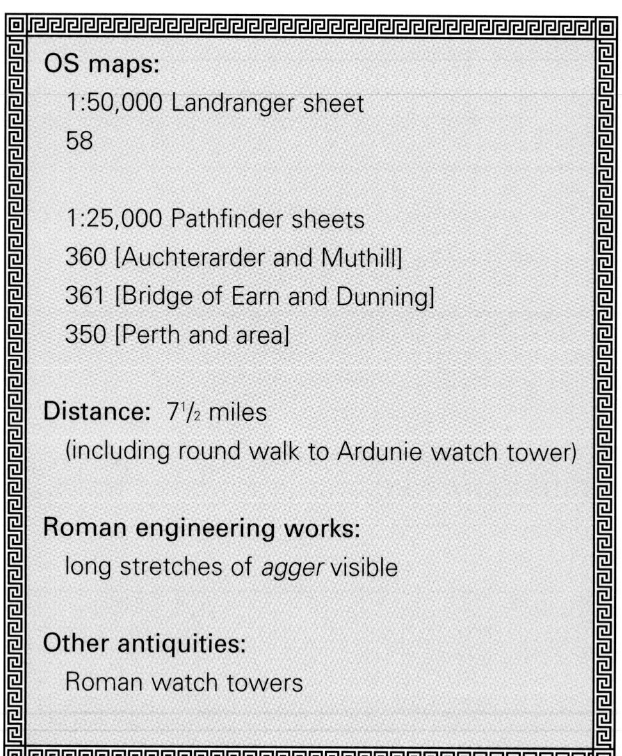

OS maps:
1:50,000 Landranger sheet
58

1:25,000 Pathfinder sheets
360 [Auchterarder and Muthill]
361 [Bridge of Earn and Dunning]
350 [Perth and area]

Distance: 7½ miles
(including round walk to Ardunie watch tower)

Roman engineering works:
long stretches of *agger* visible

Other antiquities:
Roman watch towers

towers surrounded by an earth rampart and ditch with an entrance facing the road.

The Gask frontier was a short-lived phenomenon, of three years' duration at most. The towers were constructed in AD 86 or maybe later, and yet by AD 90 the Romans had abandoned Scotland north of the Forth-Clyde isthmus, dismantling and burning their forts and watch-towers.

The little lane along the Gask Ridge is the best preserved stretch of this road, which almost everywhere else has been lost. It has a typically Roman character, open and on top of the world, with dream-like views to the mountains beyond bathed in dappled light. Past Ardunie it is carpeted with wild flowers and overhung by a venerable avenue of beech and oak trees.

50 A WALK FROM CROSSGATES TO ARDUNIE

This exciting walk follows the northernmost walkable stretch of Roman road in the Roman Empire, commanding wide views to the north.

Instructions

1. Start at Crossgates. Head west along the lane past Thorny Hill Roman watch tower. Carry on past Roman Park and the site of another watch tower, Mossside.

2. Go over the crossroads and past the Witch Knowe watch tower on the right and the Gask House watch tower on the left.

3. Carry on along the track through the gate where the modern road turns off to the left.

4. Continue along the lane.

5. Either carry straight on to Ardunie watch tower. The green lane is impassable at the far end, so you will have to retrace your steps, or leave the Roman road and turn left to the lane.

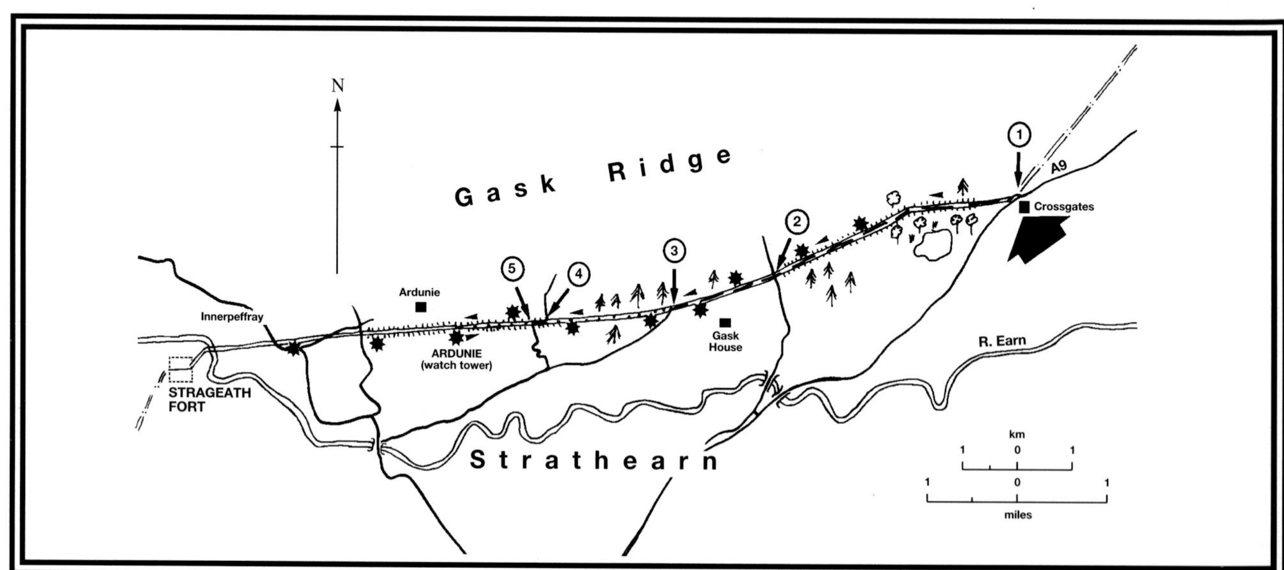

APPENDIX

ENGLISH-ROMAN PLACE NAMES

English	Roman
Abergavenny	*Gobannium*
Aldborough	*Isurium*
Ambleside	*Galava*
Ardoch	*Alavna*
Badbury Rings	*Vindocladia*
Bath	*Aquae Sulis*
Baylham House	*Combretovium*
Birrens	*Blatobulgium*
Brecon (Y Gaer)	*Cicucium*
Brougham (Penrith)	*Brocavum*
Brough-by-Bainbridge	*Virosidum*
Brough-on-Humber	*Petuaria*
Caerhun	*Canovium*
Caerleon	*Isca*
Caernarfon	*Segontium*
Caerwent	*Venta Siluram*
Caistor St Edmund	*Venta Icenorum*
Cambridge	*Duroliponte*
Canterbury	*Durovernum*
Carlisle	*Luguvalium*
Carmarthen	*Moridunum*
Chelmsford	*Caesaromagus*
Chester	*Deva*
Chichester	*Noviomagus*
Cirencester	*Corinium*
Colchester	*Camulodunum*
Corbridge	*Corstopitum*
Dorchester (Dorset)	*Durnovaria*
Dover	*Dubris*
East Anton	*Levcomagus*
Exeter	*Isca*
Gloucester	*Glevum*
Godmanchester	*Durovigutum*
Great Chesters	*Aesica*
Hardknott	*Mediobogdum*
High Cross	*Venonis*
High Rochester	*Bremenium*
Housesteads	*Vercovicium*
Ilchester	*Lindinis*
Kenchester	*Magnis*
Leicester	*Ratae*
Leintwardine	*Bravonium*
Lincoln	*Lindum*
Littlechester	*Derventio*
Llandovery	*Alabum*
London	*Londinium*
Low Learchild	*Alauna*
Lympne	*Portus Lemanis*
Malton	*Derventio*
Mildenhall	*Cunetio*
Millington	*Deleovicia*
Neath	*Nidvii*
Newstead	*Trimontium*
Old Sarum	*Sorviodunum*
Ravenglass	*Glannaventa*
Richborough	*Portus Rutupiae*
St Albans	*Verulamium*
St Asaph	*(?) Varae*
Sandy Lane	*Verlucio*
Silchester	*Calleva Atrebatum*
Towcester	*Lactodorum*
Usk	*Burrium*
Wall	*Letocetum*
Water Newton	*Durobrivae*
Whitley Castle	*Epiacum*
Winchester	*Venta Belgarum*
Wroxeter	*Viroconium*
York	*Eboracum*

INDEX